11·15·79

SLAVE TRADE TODAY

They come from Europe and the Orient
as stowaways on freighters, from Haiti in
tiny boats held fast by baling wire, from
Mexico and Canada in death vans and
coffin trucks. Every year over 350,000 of the
world's poor cross U.S. borders illegally,
lured by the promises of smugglers who
paint a vivid but false picture of the good
life. These immigrants' misery is abetted by
corrupt border police and customs officials,
who are making human bondage one of the
cruelest realities of the twentieth century.

In *Slave Trade Today*, investigative reporter Sasha G. Lewis uncovers the international network of cutthroat businessmen
—farmers, restaurateurs, industrialists, and
their front men—who thrive on the exploitation of America's 6 million illegal
aliens.

The story of Guillermo Valdiva and Jesus
Hernandez is typical. At seventeen both
young men worked long hours for less than
a dollar a day in the citrus groves outside
their hometown in southern Mexico. That
is, until a well-dressed American pulled up
in his Chevy van and offered them six dollars an hour for work in the States—if
they'd meet him next week 1,000 miles
north in Tijuana. Jesus and Guillermo never
saw that man again—not in the flophouse
in Tijuana, nor when they were herded with
23 others into the back of a truck, where
they would spend days hungry and thirsty
in the stifling heat as their captors drove
wildly through the mountains into California. Once in the U.S. they met men who
exacted high prices for the bread they ate

and the water they drank and men who deducted so much for "expenses" from their
pay that they became virtual slaves.

Guillermo and Jesus never received six
dollars an hour. Like the more than 700,000
illegals in New York City, the 700,000 in
Los Angeles, the 300,000 in Chicago, the
100,000 in Washington, and the 25,000 in
Boston, they were victims of the modern
slave trade: the multi-billion-dollar business of providing cheap labor on demand to
companies both large and small.

Sasha Lewis assesses the effect these
immigrants have on American society and
examines the immigration laws and socioeconomic forces that create this illegal population. A searing documentary on a national issue of growing concern, *Slave
Trade Today* makes a strong case for a
more humane immigration policy.

SLAVE TRADE TODAY

American Exploitation of Illegal Aliens

Sasha G. Lewis

BEACON PRESS Boston

Beacon Press books are published under the auspices
of the Unitarian Universalist Association
Published simultaneously in Canada by
Fitzhenry & Whiteside Limited, Toronto

Library of Congress Cataloging in Publication Data
Lewis, Sasha Gregory.
  Slave trade today.

  Bibliography: p.
  Includes index.
  1. Alien labor—United States. I. Title.
II. Title: Illegal aliens.
HD8081.A5L48   1979   331.6'2   79-51151
ISBN   0-8070-0489-8

2079052

For

my grandmother, **Anastasia Sergeyevna Ivanov,**

who came to this country with her son and could not speak English and who supported him by working as a seamstress at some of the same sweatshops that today hire undocumented workers;

and

in memory of

my other immigrant grandmother who did the same to support her immigrant daughter;

and

in memory of

Otto Hagel, an immigrant too, who worked in the same fields that today hire undocumented workers.

I think he would have liked this book.

Acknowledgments

First I extend my deep gratitude to the people in hiding, who at great risk spent several hours talking with me about their lives and experiences as part of the underground labor market. They were only a dozen, but their stories have shaped every element of this book. Also I thank the retired gringo coyote who told me things about his one-time trade that aren't ordinarily known. And I thank the supervisor who explained to me how things went when his boss wanted some "wetbacks" for his union plant. Also I thank the various people I met in border regions, both citizens of the United States of America and of the United Mexican States, who gave not only their off-the-cuff observations, but the specific and tiny facts about border life as they lived it. These people made an overwhelming situation comprehensible.

Also I thank those people who probably never knew they were contributing to this book, the people who talked to me before this book was even an idea: visa abusers from Canada, Great Britain, South Korea, the Philippines, and Iran; and community organizers who built unions in the fields when everyone else said it couldn't be done, who worked with refugees from Haiti in Florida, from Guatemala in Boston, from Ecuador in Brooklyn, and from Chile in the San Francisco Bay Area.

Next I thank the hundreds of women and men who are seldom acknowledged in a project such as this: assiduous workers who read, search, clip, and label for the clipping services that digest every newspaper in the country.

Then there are some people whom I would like one day to tell how hard they made it for me to obtain public documents from the government in Washington, D. C. But here, instead, I thank the people who helped me circumvent my troubles with those other people. They are the members of the staff of U.S. Senator Edward M. Kennedy and U.S. Representatives Don Edwards, Cecil "Cec" Heftel, and Elizabeth Holtzman.

Also, for going beyond what their jobs required of them, I thank: Elizabeth Benedict, media coordinator for the Mexican-American Legal Defense and Education Fund; Herb Berkowitz, director of public relations for The Heritage Foundation; Frank Galván of the American Friends Service Committee; and Joyce C. Vialet, an analyst for the Congressional Research Service of the Library of Congress.

The above acknowledgments do not imply that these people, or the organizations and people they represent, necessarily endorse or support any word of what is written in this book. In any case, I thank them for the help they extended to me.

Additionally, I thank the editors of Beacon Press who believed in this book and decided to publish it. Also I thank all the people at Beacon, from editorial assistants to switchboard operators, who make a book, try to find readers for a book, and who contribute to it in every capacity.

Finally, I thank two very special people: George Mendenhall, who helped me with my research, and Mary E. Lewis, without whose support—both moral and material—this book would not have been possible.

Preface

There are several difficulties in trying to write a book about "illegal aliens" at this time in U.S. history.

The first of these is a semantic treachery forced upon author and reader alike by other media. The phrase "illegal alien" is doubly negative in connotation. *Alien*, standing alone, is a scare word that dredges up old phrases like "alien hordes," or, in the post-"Star Trek" era, images of strangers from some other galactic system. Sticking the word *illegal* in front of it as an adjective is an affront to all that America stands for. One of the things we enjoy in our nation is the right to be presumed innocent until someone proves us guilty – even if we are arrested and charged with a crime and all the circumstances surrounding the arrest make us appear to be guilty of it. Using the adjective *illegal* in reference to someone arrested, but not yet found guilty of the misdemeanor of crossing our borders without proper inspection, is as unconscionable as using the noun *murderer* in reference to someone arrested, but not yet tried and found guilty of that crime. But thanks to headline writers, some reporters and television newscasters, and many law enforcement officers across the United States, if a book such as this were subtitled "suspected foreign nationals working without proper certification," or something else approaching accuracy, no one would know what it was about. Nearly everyone, however, has some idea of what an "illegal alien" is, and that is the purpose of a book's title – to give the reader some idea of what she or he is going to find inside. Within the pages of this book I have tried to correct this semantic treachery by using more accurate and less fright-provoking terms to describe the people who toil in the depths of America's underground labor market. When I do use the term "illegal alien" – unavoidable in certain contexts – it is enclosed in quotes.

The second problem in writing a book like this is a latter-day xenophobia that has crept into American reportage and studies of immigrants and migrant workers who enter the country without proper authority. That xenophobia is a contemporary "wetback syndrome," a preoccupation with Hispanic peoples, especially Mexicans. In earlier times our xenophobia focused on Asians, and later on peoples from southern and eastern Europe. But the last three decades have generated the wetback syndrome, and therefore most reportage, enforcement, debate, and sociological study have focused on Mexican and (more recently) other Hispanic immigrants in the underground labor market. Additionally, vocal lobbying and civil rights organizations actively work to better the lot of Americans of Mexican descent and their near and distant relatives in America who are citizens of the United

Mexican States. These combined influences have worked to provide a substantial amount of information about Mexican nationals in the U.S. However, the underground labor market is composed of people from almost every nation of the world, and there are few who speak for them. So there are virtually no resources to draw upon to learn about Poles living and working in violation of U.S. law in New Jersey, nor the Chinese in San Francisco and New York, nor the Koreans in Los Angeles, nor stateless Armenians, Italians, and Irish in California, nor Canadians in San Francisco and Hawaii, in fact, not much about anyone except the "wetbacks."

While it is probably correct that more than half the people who come to work in the U.S. the only way they can—by violating one law or another—are currently from Hispanic nations, I find it troublesome that when we speak of "illegal aliens" most of us somehow automatically think of Mexicans. In this book I have tried to correct, as much as possible, the defects in information about other immigrants in hiding, but not as successfully as I wished.

The third difficulty with a book such as this is, I hope, not inevitable. Exposés of the plight of the slave laborer—whose immigration American institutions are in part responsible for—have in the past been used as excuses to enact laws and policies that have done little more than worsen the lives of the workers involved. So it is with some fear that I describe this trade in human flesh, a fear that some readers may use the information to create some form of legalized slavery such as the old Bracero Program. I have tried as best I could to mitigate this reaction by focusing on the historical roots of our contemporary underground labor market; by attempting to show how American special interests have encouraged it by their actions both at home and abroad; and by exposing some of the ailments that need curing if the symptom—slavery—is to be ended.

The misery of those who live and work in the underground labor market is something that the American conscience, I believe, cannot tolerate. Realistic forms of protection for these workers must be found and enforced. If new policies are needed, then we should have them. But these policies should not be molded by emotional heat, because that makes bad policy. If new laws really are needed, then they should be enacted. But neither should these laws be based on emotionalism, for that makes bad law. I hope that those who read this book are encouraged to support decent and humane and good policies and laws that will not result in increased discrimination against one race or group of citizens and permanent residents, but will ensure that people need no longer come to our country in search of hope, only to find slavery and humiliation and degradation. As we try to forge a foreign policy that considers human rights, so should we create domestic policies that ensure, at least within our own borders, that human rights prevail for all, regardless of their status or position.

CONTENTS

SLAVE TRADE TODAY

1: DIMENSIONS AND BACKGROUND

> He has waged a cruel war against human nature itself,
> violating its most sacred rights of life and liberty in the
> persons of a distant people who never offended him,
> captivating them and carrying them into slavery . . . or
> to incur miserable death in their transportation thither.
> —*Thomas Jefferson, from original draft of the Declaration of*
> *Independence. This charge against King George III was*
> *dropped in a compromise with slave-holding states*

Father Miguel Hidalgo y Costilla walked slowly down the steps of his church after Sunday morning mass to talk with his parishioners about the harshness of colonial rule and the poverty and desperation it imposed on the people. He urged the townspeople, on this mid-September morning of 1810, to take up arms to win their freedom. With this solemn homily Mexico began her war for independence. Father Hidalgo and his freedom fighters marched next to the town of Atotonilco, a place known for its healing hot springs. There he went to the church and took from it an embroidered tapestry of Mexico's patron saint, the Virgin of Guadalupe, and made it the banner of Mexico's cause.

Nearly 170 years later, after Mexico had fought several wars for freedom from her oppressors, another man came to Atotonilco, a town of substance now renowned for its citrus groves, but still remembered as the town that gave Mexico its banner of freedom. The man spent some time talking to local youths. He promised them work in El Norte, where, for picking the same citrus fruits that surrounded Atotonilco, the wealthy gringos would pay them six American dollars an hour. To teenagers Guillermo Valdiva and Jesus Alvarez Hernandez this was a promise of wealth beyond their furthest aspirations. They had worked for almost a year in a furniture factory where they earned seventy-five cents an hour. Each of the seventeen-year-old friends had nine brothers and sisters and knew what such a fortune as the man promised them would mean to their families.

The recruiter gave Jesus, Guillermo, and some others the address of a hotel in Tijuana, where, he told them, they would be met and taken to their jobs. They did not even have to pay the recruiter any money for the costly business of crossing into the United States. This, they were told, would be deducted from their wages at the rate of $25 a week. The rest would be free: food, water, shelter, work clothing, and equipment.

And so Guillermo and Jesus agreed to make the arduous trek of more than one thousand miles from their town: west to Guadalajara, then north, then west again to Tijuana, then north again to their work in El Norte.

When they reached the dingy Tijuana hotel, they waited with some fifty others hoping for work in El Norte, until a boy took them to two guides who were to lead them across the border. They tried three times, and on the third night they crossed successfully, walking through damp fields and over a freeway. At a prearranged spot on the side of the freeway, Guillermo, Jesus, and about twenty-three others were quickly hustled into a van. After a forty-five-minute drive they reached a tomato field south of San Clemente, where they were unloaded to sleep the rest of the night in a house.

The next day, a Saturday, they climbed back into the camper and rode for several hours until they stopped at a packing shed near Riverside, California. They were told to sleep there until morning, when someone would come to take them to their work. There was no heat in the shed, nor were there blankets, water, or a toilet. They slept poorly in the cold on the rough bare floor, despite their weariness from the crowded trip in the van. At 5 A.M. they were awakened and taken to an orange grove and led some four to five hundred yards from the road until they reached a place where a sheet of plastic had been spread out on the ground. This, they were told, was to be their shelter. Each was issued a blanket, its cost to be deducted from their earnings, and it was explained that they could do their cooking over open fires. They would work, they were told, from 7 A.M. to 4 P.M. and would have a half-hour break for lunch.

The first day they were not given enough water to quench their thirst. At night they ate bread and bologna brought to them by a field boss. The next morning they finished the bread and bologna and complained to the field boss about the lack of water and the inadequacy of a plastic sheet for shelter. The boss brought them tortillas, eggs, and beans. This too, they were told, was to be charged against their earnings. The third day it rained. The January night brought frost with the rain, so that when they woke up the next day, wet and muddied from the rain, their blankets were covered with ice. They rose, cramped and cold, and tried to make a shelter from the orange bins, which they covered with their plastic sheet. They could not make a fire to cook the eggs or warm the tortillas and beans. As they huddled there together trying to hide from the cold and the rain, a rock they had used to anchor the plastic above them was tugged free as the weight of the water collected in the plastic sheet. The rock fell and struck one of the workers on the head. There was no doctor or nurse to care for him.

The workers complained to the boss. Two of them had swollen legs from the cold and the wet and could barely walk, much less climb the slippery wet ladders up into the trees. The boss ordered them to pick anyway. They complained again to the boss and asked for their pay. But, recalled Guillermo and Jesus, the boss told them they could not be paid because they still owed for their transportation. No more food was brought to them until the following Saturday.

On Sunday evening some members of the crew decided they would not go back to work until they were provided the shelter and water that had been promised them. On Monday morning a new boss came and listened to their complaints. He told them they could have a house, but it would cost more money from their wages, and that a house would put them in danger from immigration agents. He angrily reminded them they still owed money for their transportation, their blankets, their equipment, as well as $218.56 for food. Guillermo, Jesus, and the others insisted they would not work until they were given what was promised them by the recruiter in Atotonilco. The boss took away their blankets and canvas sacks and they knew then that they must escape and hide. They ran for the nearby hills, without even a penny among them all.

Some friendly Spanish-speaking legal service workers finally coaxed them down from the hills. Most of the crew were happy enough to return safely to their homes in Mexico, but Jesus, Guillermo, and four others stayed behind to testify as witnesses against their one-time bosses in a suit charging the bosses and citrus-ranch owner with peonage and false imprisonment—contemporary legal jargon for slavery—two among a dozen charges.

Roots of Contemporary Slavery

America has always hungered for laborers to plough, hoe, plant, and harvest cotton, fruit, vegetables, tobacco, sugar cane; hands to turn cotton and wool into textiles, and those into clothing; arms to swing the pickaxes that cracked open roadbeds for railroads and ditches for canals; hardy men to blast and dig and drag the minerals out from the earth—laborers, nation builders. And laws were written in bits and pieces to accomplish these things, immigration laws.

America's first immigration law was slavery. Her second immigration law was a prohibition of the African slave trade after 1807. No law, however, can really end the supply of a commodity in demand, and more slaves were brought into the country during the fifty years after 1807 than were brought before the trade was driven underground. The African slave trade was finally ended by the Civil War.

Still, America hungered for good, cheap laborers. The hunger was

insatiable; men and women were needed to do the jobs that needed doing. The hunger went abroad to foreign lands in search of strong arms
and backs and hands, and contract laborers replaced the slaves:
Chinese, Filipinos, Japanese, Irish, Poles, nearly a world of
nationalities. And the poor and starving and homeless came to feed the
insatiable American hunger for labor at cheap prices, doing all the jobs
that needed doing, filling her cities, spreading out from both coasts
until they met where a golden spike was driven into a railroad tie that
joined two halves of a nation. But as laborers already working in the
U.S. saw what was happening—that more men were contracted for than
there were jobs, just to drive the price of labor down even lower—Congress added to its immigration codes prohibitions against labor contracted in foreign lands. But the hunger for cheap labor found its way
around the law, as Ann Novotny describes in her book on American
immigrants, *Strangers at the Door*:

> Even after prearranged employment was forbidden, many an im-
> migrant went directly from ship to construction camp or mine.
> Labor contractors continued to recruit work gangs (and strike-
> breakers) in the immigrant lodgings of every port. . . . Wages there
> sounded attractive—but the disadvantages soon became clear. The
> work gang's boss or padrone, a middleman of the same nationality
> as the crew he hired, often turned out to be a parasite rather than
> an ally to the immigrants. When he arbitrarily lowered wages to
> increase his personal profit, who was in a position to argue with
> him? The workers, housed in ramshackle huts or ancient railroad
> cars, were crowded, uncomfortable and usually dirty. The men
> often found themselves owing money to the company store where
> they were forced to buy supplies. . . . It was very hard to save a
> dollar, and they owed the padrone the cost of their transportation to
> the camp. They felt the despair of trapped men.

And then America hungered for settlers to people the land along the
rails; shopkeepers, farmers, ranchers, preachers, to build up towns that
would make it profitable for a railroad to cross a nation. But America
did not want the kinds of laborers who had earlier built up the nation.
This was the preserve of white men, and, later on, only certain breeds of
white men. And so, added to the immigration laws were statutes that
would exclude the poor and hungry and encourage the storekeepers and
bankers and citified people to cross to her golden doors. Laws were
added making it hard for the black people and the yellow people and the
red and brown peoples to be part of the nation as citizens. As America
sank under a nineteenth-century depression, her workers looked to the

"aliens" among them, and blamed the depression on them. And Congress added to its laws, creating the Chinese Exclusion Act, to bar the importation of Chinese coolie labor.

But still American bosses hungered for cheap laborers. The Chinese Exclusion Act left a vacuum on the West Coast and further inland, and the bosses looked south for backs and arms and hands to replace coolie labor. They found their labor in Mexico, the nation that had once owned much of the land they now claimed as theirs: California, Arizona, Texas, New Mexico, Utah, Nevada, and parts of Colorado.

In 1917 Congress tacked on another law to its immigration codes—the literacy law—to further limit the hungry, the poor, the huddled masses who would work for next to nothing in America. The literacy law helped to cement the foundations of what is a large chunk of today's slave trade. It forced the poor and hungry and illiterate people in search of work into a brutal reliance on the pact between the employer, who needed cheap labor, and the trader, ready to supply it. This institution was first used primarily between Mexico and the U.S. Today it has expanded to cover the globe. The peculiar functions of this institution along the U.S.-Mexican border were described in 1930 by Manuel Gamio as he reported the results of his 1926-1927 study of Mexican immigration to the United States. He concluded that for every three people who legally entered the U.S. from Mexico, two entered illegally.

> The real forces which move illegal immigration are, first of all, the smugglers or "coyotes" who facilitate illegal entrance to Mexican immigrants, and the contractors or *enganchistas* who provide them with jobs. The smuggler and the contractor are an intimate and powerful alliance from Calexico to Brownsville. Second, indirectly, but logically and fundamentally, the origin of the illegal immigration is to be found in the farmers and ranchers, and railroad, mining, and other enterprises to which Mexican labor is indispensable. . . .
>
> Because passing through . . . official channels entails a great deal of bother and delay, and also expense . . . and since many laborers, furthermore, are not able to pass the literacy tests of the American authorities, a great number of them enter illegally . . . [some] jump the fence, usually at night, and get work on nearby ranches. Their employers, taking advantage of their risky position, as a rule pay very low wages and treat them almost like slaves. . . .
>
> The smugglers are at times employed by big commercial, industrial or agricultural enterprises in the border states and even in the interior of the United States. . . . There are a great many abuses

and many ways in which the immigrants are exploited. From the beginning they are absolutely in the hands of the contractor, and even more so if they have been smuggled by him. . . . Immigrants contracted for and taken to their place of work are often overcharged greatly for food and incidental expenses on the road and in the camp. Since the wages of the men are kept in the hands of the contractor until the debt to him is paid, generally for the first two or three weeks the laborer gets nothing, and sometimes it results that he is in debt to the contractor at the end of that time.

At every crisis point of American history immigration has been the scapegoat for economic turmoil. New immigration laws and policies have been the political palliatives offered by government to the public. And at each time there has remained the hunger for labor, and employers hungry for the cheap labor found one escape clause or another to satisfy their craving.

In the mid-1970s, as America faced both increasing inflation and unemployment rates unprecedented since the Great Depression, it was little surprise that government agencies were again ready to tackle the "problem" of immigration. But legal immigrants were no longer so destitute as those of an earlier generation, and were bound together with citizens of their own nationalities in powerful political alliances. So another scapegoat was needed as a sacrifice for the public. President Nixon's staff "discovered" "illegal aliens," as if there was something new in it. Debate centered on the new scapegoats and ranged widely. Little truth resulted from the fury except for the fact that no one even knew or could determine how many *legal* immigrants, or, for that matter, citizens, were still in the country. This finding was dropped almost as soon as it was mentioned. All agreed, however, that no one knew or would ever know how many people were in the U.S. who had not entered through legal channels. Not knowing their number, and never likely to discover it, politicians were able to speak of an "illegal alien problem" of as vast dimensions as they wished. At the peak of the Nixon-era preoccupation with the unknown and underground workforce, estimates of the "illegal" population in the country were as high as twelve million workers, who, if removed, could theoretically open up that many jobs for American citizens. (Later estimates hovered near five million.)

Among the first actions the executive branch of government took to put an end to the "problem" was to post more Border Patrol troops at the Mexican-American border. This had predictable results. The number of people caught trying to cross the border without going through proper channels rose about 20 percent per year until politicians and journalists alike observed that the "problem" seemed to be skyrocketing beyond apparent control. As government investigators and journalists began digging into the subject, they found that much of the immigration was being handled by organized smuggling rings. And for the first time in more than a century, government officials began talking about a domestic slave trade.

Slave Trade Today

Leonel J. Castillo, commissioner of the Immigration and Naturalization Service (INS), the agency charged not only with processing all legal immigrants and visitors but tracking down immigration law violators as well, in 1978 gave a general description of the trade: "It's a very extensive network . . . we think that as many as one-fourth of all people coming across have someone helping them. They are very big operations. . . . They have an office in New York, and they can find you fifty workers . . . to work in car washes in Philadelphia. . . . Some of them become a modern form of indentured servant. They pay a percentage of their salaries [to the smugglers] for years." At the time Castillo spoke, the INS estimated that about one million people were entering the U.S. illegally each year. Others put this count at half as many and others put it higher. A quarter of a million of them, by INS calculations, were thought to be the annual cargo of today's slave trade.

Castillo was not alone in his assessment. "The smuggling of aliens is an industry, perhaps the biggest industry on the [Mexican] border, and it is, if not a modern slave trade, the next closest thing to it," a California Border Patrol agent agreed.

A Texas INS investigator reiterated, "It's a multimillion-dollar business. It's really a form of slavery and there's no end to the inhumanities involved."

And, in sentencing one of those found guilty in a smuggling operation estimated to have carried about fifty people per week from Mexico to Los Angeles and Chicago, a U.S. District Court judge said, "I don't know how we can make it any clearer that the business of alien smuggling is the business of dealing in people – a form of slavery."

Today's slave trade is international in scope, involving the importation of Chinese, Japanese, Koreans, Ecuadorians, El Salvadorians, Guatemalans, Dominicans, Haitians, Argentinians, Nigerians, Mexicans, Poles, Italians, Greeks, and people from virtually every other country of the world. Smuggling schemes vary from country to country and adjust themselves as old routes and tactics are put out of operation by the INS or the police of foreign governments.

As the slave trade has reached virtually every nation of the world, the trade has spread to every state of the U.S. A decade ago Americans knew there were undocumented immigrants in such places as New York, Los Angeles, and states along our 1,945-mile border with Mexico. But today undocumented immigrants and migrant workers are working in states and at jobs where no one would have thought to look ten years ago: in Louisiana, Montana, Utah, Rhode Island. They work not only in the fields of California, Texas, Florida, and Arizona, but at farming Christmas trees in Washington and Oregon, rolling irrigation pipes in Idaho, roping cattle and mending fences and driving tractors in Wyoming, bringing in harvests of grain in Kansas, Colorado, Nebraska, and Missouri—an estimated 64,000 work in the grain belt alone.

They work in the light industries strung out along Interstate 80 near Chicago, in restaurants where the politically powerful dine in Washington, D. C., as domestics in New Jersey, at every kind of job in the San Francisco Bay Area, and they make up an estimated three-quarters of the minority workforce in Boston's metropolitan region. They harvest every American crop from avocados to tobacco. They clean the dirty laundry of Nevada hotel-casino complexes. They sew in garment sweatshops in Los Angeles and New York. There is no end to the work they do nor the places they do it, for America still hungers for cheap labor, labor that is docile, labor that will remain muffled when the hours are long and paychecks short.

This slavery has two levels. Its deepest level is that described by Jesus and Guillermo and also described by Ana Beatrix, a Guatemalan woman who said she was forced to work in Maryland as a maid for less than twenty cents an hour. She was confined, she said, to the house where she worked, and forbidden to talk to anyone outside the family. Instead of the room she was promised when she left Guatemala, she slept in a damp and dark basement corner. It was nearly a year before Ana Beatrix managed to escape and tell her story. Also able to tell their story were seven Mexican nationals, who told authorities that they had entered the U.S. illegally and were promised jobs near the Mexican border. They were taken to a poultry farm. Apparently, all was not as promised, and they wanted to leave. The poultry businessman, they said, forced them to stay on the job by threatening them with a gun. Such work as they did under threat of being shot was apparently not satisfactory, so the businessman drove them across the Texas border to

Louisiana and dumped them there, they said. They were apprehended in Bossier City, Louisiana. The Shelby County, Texas, district attorney's office launched an investigation of their charges.

The slavery has a second level—the level where the wage is a minimum wage, sometimes better, but where captivity is the same. For the worker in the U.S. without proper documents, somewhat lost in a land that speaks a different language from that he or she learned at home, there remains the threat of the INS. As one undocumented worker told a reporter, "When I asked for my pay, the boss told me he would pay me by calling immigration." And for most, immigration means deportation and return to whatever misery, poverty, or near-starvation that drove the worker to seek a job in the U.S. And, when returned, there may still be the debt to be paid to the smugglers, sometimes as much as $1,500—more than seven years' wages to the worker who is lucky enough to find a job in El Salvador, Haiti, or several dozen other nations.

While the difference between these two depths of slavery can be gauged in terms of U.S. earnings, their measure in fear is equal.

The fear is not shared equally by all ethnic and racial groups, or by those who have been fortunate enough to choose one or another of the routes of legal entry that may be open to them. For the INS agents hunt primarily for the brown people, Hispanic people. Sometimes they also search for other third world people, but spend little time or money searching for English, Irish, or Canadian men and women. The INS has all but given up its search for those who have entered illegally on student visas, and it has no means of searching for those who enter on tourist visas and do not leave. These, the alleged students, the alleged temporary visitors, the white, English-speaking people, are as "illegal" as were Jesus and Guillermo, but they are more free than slave, for they can more easily "pass" as free men, just as some blacks once passed as white.

There are few ways of judging the slavery in the underground labor market, few ways of grasping it, and fewer facts about it. How many are like Ana, Jesus, and Guillermo? How many live in fear but not in peonage? One study of 185 undocumented farm workers at their jobs in 1977 on ranches in Arizona, Texas, and California, found that 3 percent had once experienced the involuntary servitude described by Ana and the others, and, like them, escaped. Thirteen percent of the workers surveyed by Manuel De Jesus Alvarado and Theresa Medina said their bosses had turned them over to the INS before payday, and an additional 6 percent said they were fired without receiving any pay.

Nor is there a geographical map of today's slave trade. It recognizes no Mason-Dixon line, and it moves as enforcement tightens in one area or another. There may be a kind of fiscal map of this human bondage, for those who are smuggled from more distant places pay more, and those who travel farthest in the U.S. pay the most. While only one-quarter of the undocumented population as a whole was estimated by the INS to have been brought to the U.S. by the smugglers and traders in human cargo, in Chicago the INS estimated that three-quarters of the underground workforce in the metropolitan area had arrived as cargo of the trade. According to one INS investigator there, this business was a "multibillion dollar" industry.

According to Umberto Marino, head of the INS National Anti-Smuggling Program, in 1978 an estimated 18,000 smugglers worked the domestic slave trade in "rings of five, ten, twenty, and more." This figure did not include the weekend smugglers, bringing Mexicans across the border in their trunks for a couple of hundred dollars, along with their tequila and other tourist items.

Vans, semitrailer trucks, and U-Haul trucks are the coffin ships of today's slave trade. Each van carries from twelve to twenty-five people per trip, and each truckload carries about fifty. Sometimes the crowded passengers are lucky, and a loaf of bread, a package or two of bologna, and a bottle of water are thrown in with them. At other times there is nothing but stale air and stifling heat in summer or unbearable cold in winter. No one knows how many die along the way. Only in the most dramatic circumstances are the dead found, as were the bodies of two Central Americans, found in the California desert near Palm Springs after their twenty-one suffocating compatriots managed to break free from a six-by-ten locked U-Haul truck. Also replacing the coffin ships of old are boats plying the Caribbean trade, small fishing boats loaded beyond capacity with two dozen or more in a boat built for six. Again, no one knows how many are swept overboard in a high sea, or how many boats sink entirely, leaving no survivors and no record of their presence. Air travel also has become a modern adjunct to the historic trade: from the Cessna's bearing human cargo into Florida as they have carried other cargo, to crop dusters flying from Texas border towns to points inland and beyond immigration checkpoints. And, for the luckiest of all, jumbo jets, bringing people either on the first leg of their journeys—from Italy or Yugoslavia to Montreal, or from Ecuador to Mexico City—or on the final leg, where a tourist or student visa will guarantee safe entry into U.S. international ports.

Although vans and trucks and planes and fishing boats have replaced the coffin ships bringing their cargo from Africa, work conditions and living conditions remain as brutal for many of today's slave trade victims as they were two centuries ago. In citrus groves polyethylene sheets are likely to serve as both tent and blanket. Others find shelter in fruit packing crates, and others in abandoned cars. Where real housing is available it is crowded. A Texas journalist, for example, reported forty-five men living in an old three-bedroom house. Each man paid $20 a week rent. And this is by no means an isolated incident, nor is it a record of any sort. Eighty-three people were found living in a two-bedroom San Diego "drop house" while waiting for transport farther north. Perhaps this is a record, but no one keeps such gruesome records.

Nor are these short tales all of the terrors of the contemporary slave trade, for the smuggler must be paid, and the smuggler demands collateral. In some cases the collateral is the children of the undocumented, held by the smuggler until parents or friends can meet demands for payment that are raised as "interest" accumulates.

Even when brutality and inhumanity are removed by a boss who takes no joy from slavery and pays his worker the minimum wage or more for his work, fear holds the immigrant in mute bondage not only to his boss, but to the parasites who suck their livelihoods from exploitation of the trade. Landlords collect a month's rent in advance, and after a week or so call in the INS to deport the tenants, then fill the building again with a new group of renters, collecting four months' rent for every month of housing given. Runners bring food to those in hiding at twice or three times its cost. Gangs wait to rob the worker of his or her pay on payday, beating and raping in added viciousness. Racketeers posing as lawyers promise to get legal work permits, collecting their payments in advance and delivering nothing. Forgers sell fake documents on the installment plan for $1,000 a set—yet the documents are not good enough to pass inspection. Marriage brokers sell phony weddings for $1,000 that also do not pass INS inspection. And used car dealers sell junk cars at double or triple their usual price.

All of these observations, all of the stories, all of the data lead to one inescapable question. How is it that this institution can exist today in the United States, penetrating every state and every large city with its poison? Its history is as old as the nation's first immigration law, but its modern evolution can be found within the twisted practices of immigration regulation that had their beginnings in the late nineteenth century.

2: PAVING THE WAY FOR UNDERGROUND IMMIGRATION

> Our progress in degeneracy appears to me to be pretty
> rapid. As a nation we began by declaring that "all men
> are created equal." We now practically read it "all men
> are created equal except Negroes." When the
> Know-Nothings get control, it will read "all men are
> created equal except Negroes and foreigners and
> Catholics." When it comes to this I should prefer
> emigrating to some country where they make no
> pretence of loving liberty – to Russia for instance, where
> despotism can be taken pure and without the base alloy
> of hypocrisy.
> *– Letter from Abraham Lincoln to his friend James Speed, 1855*

A few miles north and west of Tecate, USA – twin town to the more
populous Tecate, Mexico – up and down a dusty road that turns to mud
in the occasional flash floods, squats a relic of Mexican history, an
adobe rancheria, now owned by a gringo couple. Its land runs for forty
acres, stopped on the south by the Mexican-American border, marked
here by only a sprawling clump of bamboo. Aside from the bamboo and
lush green trees and flowers and grass of the little rancho, the entire
vista is a view of desolation, of bare, jagged mountains and desert, even
though the water table is only thirty-five feet below ground. The kind-
est act of hospitality in this dried out place is the offer of a glass of
fresh well water.

Walking back along the dirt road down toward town, one sees the
border begin to take shape in the form of occasional posts linked by a
single rusted multi-stranded steel cable strung through the holes at the
top of the posts. Closer to town the cable is covered, here and there, by a
drop cloth of torn and mangled barbed wire. Parallel to the road, on the
other side of the cable, is an equally dusty road, a Mexican road.

It is at this place, in the mid-afternoon silence of this barren region,
that one pauses to question what a national border is, exactly. Is it a
three-foot post anchored in a plot of desert that no one apparently
wants?

One asks if the creosote bush, rooted on the south side of the post but
sprawling over into the north, is an American bush or a Mexican bush.
And the occasional bird crossing high above without even pausing for
the tiny post and cable below it. Does it change from an American bird
to a Mexican bird as it crosses, and on which side of the cable is it a
"legal" bird? And the shadow cast by the pole like a sundial. Is it Mexican at one hour and American at another? The questions are as ridicul-

ous as they seem, until one looks more closely at the land around the post and the cable.

On the Mexican side are rows of dusty, tiny wooden houses. It is afternoon and there is little activity around them. In front of one of them a recent-model dust-covered Cadillac sits empty and still.

And on the American side, looking up into the desert foothills that no one seems to want, are footpaths twisting through the weeds and scrub brush, ground down into sand from many travelers. The paths lead off into the rocky mountain clusters that separate this stretch of desert like a horseshoe from the agricultural belt of San Diego County a few dozen miles to the west, and from the heartland of California winter harvests in Imperial County farther to the east. Along nearly a dozen sandy footpaths are strewn everything from plastic water bottles to a torn child's sweater, from a pair of worn down women's heels with a hole in one sole to a single child's shoe missing its laces: a litter of human relics leading up the paths. And then one understands that the posts and the cable have meaning, that a border is something after all; for the remnants of human usage dropped along the paths mark the desperation of border crossers, running at night from the Border Patrol. Only in desperation would a person leave behind a plastic water bottle in this desolate land, or a woman her shoes, or a child a sweater against the cold night and chill winds that howl down from the mountains.

One takes a second look at the cable and sees that everything may cross it without interruption – water from flash floods, dust kicked up by winds or cars, snakes, the shade made by the sun striking the post. Even money may cross the border without interruption through telephone transactions – multi-million-dollar currency deals that pass back and forth with as much ease as the buzzard circling in its search for food below.

Only one of nature's creations must stop on account of a post and a cable no thicker than a good-sized rope: people. Men and women and children who are looking for work, or maybe trying to join their families somewhere farther north.

What is it that caused men to bring this heavy cable, and anchor the posts, and stretch the cable between the posts to mark an invisible line? What is it that caused men to make a line where nature had no reason for one?

By early evening, as the midday sun stretches its shadows longer across the land, the reason for this rusted cable and its barbed wire drop cloth reveals itself as the people living both north and south begin coming home. Kids on the south side are playing on the dirt road, and later their parents come home and shout at some of them. The rows of wooden houses are now homes, full of people and activity. And the people are all brown people. On the north side, where some have brought mobile homes and planted them in the foothills so they have quiet and clean air for their retirement, men and women have come out to enjoy the evening air. And other people come by car to small houses, back from a day's work. And on the north side, most of the people are white.

Immigration to the U.S. was impeded only by nature's boundaries until there were enough white people spreading out from the Atlantic Coast to think they made a nation, enough of a nation to declare their independence from foreign rule and make up boundaries of their own. And then immigration became a fight between the white people already settled as citizens and new people from other countries recruited to the land by employers hungry for cheap labor. And the founders of the new nation began to think there were enough people already in the land. In 1797 their Congress deliberated and decided that since the country was already sufficiently well populated, new people who might want to become citizens and have a voice in the governing of their lives should be discouraged. The Congress passed a law that required fourteen years' residence before a newcomer could become a citizen. The law expired after two years and future Congresses moved on to more important things. New immigrants were left unharmed by Congress for almost a century, despite the agitation of the country's founders, their sons, and grandsons who continually campaigned against the newcomers. Later the nativists were joined by labor groups, but the two combined were on the wrong side of the nation's hunger for workers. In 1864 Congress passed an immigrant labor act to encourage even more workers to come to do the job of nation building.

None of the petitions and riots of citizens could bring Congress to stop the immigration until the depression of 1873-1877, when Congress made its first concession and barred convicts, prostitutes, and mental and physical "incompetents" from entry to the U.S. But not much can stand in the way of a hungry market, and on the West Coast prostitutes continued to be imported, where they avoided contact with the law by entering overland from British Columbia and Baja, Mexico, to become a nation's first "illegal aliens."

Nativists and labor organizations increased their demands and won further concessions in 1882. Congress placed immigration law under its control and removed it from the hands of the several states, levied a head tax of fifty cents per immigrant to pay for federal inspection, and added a new class of people who could no longer enter the country legally – the poor and the hungry, "persons likely to become public charges." Congress locked the official door on the once-welcome. The law had little real effect as immigrants soon learned their way around the laws to become the nation's second class of "illegal aliens."

The emerging alliance between nativist and labor leaders was finally successful, in 1882, in getting Congress to act against Chinese immigrants. They had been recruited to do the heavy and dirty work of building railroads and washing white men's laundry, but had saved their money and began to settle down and open up businesses of their own and began to look more like permanent residents than just cheap, coolie labor who could be kicked and shoved around. When a shoe manufacturer in North Adams, Massachusetts, tried to break a strike with imported Chinese labor, Congress acted. It gave nativist and labor leaders the Chinese Exclusion Act to bar new Chinese immigration to the U.S. Meanwhile, in the West, employers still hungry for cheap labor took a clue from the wealthy Yankee entrepreneurs of Hawaii and began importing Japanese to replace the Chinese.

And, as organized labor finally, in 1885 and 1887, won real concessions from Congress – contract labor laws "aimed at the practice of certain employers importing cheap labor from abroad" – employers not only found their way around the law, but successfully lobbied for loopholes in the law for future use. Exempt from the contract labor laws were, among others, "foreigners temporarily residing in the U.S." The exemption became an early precedent for the recruitment of Mexican nationals.

Exclusionary immigration acts continued to proliferate through the beginning of the twentieth century, expanding the class of "undesirable aliens" and extending the time after which the immigrant who became a "public charge" could be deported.

In 1913, unions, in a strange alliance with Yankee business owners who saw their ethnic hegemony jeopardized, succeeded in getting Congress to approve a bill excluding illiterates from entry, but it was vetoed by President Taft. But nativist pressure and labor pressure were building against Japanese immigrants, against Hispanic immigrants, and against the increasing number of "racially inferior" persecuted Jews and Poles and Slavs who sought the promise of a new land. By 1917, unions and Yankee racism prevailed, and the illiteracy law passed over President Wilson's veto. And, to reinforce the ban against the "yellow peril," Congress created an "Asiatic Barred Zone," providing that no Asian could become a U.S. citizen.

But the 1917 laws again had a loophole for employers in search of cheap labor. This one provided that the commissioner general of immigration could admit, for temporary employment, various classes of foreign workers. Among these were agricultural workers. An alleged wartime shortage of labor gave employers the excuse they needed, and in 1918 the commissioner general opened the gates to such temporary workers, exempting Mexican nationals from the head tax, the literacy laws, and the contract labor laws. Employers managed to hold onto their exemption until 1921, despite the fact that the U.S. faced a brief postwar depression as factories and the military discharged their workers and soldiers to unemployment, or to jobs that paid less than they had before the war began.

This exemption became the first "bracero program," and when it ended, employers continued to hire cheap labor shipped to them from Mexico. The exemption set a pattern of labor migration from Mexico to temporary work in U.S. fields and ranches that continues virtually unchanged to this day. The same Mexican villages that sent temporary workers in the 1920s sent them again in the 1940s, and still continue to send them to satisfy the craving for cheap workers.

By 1924 the nativists, the restrictionists, the isolationists, and the racists held control of Congress. And the sentiment against immigrants was widespread in the public. Just as the Know Nothings had earlier marched, and rioted, and attacked an earlier wave of Irish immigrants, new nativists, protesting immigrants from Slavic nations and Jews fleeing persecution, swelled the ranks of the Ku Klux Klan to more than three million. Congress finally shut the door on immigration, to preserve the nation's "ethnic and racial balance" and its white majority by restricting not only the numbers of people who could enter the country, but by setting "national origins" quotas for the immigrants as well. The 1924 Immigration Act set quotas for immigrants from each country based on their presence as reflected in the 1890 census, and allowed for a revision of these quotas in accord with the "national origins" of American citizens as recorded in the 1920 census (the numbers of which were finally calculated and passed into law in 1929). The 1924 Immigration Act prohibited the immigration of all those ineligible to become citizens (including Asians, as a result of the 1917 Asiatic Barred Zone law) and gave no quota to Africa, thereby excluding black immigrants.

The law maintained the classes of inadmissible immigrants from all the earlier laws and added additional ones. These included persons falling under the post-World War I Alien and Sedition Acts, and a general class of people who could be banned on the grounds of "moral turpitude." As an additional disincentive to keep foreigners from landing on U.S. shores, it charged U.S. consular officials in foreign countries with distributing visas to would-be immigrants who had to supply not only proof that they weren't anarchists or revolutionaries, but also a statement from police attesting to their good "moral character." In addition, they had to prove to the satisfaction of the consular official that they would not become "public charges" after landing in the U.S. In a compromise move with those who demanded that national origins quotas also be applied to limit Hispanic immigrants, the border between the U.S. and Mexico was strengthened, marked with fences, wires, and cables, and patrolled by a newly created Border Patrol.

The 1924 law provided not only legal justification for the exclusion of racially and otherwise "undesirable" persons, but for massive deportations of those who, once here, became public charges, violated U.S. law, or engaged in alleged anarchist or seditionist acts. The law, which remained the basis of U.S. immigration law until 1965, kept the imported cheap laborer and the nonwhite and non-Christian foreigner in his place—protected by few civil rights while in the U.S. and tossed out when he was no longer wanted. As a result of the 1924 law, thirteen states passed legislation stating that "aliens ineligible for naturalization" (primarily Asians) were prohibited from owning property. In 1929, bowing to still rampant nativist pressures against Mexicans, Congress made it a misdemeanor to enter the U.S. without government permission.

The onset of the Great Depression proved the value of the law to its supporters. When a zealous secretary of labor told President Hoover that there were 400,000 "illegal aliens" in the U.S. who could be arrested and deported, Hoover ordered them found and kicked out. Police and federal authorities carrying out the Hoover plan pursued the foreign born with vengeance, raiding rooming houses, public restaurants, and immigrant clubs. They swept the streets for anyone who could be labeled an anarchist, a possible public charge, and those who could not prove citizenship.

Some states followed suit, even though states were supposedly barred from acting in immigration matters. California was among the first to rise to the challenge, as a Los Angeles County supervisor told reporters that "If we were rid of all the aliens who have entered this country illegally since 1931 ... our present unemployment would probably shrink to the proportions of a relatively unimportant flat spot in business." California and other states began their own "repatriation" programs, sending their police to raid primarily Mexican neighborhoods and towns to find people who could be shipped "back where they came from." No tabulations of the success of such state and locally sponsored "repatriation" programs exist, but some historians estimate that more than one million undocumented Mexicans were either deported or left voluntarily, and that more than 400,000 Mexican-American citizens were also returned to Mexico. The state programs proved much more effective than the lawful federal program. Only about 200,000 were deported by the federal government during the entire Depression.

Another of President Hoover's acts was to order consular officials to deny a visa to any person who was *ever likely* to become a public charge. The Hoover order was carried out enthusiastically and immigration came to a virtual end. This order stayed in effect even during the Roosevelt administration. As a result, tens of thousands of Jews and others fleeing Nazi persecution were denied visas. As the plight of the Jews under Hitler's regime became apparent to all who could read a newspaper, some members of Congress tried repeatedly to overturn the Hoover order, but they were outnumbered by those who preferred to outlaw immigration altogether. Summarizing the sentiment of Congress during the decade, U.S. Representative Martin Dies—the pre-McCarthy communist hunter—said: "We must ignore the tears of sobbing sentimentalists and internationalists, and we must permanently close, lock and bar the gates of our country to new immigration waves and then throw the keys away."

America's entry into World War II in 1941 was immediately followed by the internment of more than 100,000 Japanese in concentration camps and the confiscation of their property, as prejudice against Asian peoples again surfaced in California. The biases inherent in the 1924 Immigration Act and the laws following it had set the tone that allowed for the incarceration not only of Japanese ineligible to become citizens, but their Amercan-born-citizen children as well. And, as China was now technically an ally, the Chinese Exclusion Act was rescinded in 1943 and a quota was given to Chinese immigrants: 105 people per year.

The war once again gave employers of cheap labor the excuse they needed to legalize the de facto practice of recruiting Mexican nationals whenever needed, lawfully or not. In 1942, under U.S. pressure, Mexico signed a treaty with the United States allowing for the importation of Mexican laborers for American employers. One year later, however, appalled at the treatment her citizens received in Texas, Mexico forbade them to work there under the treaty. Texas farmers and ranchers again returned to their de facto practice. In 1947, Mexico declined to renew most parts of the treaty, and the rest of the American employers in search of cheap labor also returned to their underground employment practices. Meanwhile, as postwar anticommunist hysteria blossomed, so did the fear of "illegal aliens." Using this fear, and the excuse of a labor shortage because of the Korean War, Congress enacted Public Law 78, the Bracero Program, entitling employers to contract for as many Mexican farm laborers as they wanted. Employers, however, did not trust the permanence of PL 78, and so, in early 1952, persuaded Congress to exempt them from penalties for hiring "illegal aliens," an exemption that was known as the Texas Proviso, and was included in the subsequent 1952 Immigration Act.

Amidst the growing national anticommunist hysteria, and sensing an oncoming recession, the federal government once again used its power to deport "illegal aliens." In 1954, federal agents, assisted by the military, began Operation Wetback, and by the conclusion of the year, more than one million Mexicans, many of whom were American citizens, were deported.

The Bracero Program again provided evidence that nonwhites were welcome in the U.S. as cheap labor but not as citizens. During the twenty-two-year history of the program, some five million temporary workers were imported, while fewer than one-tenth that number were admitted as permanent residents. The Border Patrol became the gracious enforcer of the "worker-not-resident" thesis by ensuring that all Mexican temporary workers were deported at the end of the harvesting season.

In 1964, domestic farm workers finally won the sympathy of Congress. They testified that PL 78 not only excluded them from jobs but held wages down and prevented them from organizing unions, and Congress ended its traditional biennual renewal of the law. Wages of domestic farm workers rose more than 5 percent in 1965 and their unemployment rate dropped significantly. Within a year, however, farmers in search of cheap, captive labor returned to their earlier, de facto practices, with full protection of the Texas Proviso they had so providently maneuvered through Congress more than a decade earlier.

One cornerstone of the contemporary slave trade was cemented in place.

As night comes to Tecate, the darkness provides some measure of security for the people on the south side of the cable marking the line between two races, white and brown. The people begin to come across the steel cable, grinding down the sand of the footpaths further, and running in fear if they hear the sounds of the Border Patrol, dropping their small belongings as they try to hide. By morning, many have reached safety.

In the morning, east and north of Tecate, a van pulls up to a backroad house where a nondescript semitrailer truck waits. As people sneak from the house to the truck, the doors of the somber dark green van open and a dozen brown-skinned people climb from its crowded quarters to join the others in the semi. Not all of them are Mexicans. Some are from South and Central America. And not all of them are being shipped to jobs on farms and ranches. Many are en route to jobs in Chicago-area light industries, or to restaurants in Washington, D. C., or to Los Angeles garment factories. For in the mid-1960s, America's hunger for cheap labor had grown and spread to other industries besides agriculture. And her foreign policies had created new sources of cheap and captive labor.

3: OPENING NEW ROUTES FOR UNDERGROUND IMMIGRANTS

Four years after Rafael Trujillo grabbed power in 1930 over the Spanish-speaking two thirds of the Caribbean island that shares a boundary with Haiti and looks across a channel to Puerto Rico, a boy was born in a small village of the Dominican Republic. The boy's father and mother rejoiced, for the boy was healthy and strong. Even the child's seven older brothers and sisters felt the happiness of the birth, for they knew already that not all babies were born healthy and strong, and that many had come into the world stillborn. The family held a small party at his baptism, and, in the poverty and harshness of the land huddling in the southern side of the mountains that cross the country from east to west, the neighboring people and relatives brought such small gifts as they could to help celebrate the arrival of a sixth healthy son.

The boy grew to be a man. And, as a man, he asked the reporters who wrote about him not to use his true name, so the reporters gave him a name of their own making. It is just as well that he remains without a name, an unknown immigrant much like an unknown soldier, a symbol of so many things bigger than one man alone. This man – standing five foot eight, with penetrating dark eyes that look straight at the people who talk with him, and a body that, though slim, is built of strong muscles from heavy work – is now one of New York City's undocumented workers. His story symbolizes the forces of his own country and the forces of the United States that not only shaped his own life, but built a new route of underground immigration to the United States.

The boy's father died when he was only two, leaving his mother alone with six sons and two daughters to feed and care for. The family was not rich, but it was not entirely poor, for there was one pair of shoes that was shared among the brothers. Since it was a law at the time that no child could attend school without shoes, the boy missed most days of school. "I was lucky if I went one day a week," he explains. "There was no breakfast, there was no money for lunch." When he and his next-oldest brother did go to school, they used the single pair of shoes between them. "My brother used to wear one and I'd wear the other, and my mother would wrap a bandage around the other foot and claim we'd hurt our feet and couldn't wear a shoe."

When the boy was twelve he began working full time, as had his other brothers and sisters before him, to keep the family going. His first work was sewing trousers for fifteen cents a pair. With his money, he recalls, the family would buy green bananas, wheat, and some vegetables. By the time he was sixteen he gave up on sewing pants. "It was no sense. Everyone was making pants. Jobs were so scarce that when one came up everyone would dive for it. You learned how to be a scavenger."

But the young man had ambitions and thought that if he left his village for the capital, Santo Domingo, surely he could get a job. Once there, one of his cousins took him on, and he helped his cousin run a taxi service. "Soon everyone was running a taxi service, so that didn't pay either."

By then one of his sisters had married a general repairman who took him in and began teaching him how to do odd jobs. Soon, though, his brother-in-law got sick and the business ended. But while he had been working with his brother-in-law, making $1.50 a week, he had begun to save pennies for a passport. He finally got his passport, but was not able to get a visa to come to the United States. America was growing restive about Trujillo, the Butcher of the Caribbean, who had begun to try to compete with American-owned companies. Exiles from the island were already planning a revolution.

A friend from his home town worked for the local police force and managed to get him a job with Trujillo's police. He did not question the politics or morality of working at such a job, for even the church continued to praise Trujillo. The job paid $74 a month, enough to make a life with some left over to send back home to help his mother, and even enough to begin to save until he could find another way to come to the United States. After two years his boss on the police force told him he should get some education and study to become a priest. The officer sent him to the mission. He went, even though he earned nothing as a student at the mission, for no one questioned such an order. At the mission one of the teachers helped him with small gifts: soap, food, and even a little money for clothes.

In 1960, the U.S. broke off diplomatic relations with the republic, for, as anticommunist as Trujillo claimed to be, not even the U.S. could bear the stink of his bloody and corrupt regime. In 1961, with help from the CIA, Trujillo was assassinated. The United States again opened its doors a small crack to immigrants from the republic, and after the assassination, 3,045 immigrants were granted permission to leave for the United States. But these visas were for the literate and the educated.

Trujillo's death left a power vacuum with three groups struggling for ascendancy: the elite of Trujillo's creation, the more traditional elite, and a third group—reformers who succeeded in installing Juan Bosch in power as head of the republic in 1962. It was no longer a time for a former policeman who had worked for Trujillo to stay at the mission, and the young man married the teacher who had helped him. The woman supported him, for she still had a job, and the man went back to scavenging. From the pieces of junk he was able to sell or trade, and the occasional odd job he could pick up, he continued to send a bit of money to his mother, who was now supporting one of his brothers and the brother's two children, as well as one of his sisters.

After seven months Bosch was deposed by his military, who, as part of an American aid package, had received special training and new equipment. The doors to the U.S. opened a bit wider, and 4,603 immigrants were admitted from the republic in 1962, and 10,683 in 1963. But the republic was still not stable, and reformers continued their plans, in exile, to reinstate Bosch. By 1965 they had built enough power, and civil war broke out. This time the U.S. turned its back on Bosch, openly declaring it didn't want "another Cuba, another communist country," in the Caribbean. Twenty thousand U.S. Marines were sent to restore order and to ensure the election of a person more to America's liking, Juaquin Balaguer. Members of Balaguer's first government were even briefly paid with U.S. funds. And the nation finally appeared to be stabilized. The U.S. then opened its doors wide to immigrants from the republic, and to tourists as well. In 1966, it granted 16,503 immigrant visas and thousands of tourist visas.

When Balaguer was installed, the man, born thirty-one years earlier in a poor village, was finally able to get a tourist visa to the United States. With the money he had been saving all these years he took the passport and the one-month tourist visa and flew to New York, landing there with only eleven dollars and the address of some Dominican women there his wife had known. The women were in the U.S. illegally and had learned how to get jobs and where to go. They helped the man and he got the first of many jobs, putting his general repair skills to good use, continually telling his bosses that his immigration papers would be coming soon. When the papers did not come, he was fired. He finally went to an employment agency that spotted him as an "illegal alien" and directed him to the kind of places that wanted such workers. On his last job, he worked as a general repairman at a motel, doing the heavy work and the cleaning. He was given a room in the basement. After a week, he asked for his pay and the boss told him that if he wanted his money he should call immigration. There were no jobs after this and the man decided, in 1967, to return home, to see if things might have improved. As he left New York he was warned that he could never come back because he had broken the law by overstaying his tourist visa.

"Things were even worse than when I left," he recalled to the newspaper interviewer. "Once I borrowed ten dollars to go from Santo Domingo to my mother's house. Of that, three dollars was for the carfare. When I'd spent all but the dollar fifty it takes to get back to Santo Domingo, I had to use it to buy food for the little girl next door. She was starving to death. I had to."

He tried to get any job he could in Santo Domingo. There was an ad for insurance salesmen and he got a job, but nobody could afford to buy insurance. Finally he returned to the mission where the priest took him on, giving him room and board in exchange for his work. As he grew more desperate, he went back to the American consulate to try to get a visa. But they knew he had violated the terms of his first visa, and denied him a new one.

After three years he made friends with a Puerto Rican who sold forged documents and agreed to take an IOU for $1,000. For this the man received a forged Puerto Rican birth certificate and help to get back to New York. When he arrived, standing his full five feet, eight inches, he weighed only 98 pounds. By 1971 he was again doing odd jobs at less than the minimum wage for bosses who took advantage of his illegal status. But he considered himself lucky. At least he had a bit of money to send home, and he weighed 112 pounds. He was trying to save money to help others from his family leave their desperation and join him in New York's underground labor market.

By 1971, the routes of entry to the United States for those who were too poor, for all those whom the United States would not accept as immigrants, were well established. And, by 1971, the U.S. knew that many of those who got tourist visas were staying permanently and ordered its consular officials to clamp down on the number of tourist visas they issued, and to tighten their screening of applicants.

But for the person who had been rejected by the consulate, there were travel agents in New York, Puerto Rico, and the Dominican Republic who acted as brokers and provided false papers, housing, and even jobs. Along the Avenida Maximo Gomez, just outside the U.S. consulate in Santo Domingo, a number of people were available to provide false passports and papers for $350 to $1,000, depending on the ability to pay. Alien registration cards and social security cards were the best of the documents available, and the market for them flourished.

And if the emigrant did not like these, he or she could go to the "consul of Bella Vista," the man known by the name of the Santiago neighborhood where he lived in his sixty-thousand dollar house, and whose specialty was visa fixing. The consul of Bella Vista employed an array of hustlers and couriers in New York and Puerto Rico. And in

New York one could get credit, for the consul also employed collectors there.

Among the biggest operators was one known as Doña Mercedes, who, because she was over seventy years old, was never jailed. Neither were the other big operators jailed because they had become wealthy and respected.

By 1971, a decade after the exodus began with Trujillo's assassination, a local police official was able to comment that "next to sugar, the biggest export of the Dominican Republic is people."

The exodus had not stopped by 1974 because as old routes closed, new "consulates" opened. Tourist visa rejection rates ran as high as 50 percent. A new "consul" had opened operations, the consul at Miches, a northeast coastal town where, among the ramshackle clutter of seemingly untended pigs, and among horsemen traveling through town with machetes for the sugar crop, the "consul" arranged, for $150, trips on fishing boats to Puerto Rico across the Mona Channel. Once in Puerto Rico, the document fixers provided papers proving Puerto Rican birth, and one was free, as an "American citizen," to travel to New York on one of the jumbo jets in relative peace.

Nor had the industry stopped several years later, for the cause of the emigration—the desperation of poverty—was even worse than it had been.

Balaguer's regime brought stability to the Dominican Republic, and American investment followed. It opened up four "free zones," where business need not pay taxes for twenty years. Wages were low, a further incentive to business. Gulf and Western, in 1967, opened the largest sugar refinery in the world, and by 1977 directly controlled at least 8 percent of all the cultivated land in the country. By 1977, a quarter of the land under cultivation went into sugar production, as Gulf and Western contracted with local farmers for their sugar crop, a cash export that was thought good for the development of the national economy. But the early Gulf and Western contracts obliged the farmers to plant every inch of their land in cane, leaving no room to grow food for their own tables. Balaguer cooperated with the investors. In 1974, when the people of a village seized some land that was about to be planted in cane to plant food with seeds supplied by sympathetic merchants, the army was called in and the people's food crops were plowed under so the landowners could plant cane.

Per capita income in the nation increased, but most of it stayed in the hands of the elite landowners who increased their income. The poor, meanwhile, paid twice as much for food, and per capita production of food decreased as more and more land was taken for cash crops.

Eighty percent of the workforce found jobs in sugar, but this is only seasonal work, and earnings from it, in 1977, were only three dollars per ton of cane harvested. Mill workers, meanwhile, earned thirty to forty cents per hour. By the end of 1977, inflation had topped 16 percent and unemployment in some areas exceeded 40 percent.

When Balaguer was deposed in 1978 with the help of the U.S., the republic had a billion-dollar debt and a balance of payments deficit nearly half as large.

The Dominican Republic is a land rich with minerals and fertile land, but few of the people share the wealth. Indeed, the vast majority grow poorer.

The story of the unknown Dominican symbolizes more than those things that brought an underground workforce to Brooklyn, Queens, Manhattan, and New Jersey. It is also very much the tale of the development of many routes of underground migration to the U.S. from many nations. Where the U.S. has gone in the developing world (or in supposedly developed countries) with its armies, or with its extraordinary CIA activities, or with its industries in search of both cheap labor and new consumer markets, there have followed legal emigrants believing that life would be better for them in the land that is the source of such apparent wealth. And along with the legal immigrants have come those who are forbidden to come, either because they are too poor or because they have tried legal channels only to learn, for one reason or another, that legal immigration to the U.S. was somehow not meant to include them. The latter are often the castoffs of two societies: their own developing domestic economy, which increases the wealth of the rich and often the poverty of the poor, and the United States', which officially has proclaimed she does not want the poor.

As much as she sells her corporate products to consumers here and abroad, America also sells an image of herself to foreign nations—a lure for anyone with access to a television set or U.S. publications and films. An El Salvadorian, for example, was drawn to the U.S. not only by the stories that his friends told him, which he was wise enough to know were often exaggerated, but by the American magazines and movies he saw in San Salvador. From these, he gauged, the United States was his best hope for a better future. Ineligible for legal immigration, and denied a tourist visa, he became the first of his family to join the underground immigration from El Salvador to the U.S.

American media, especially television, are so compelling that, in an isolated Mexican town where most of the men already migrate to seasonal jobs in the U.S. — a town of about 2,100 souls, forty miles from any real road save a rock-strewn creek-bed path, connected to the rest of the country by electric cables and a two-way radio (but no telephones) — the first American gift brought home by one of the migrant workers now sits where all can view it: a television, on which are broadcast all the supposed wonders of the U.S. and its values. Regularly advertised on this and other Mexican television sets are General Motors and Ford autos, and to accompany the cars — advertised in a mountain town that no car can reach during most of the year — are such wonders as Goodyear, Goodrich, Firestone, and Uniroyal auto products. American foods are also advertised: both Coca-Cola and Pepsi, Heinz ketchup and baby food, Kraft mayonnaise and processed cheese, and the range of General Foods consumer items. The television, as it has in so many towns and cities throughout the world, has changed not only people's aspirations, but their eating habits as well. The extra pesos, once spent on a little extra corn or milk, are now spent on Pepsi or Coke, the status symbol of the day, even among the poor.

Not only advertising spreads the word about a better world in the U.S. Programs broadcast throughout the free world do also. As one Mexican observer put it, "It is possible for the children of our country to know more about the virtues of the Marines, the wonders of Walt Disney, Jefferson's advanced ideas, the acts of Superman, than of the history of Mexico, the life of Juárez, the political significance of Zapata, or the needs of our country." Companies such as CBS have "sold" the U.S. to the emerging middle class and marginally poor alike in one hundred or more nations.

The measure of underground immigration to the U.S. can in part be taken by the extent of her interests, both political and economic, in foreign lands. Typifying the development of new routes of underground emigration to the U.S. have been American activities in both the Philippines and South Korea, major sources of our underground and undocumented population.

The Philippines, for years under a brutal martial law imposed by the regime of Ferdinand Marcos, and an outpost against the alleged threat of communism, has been the recipient of millions of dollars in American aid. The aid was used to train and equip Marcos's military and police, maintaining a climate of political stability. Foreign investments were encouraged, as were economic aid projects that sought to create financial stability in the nation by turning production to exports. Virtually her entire agricultural production is now devoted to cash export crops: sugar, bananas, coconuts, rubber, coffee, and cocoa. As a result, land has been removed from food production and the type of subsistence farming that once fed the Filipino poor. Much of the land has gone into production for American-owned companies such as Del Monte and Dole. The average Filipino diet now stands at just one hundred calories more per day than the average in Bangladesh. There can be little question that those who seek to leave the Philippines, where 60 percent of the television programming is provided by American companies, will choose the nation of "Bonanza" and "I Love Lucy" as his or her economic refuge from poverty. The Filipinos excluded from legal emigration to the U.S. come by illegal channels across a new route, the Pacific route to Hawaii, San Francisco, or Los Angeles.

Corporate and U.S. government presence bolstering the anticommunist regime of South Korea has had similar effects. Little more than a decade ago South Korea was the only noncommunist Asian nation, one of four Asian countries listed by the World Bank as able to supply adequate food for her own people, despite the fact that it has one of the lowest ratios of arable crop land per person in the world – one-tenth of one acre. Additionally, South Korea has one of the lowest population growth rates in the developing world. In other words, after recovering from the devastation of the 1950s war, South Korea has been doing quite well for her people. Within the "stabilized" political and economic climate, America has found a source not only for wise investment, but for cheap labor as well. In 1969, after American corporations began to develop South Korea into an export-producing nation through the U.S. Food for Peace program, South Korea was no longer food self-sufficient. Per capita daily wages averaged $1.76 for those employed. Her exports of livestock, now raised on what once was farmland, have increased. South Korea began exporting her people along another American-made Pacific route.

Apparently, the first Korea-to-U.S. smuggling route was ferreted out in 1972, just after President Park Chung Hee had placed South Korea under martial law. Charged with running the smuggling ring in 1973 were three West Virginia residents and one Maryland resident, who operated from Maryland, New York City, Philadelphia, Los Angeles, Dallas, Atlanta, Newark, and Trenton, New Jersey. The team, which included a former member of the South Korean embassy staff, arranged bogus job offers which were then used by the immigrants to obtain entry into the U.S. under provisions of the immigration act providing for the entry of specially qualified people under a special visa. It was charged that the team had helped more than three thousand aliens into the U.S. at fees ranging from two hundred to fifteen hundred dollars. Most of the fraudulent entrants were said to be Korean, although further investigation showed that the team also assisted Caribbean immigrants.

In 1979, Argentinian police broke up a Korean smuggling ring operating with the help of employees of the U.S. consulate in Buenos Aires, which may have been in continuous operation for six years. In this scheme, refugees from both North and South Korea entered Argentina with fraudulent documents. They then went to a small section of Buenos Aires called Koreatown, where they located travel agents who steered them to an underground "consulate" operating only four blocks from the U.S. embassy. This "ring" was run by an employee of the official U.S. consulate who had access to the American embassy's visa stamp. The Koreans paid between one and three thousand dollars each to have their passports stamped, and then, apparently, left for the United States. Argentinian police speculated that the ring might have taken in as much as five million dollars from as many as three thousand Koreans before it was closed down.

Yet another "consulate" for Koreans was based in Miami and operated by two unidentified Koreans, who wrote letters to the U.S. consulate in Seoul requesting transit visas for certain Korean sailors who supposedly were scheduled to join ship crews in Miami. Once the Koreans arrived in Miami, the "sailors" boarded ships for short periods until contact could be made with smugglers, who flew them to Los Angeles where they were inducted into the U.S. Army, allegedly by five Army recruiters who were later arrested. The Army scheme had run from some time prior to 1977 until 1979 when it was finally cracked. U.S. authorities learned about it by reading a translation of a *Korean Times* article on fraudulent enlistments.

The Army was not the lone haven for foreign nationals seeking entry into the U.S. The Marines, in 1978, began a large-scale investigation of Panamanians who had fraudulently enlisted with the alleged help of four New York Marine recruiters. A Navy spokesman, meanwhile, revealed that, since 1974, 450 nonresident aliens had been discovered within its ranks. The spokesman would not speculate on how many went undetected.

Similar stories and data apply equally well to other routes of immigration, where others have made the poor more poor, and where American consuls cannot let them immigrate because they are too poor. Data from Nationalist China, India, Hong Kong, and Thailand; Colombia, Ecuador, Peru, and Argentina; Haiti and Jamaica; from Greece and Iran; and from Central America—all are similar. And all, in the early 1960s, had already established the "consuls," visa fixers, passport forgers, smugglers, and others who gave the poor and the persecuted entrance to a country that would not legally accept them.

Four women who tried to get jobs in the U.S. by the underground route from El Salvador, who were caught in 1978 soon after they crossed the U.S. border, perhaps speak best for all of the poor and hungry who have sought work in the American underground labor market.

Antonia Martinez left her sixteen-month-old daughter with her mother in the fishing port of La Union, where the family tried to make a living feeding fishermen. As she explained, when no boats came in there was no money. "Poor people have no chance at all."

Rosa del Carmen Romero, twenty-four, left her two children with a grandmother in Cantonamata, and left her job in the corn fields. "I am poor. The only work is with the corn in the summer. It's very hard work. They pay one dollar American to pick one hundred pounds of corn. If it's a good day, I can make between eighty and one hundred pounds."

Rosa Urbina, twenty-nine, earned about fifty cents a day working as a seamstress. There are no public schools for her children, a girl, seven, and a boy, ten. The cost of their tuition and books at a private school, sixty dollars a year, thinned her already pitiful earnings. "The law, the government, the people who have the money just take advantage of the poor people," she said.

Lucia Hernandez, thirty-five and the mother of six children, was a sharecropper whose husband had long ago abandoned them. Her mother is fifty. When the harvest was good, she could make between one and two dollars a day. But there were no earnings when the cash harvest was brought in. Meanwhile, said Lucia Hernandez, her mother will not live much longer if all she has to look forward to is the hard work of sharecropping.

The journalist who interviewed the women praised them for their courage in trying such a long trip to a country where, they said, they knew no one. Lucia Hernandez explained, "It is not an act of courage. It's an act of anguish."

As the U.S. embassy spokesman in San Salvador, Vytas Dambrava, explained, "Poor people try to get to the U.S. just to have some kind of future."

4: IN SEARCH OF SOME KIND OF FUTURE

A reporter asked a Catholic nun who manages a volunteer immigrant service center in a Laredo, Texas, storefront office a question she has heard hundreds of times. "How many of them are there? How many illegals?" She settled back in her chair, chin on crossed hands, elbows propped on the chair's wooden arms, and wearily responded, "Who can count them? They are like the pigeons in the park."

In fact, no one is ever likely to count them. They are a population in hiding. Every attempt to count them in the past has been a numbers game played by lobbyists, politicans, and government agencies, each using numbers for their own agendas: more restrictive laws, more money for local hospitals and services, and more money for enforcement of laws already in the Immigration and Nationality Act. Estimates made during the Nixon administration went as high as twelve million. Under the Carter presidency the number also first fluctuated at around ten to twelve million, then it gradually edged down to "somewhere between two and six million," and finally, to the truth of the matter, "we don't know and we won't pretend to know."

Finding a total number of "illegal aliens" living in the U.S. has been a body-count game, much like the body count of "kills" during the Vietnam War. There are three mistakes in the way the government has played its game over the years. The first of these is that the number of undocumented immigrants was somehow thought to be tied to the apprehension rate of so-called deportable aliens. The number of these apprehensions, however, is not a total of individual people. Some of those who cross the U.S. border clandestinely from the south admit that they have been stopped two, three, even as many as twenty times. So, one million border apprehensions may have actually represented half a million people caught twice, a quarter of a million caught four times, or one hundred thousand caught ten times. No one knows and there has been no way of knowing.

The second error in the body-count game is that the U.S. has no way of knowing how many of its underground immigrants leave the country each year (or even how many U.S. citizens emigrate each year). A large segment of the workers in the underground market are apparently migrant workers, who leave either to return home once or twice a year (especially in the case of agricultural workers who leave once the harvest season is over), or who stay only long enough to build a grubstake to buy a small business or a decent house back home, or to pay off debts from some emergency. Estimates of the number of Mexicans who migrate both to and from the U.S. each year range from 70 to 90 percent of all the Mexicans in America's underground labor market.

31

The third and perhaps most damaging flaw of the body-count game is that when enforcement activities are stepped up in one area, the number of apprehensions in that area rises. The danger of basing underground population estimates on this faulty foundation is that it builds a false model of who it is that seeks to enter the U.S. clandestinely. As the House Judiciary Committee concluded as early as 1973, the reported number and source countries of undocumented immigrants are "primarily a function of [the] manpower and funds which are available to the INS." In recent years, in an effort to apprehend more "deportable aliens" for each dollar of the INS budget, as if there were some kind of scorecard that measured its performance, enforcement activities have been concentrated along the border with Mexico–where apprehensions are less costly than seeking out the "deportable aliens" entering through airports, through Canada, or those living in U.S. cities and towns. As a result, recent apprehension data report locating about 87 percent deportable Mexican nationals. This type of figure is too often translated by the media as meaning a "Mexican tide flooding across our borders," and builds a wetback syndrome of anti-Mexican sentiment. If enforcement were stepped up along the Canadian border, it is likely that the number of Italian, Eastern European, Asian, and Caribbean clandestine immigrants apprehended would rise. Were enforcement stepped up at airports, an entirely different statistical picture would be painted.

And these are just the beginnings of the statistical nightmare of the body-count game.

The Under-Counted

Under-represented in virtually every study of foreigners not legally allowed to live in the U.S. are those who have passed through an immigration point with documents that, on their face, entitle them to enter the U.S. legally. The variety of such documents is endless, but the one most frequently issued is the tourist visa. If, by renting new clothes, borrowing documents substantiating sufficient wealth, or by other means, the would-be immigrant can convince the consular official that he or she is prosperous enough to want to come to the U.S. only to spend money and not to stay, the tourist visa is among the easiest routes of entry to the U.S.

The U.S. government officially began encouraging tourism as a source of foreign exchange in 1961. As evidence of the success of this program, tourist entries to the United States were up from 2.6 million in 1967 to 7.6 million nine years later.

However, as the U.S. House Select Committee on Population reported in 1978, there was "no record of departure for 10 percent of the 7 million nonimmigrants arriving each year," a fact that buttressed the committee's estimate that "about 40 percent of the illegal aliens in the United States, slightly more than half of whom are female, are believed to be visa abusers."

The Immigration and Naturalization Service, in its own investigation into visa abuse, assigned a special team to investigate visa entrants at selected ports of entry to the U.S. The team found "twelve to fourteen" times the number of fraudulent entries than were found "during the routine operations of these ports." Based on these findings, the INS reported that "in excess of 500,000 malafide entries were projected to have successfully entered through the studied ports during fiscal year 1975." Fifty thousand of these entered through airports.

Who are the visa abusers? It is difficult to tell. The INS reported on a tiny sample of 185 applicants who had obtained visas but were denied entry at U.S. international ports. Their sample of ports was biased toward the land-entry points along the U.S.-Mexican border, which affected their results. In any case, according to the INS, "27 were from the Dominican Republic, 25 were from Mexico, 21 from Haiti, 20 from Jamaica," and "17 percent" were from Europe. The rest were from "other" countries. It was an intriguing way for the INS to present its findings. Alternately, and perhaps more sensibly, they could have been presented: Caribbean, 37 percent; Asia, Africa, Central America, and South America, 33 percent; Europe, 17 percent; and Mexico, 13 percent. The selection of Miami as one of the few international airports studied probably enhanced the number of Caribbean visa abusers found.

Visa issuance is at the sole discretion of the American consul of a foreign country, an employee of the U.S. Department of State, and therefore guided by U.S. foreign policy decisions as much as by immigration law. Such discretionary power was considered to be behind a demand from the Council on Hemispheric Affairs, a human rights organization, that the issuance of a tourist visa to a former Paraguayan police official, who has been accused by human rights groups of political torture-murders in his home country, be investigated by Congress. The man in question, Américo Peña-Irala, was arrested by federal agents after he was recognized in Brooklyn by a political refugee from his country. He had been issued a tourist visa in 1978 and had overstayed its term by nine months before he was recognized.

Foreign policy considerations are also often behind the issuance of a second type of frequently abused visa, the student visa. A 1975 General Accounting Office (GAO) report made this conclusion after a study, ordered by Congress, on the use of student visas: "As long as the law provides a means for various classes of nonimmigrants, such as foreign students, to proceed to the United States and provides administrative means for them to acquire lawful permanent resident [immigrant] status within the United States, an appreciable number will come ostensibly as nonimmigrants and attempt to acquire permanent resident status." The study further concluded that about 42 percent of the foreign students then present in the United States "are in illegal status because of overstaying their period of admission."

Not among their conclusions, but buried among their findings, was the fact that some foreign consular officials were aware that the students they admitted were fraudulently stating their intentions, but admitted them anyway. These were "students" from those nations then considered friendly to the United States. The GAO studied consular practices in Iran, Pakistan, Thailand, Brazil, Colombia, and Venezuela. The results were intriguing. The consulates issuing the most student visas were in Iran and Thailand which, during 1974, the fiscal year studied, were generally given favored treatment by the U.S. as alleged buffer zones against communism. The Tehran consulate issued 6,033 student visas and the Bangkok consulate 4,479 – a total of 10,512 visas. The four other nations studied accounted for only 4,555 student visas, 3,702 of these going to the three South American countries.

Consular officials in both Iran and Thailand admitted that student visa abuse was a common phenomenon. In Tehran, "the consular officers said there were about 16 [student visa brokers] in Iran. . . . Consular officers said that brokers would get a school for anyone and charged according to the student's need." In order to prove that they would be able to support themselves while studying in the U.S., a requirement for the visa, consular officials told the GAO, "It was very common for Iranians to borrow money for 2 or 3 days, just long enough to show proof of financial support." About half the sampling of visa applicants approved by the Tehran consulate and located in the U.S., according to the GAO, worked in violation of their visa status, indicating that consular officials, while aware of the fraudulent entry practices, did not enforce the laws rigidly.

Abuses were also reported in Thailand. According to the GAO, consular officials there said that "students can easily obtain certificates of eligibility from certain airlines, travel agencies, and businesses set up for this purpose. One student told a consular officer that he paid $500 to a travel agency to arrange everything. Consular officers also pointed out that one school in the United States issued a blank certificate to a Thai in the United States who sent it to a student in Thailand." Also, "During our interviews with 13 [Thai] visa applicants, we found that 12 had received their certificates of eligibility from friends or relatives in the United States and not from direct contact with the school." The story appeared the same. Consular officials seemed to be aware of abuses, but issued visas nonetheless. About half the sampling of Thai student visa users in the U.S. interviewed by the GAO worked in violation of visa stipulations.

As such practices as these are made public, they are inevitably halted, at least temporarily, and the would-be immigrant is forced to find alternate routes of entry, what is often described in INS terminology as "entry without inspection," or EWI. The EWIs include stowaways on foreign ships, those entering by small fishing boats from the Caribbean, those sometimes flown in by small aircraft, and those crossing land borders with Mexico and Canada as cargo of the slave trade.

Leading the list of EWIs who were apprehended by the INS crossing the Mexican border in the fiscal year ended September 30, 1978, were Mexicans, as might be presumed. Also crossing were nationals from the British West Indies, Belize, the Dominican Republic, El Salvador, Guatemala, Colombia, Ecuador, the Philippines, and Africa. While these nationalities were also reported as EWIs entering from Canada, more heavily represented among EWIs crossing from Canada were, as would also be expected, Canadians. Apparently preferring the Canadian border to the Mexican border, however, were Chinese, Greeks, Italians, and nationals of Great Britain. "Other Europeans" were represented about equally on both borders.

EWIs entering from Mexico outnumbered EWIs apprehended entering from Canada during fiscal year 1978 by about 250 to 1. This imbalance can be partly credited to the INS strategy of concentrating its Border Patrol agents along the Mexican border. It is probable that as long as this strategy persists, the Canadian EWIs will continually be among the under-counted in INS logs, as are visa abusers.

Having avoided apprehension by the INS, by whatever means, the clandestine foreign immigrants move on to work throughout the U.S., either to jobs that have been prearranged or to those found on their own.

Estimates of their population are usually erratic. The INS, for whatever reason, estimates a greater number than do local governments and agencies who work with immigrants, whatever their legal status.

Some population estimates, perhaps among the more reliable of the guesses in circulation as of 1979, included these:

Boston, metropolitan region	75,000	including Haitians, Guatemalans
Chicago, metropolitan region	300,000	apparently predominantly Hispanic, with a small community of Haitians
Detroit	——	no estimate, but known to include Canadians, Indians, and citizens of Great Britain and Caribbean countries
District of Columbia, metropolitan region	100,000	an area with probably the greatest variety of foreign nationals represented among its underground population. The figure also includes Northern Virginia, estimated to have an underground population composed of 40 percent from Central and South America, 40 percent from Europe and Africa, and the remainder including Caribbean islanders and Asians
Las Vegas	10,000	apparently mostly Hispanic
Los Angeles County	700,000	a melting pot of Hispanic peoples and Asian peoples with small pockets of Europeans
New York City	750,000	an early refuge for Dominicans, Haitians, Italians, Greeks, and Chinese. Another melting pot.

San Francisco Bay Area	75,000	including Hispanics, Chinese, Koreans, Canadians and others
Arizona	150,000	probably a grossly inflated figure, predominantly Hispanic migrant laborers
Colorado	26,500	
Florida	——	no reliable estimate, but includes Haitian refugees, other Caribbean natives, Hispanics, and Canadians
Hawaii	10,000	mostly Filipinos, Koreans, Canadians, and Pacific islanders
Iowa	4,000	
Kansas	12,500	
Louisiana	——	from at least 21 nations
Missouri	10,000	
Nebraska	3,000	
New Jersey	300,000	including Poles, Colombians, and others who have left New York in search of work
Rhode Island	2,500	

South Dakota	1,400	
Texas	——	only unreliable estimates are available, the highest being 800,000; most are apparently migrant workers
Utah	——	no estimate, but farm owners have been known to employ Mexicans en route to other states
Washington	5,000	mostly migrant workers, plus an unknown number of Canadians in Seattle
Wyoming	5,000	

Such are some population guesses. Somewhat more is known about the structure of the underground labor market itself. In the fiscal year ended September 30, 1978, the INS located a total of 230,530 "deportable aliens" who were employed at the time of their apprehension (686,137, meanwhile, were seeking work). The gross number of employed apprehendees was about equally divided between agricultural workers and "industry and other." Again, these INS data should be read with caution, because one apprehension may be equal to one person caught two or more times.

The previous year, the INS apprehended 268,000 employed "deportable aliens." One third of these, statistical review showed, were earning less than $2.50 per hour. Forty-five percent worked in agriculture, 31 percent in light industry, 5 percent in construction, and 2 percent in heavy industry.

Such is the lot of those who come to the U.S. in search of work. As the U.S. Department of State orders its consuls to restrict the number and types of visas they issue, closing one artery of escape from the kind of poverty that slowly sucks the spirit and strength from a people, would-be immigrants are forced to go to other "consuls," who, more frequently, resort to sending their clients via EWI routes. Along the EWI trail, there is an ever-increasing risk of being apprehended. The INS, for example, made more than one million apprehensions of "deportable aliens" in the U.S. in fiscal year 1978. Of these, nearly 70 percent were made within seventy-two hours after entry.

What kind of odds does the clandestine immigrant have of building a future once in the United States?

5: THE MEXICAN
CONNECTION—*POLLEROS* **AND COYOTES**

The odds of making it to a job in the United States without being caught by the U.S. Border Patrol are probably better for underground immigrants who can afford the services of a smuggler, or "coyote," than if he or she tries crossing into the U.S. without any help at all. In 1977 two students at the University of Arizona in Tucson interviewed 185 undocumented farm workers in California, Arizona, and Texas. Almost all were Mexican nationals. Of these, 89 reported they had no help at all, and had crossed the border on their own. These, the students said, "faced the highest apprehension rates and danger as they walked the one to eleven day journey northward across the harsh and barren desert in search of work. It was not uncommon, some of the undocumented reported, for the Border Patrol to find them lost in the desert, sometimes without food and water. Some of them reported having found dead human bodies along the route to the north."

Those who are not Mexican have little choice but to pay a smuggler, for they must not only leave their own town or village, they must cross Mexico and sometimes other foreign countries as well before they even have a chance of crossing the line that is their final barrier to hope for a better future.

There is, after all, little dishonor in paying a smuggler to help one flee from one country to another. Many thousands of people during the wars and revolutions of the twentieth century have bribed their way out of countries where they thought their lives were imperiled. As Germany prepared for World War II, many Jews and political dissidents who could manage to buy their way out of the Reich did so. In the early 1970s Switzerland was a haven for several specialists who smuggled people out of East Germany and other iron curtain nations to the West for a fee of about $10,000 per person. And by 1978 it was proven, at least to the satisfaction of Hong Kong officials, that many of the thousands of "boat people" fleeing Vietnam bought their way out with several thousand dollars' worth of gold per person, part of which went to the government and the rest to the shippers. Money for safe exit from one country to another—smuggling—is a business, a dangerous business but one with a long and mostly honorable tradition.

Smuggling people from Mexico to the U.S. began as early as the beginning of this century when the border between the two nations was first officially closed. Even today, in some Mexican villages, men are old enough to remember paying a coyote to get them across the border for work in the early 1900s, just as their sons did in the 1920s, and their grandsons and great-grandsons do today.

But in earlier times the Mexican routes were much safer than they are today, and chances of capture much less than now. What changed all this was the installation, in 1968 and 1969, of technological devices first developed for the Vietnam war. A variety of sensors were set up to spot would-be border crossers–heat sensors, vibration sensors, sound sensors, even visual sensors–all linked to computer terminals at central locations to give the U.S. Border Patrol computer read-outs of traffic on the U.S. side of the border. Aiding them today are helicopters and light aircraft carrying spotlights to illuminate the countryside, turning it all into what some Vietnam veterans have described as being more like a military combat zone than a border between two friendly nations.

As the conditions of border crossing became more difficult, the coyotes grew more sophisticated. The coyotes have now become extended, multinational business operations of their own. These rings not only operate on both sides of the border, but have contacts in Central and South America and in the Caribbean, as well as knowledge of whom to bribe in between. The network is so effective that when nighttime border checks in the U.S. were first accompanied by helicopters equipped with powerful spotlights, would-be immigrants in Quito, Ecuador, were told, just one week after the first chopper had made its test run, to bring dark clothes to help escape detection.

And, as conditions along the border turned into a war zone, smugglers began to develop a wartime mentality (as did the INS with its body-count game). The smuggling trade became a dangerous and dirty business. As a representative of Ecuador's ministry of government, Dr. Xavier Manrique Trujillo, explained in 1977, "Little by little, the smuggler takes the person for everything he has. It is a grim business. Most of the people mortgage what they have and sign contracts to continue to pay after they reach the United States . . . many of them are women, some with children. They are vulnerable."

After the Ecuadorian government had received several complaints from relatives of smugglers' victims, including one from a father who wrote that his daughter had been raped by the smugglers and arrived in the U.S. so badly traumatized that she could not even talk, it cooperated in a three-nation effort to put one multinational smuggling business out of operation. The Ecuadorian government put two undercover policewomen on the trail of the smugglers. The policewomen's story shows how one international ring operated.

The letter describing the young woman's rape mentioned a specific travel agency in Quito that had arranged her trip to the U.S. The policewomen went to the agency and were told, "The easiest way to get into the United States is illegally." They agreed, and paid $1,150 each to the travel agent for the trip, aware they they would need several hundred dollars more to cover the balance of their expenses en route. The agency arranged for the women and two dozen others to get legal tourist visas to Mexico City. They then were told to fly to Mexico City and to be on the lookout for a specific immigration officer at the airport there. Two smugglers accompanied the band on their plane ride to Mexico. In Mexico City events went as planned, and one immigration officer singled out the group of Ecuadorians from the line of tourists and gave them "royal treatment," not asking any of the questions such officers are supposed to ask in order to deter the entrance of visa abusers to Mexico. Meanwhile, one of the smugglers was observed giving the immigration officer an undetermined amount of money from a "wad of bills." Once out of the airport and in Mexico City, the smugglers apparently became wary, tipped off by someone that there were an unusually large number of Mexican police apparently watching their airport transaction, so they split the group in two. One group would take the bus inland to the north and then east to Tijuana, and the other would take a ferry ride to Baja and a bus from there to Tijuana. The groups were advised, the Ecuadorian undercover operators recounted, that they might meet Mexican immigration inspectors en route, but that they could be bribed.

In fact, when one Baja inspector did pick out one of the officers as a possible visa abuser, he refused a $50 bribe to let her pass. After several phone calls the Baja inspector managed to confirm the woman's status as a police agent working with his government's approval, and she was allowed to rejoin the group on its journey to Tijuana.

After a several hour bus ride, the women eventually reached Tijuana and were directed to a house in its Colonia Libertad district as final arrangements were made for their border crossing. In the Colonia Libertad drop house, the patron of the smuggling operation, a Mexican national living in Los Angeles, stopped by to check them out and to relieve them of all their money "for their own protection" against border bandits. As they waited for word that it was time to cross the border, they were brought sack lunches at $10 each, charged against their deposit with the patron. A lookout working for the ring saw that the American helicopter patrolling the Tijuana border had finally stopped for refueling, and the people were quickly hustled out of the drop house and smuggled across the border along a circuitous route. It was later learned that the guide had taken them along a route that had avoided all of the American border sensors.

Once across the border they were led to a cave covered with underbrush. There they waited for fourteen hours until a red van pulled up with its back facing the cave opening. They were hustled into the van which, it turned out, was driven by the patron's nephew.

Their prearranged destination was Los Angeles, and they had yet one more hurdle to cross: the inspection point on the San Diego to Los Angeles freeway near San Clemente. The inspection point was open, so the Ecuadorians were taken to another drop house to wait until it shut down. When word reached the drop house that the border inspection point was closed, they piled back into the van and were driven to Los Angeles. One of their fellow travelers, who had joined them in Tijuana and had apparently made the trip before, assisted the group in finding a cheap apartment to live in while they looked for work in Los Angeles.

The Ecuadorian undercover policewomen called their INS contacts and, eventually, between their testimony and that of the Mexican authorities who had been tracking the operation, the leaders of the ring were arrested.

The only tragedy of the story, according to the two Ecuadorian agents, was that two of the immigrants, a brother and sister, were also arrested. They were sent back to Ecuador, still in debt $1,500 each for their ride on the travel agency's underground express. In order to raise the money, their family had mortgaged their home and all of their furniture. Now there was no hope of repaying the debt and the family would lose everything.

The trip through Mexico to the United States is virtually the same for all immigrants, whether they are from Ecuador, El Salvador, Colombia, the Caribbean, or even Asia. It begins in a big city of a foreign country with either a discreet contact with a smuggler or with a local "travel agency," and ends with a guided walk or swim across the American border and on to some point north of local traffic checkpoints. Somewhere in between there is always a reliable Mexican contact to facilitate their venture. Sometimes there is a corrupt American official who also helps.

Middlemen and Women

The smuggling rings operating from countries outside Mexico rely on corrupt officials to ensure that rigged documents will pass inspection and allow the immigrant to pass to the north of Mexico. Then immigrants, Mexican and non-Mexican alike, are steered to Tijuana or some other border city, where, either by prearrangement or by simply asking, they are sent on to a contact point where the border crossing will be arranged.

If he or she heads for Tijuana, the destination is inevitably Colonia Libertad, one of Tijuana's 200 *colonias* or neighborhoods. Colonia Libertad is a smuggler's haven overlooking the U.S.-Mexican border. Dirt and gravel roads lead up the hillside dotted with small wood shingle houses whose colors match the tints of the sky as the sun sets—lavender, pink, turquoise, yellow. A few cars, mostly old American models, sit in some of the yards. From Colonia Libertad, about half a mile or so east of the official port of entry to the United States, one can look down and see local landmarks: Washerwoman Flats, Spring Canyon, and the border. A ten-foot chain-link fence reinforced by aircraft matting ends just west of the foot of Colonia Libertad hill. Only a few strands of sagging barbed wire mark the border below the *colonia*. The brush on the other side of the barbed wire is in some places so high that people can hide there safely for hours at a time, just a mile away from some San Ysidro, California, residential areas.

During the peak of the immigration season, when crops are ready for harvest in the U.S., the *polleros* (literally, people who round up chickens)—recruiters or arrangers—begin making up their loads for the evening, sending the *pollos*—the would-be immigrants—to specific houses in the *colonia* to await their *pasadore* who will guide them across the border. Occasionally, the *pollero* recruits too many immigrants for the trip and shows up in a neighborhood bar, announcing, "I have five extra *pollos*. Who wants to buy them?" He will sell his extras for $10 apiece to another *pollero* who has not yet made up a full load.

If the immigrant goes to Juárez, the story is much the same. He or she arrives, usually by bus, from Mexico's interior and heads for one of the public parks where the recruiters hang out. They steer the men and women to cheap hotels along the Mariscal—a rough Juárez street lined with cabarets and cheap hotels—where the *pollos* join five or ten others, waiting until there are enough bodies for a *pasadore* to guide across the Rio Grande River.

There are many border towns and many contacts. In San Luis, Mexico, according to one smuggler who retired in the early 1970s, the local mayor arranged the details of getting the *pollos* across to the American side near Yuma, where he and his partner would meet them and drive them to Los Angeles. In Tecate, Mexico, the drop houses are conspicuous by the presence of new and expensive American cars parked in front of them.

Payment schemes for all of those involved in the complex smuggling operation vary. A typical arrangement for a simple trip from a Mexican border town to Los Angeles, which may cost the *pollo* up to $250, breaks down like this:

$25 to $50 per person for the arranger, or *pollero*;

$30   per person for the *pasadore* or guide across the border;

$10 to $20 per *pollo* per day to the drop house operators on either side of the border, and

$20 to $50 per *pollo* for the *mule*, or driver, who transports *pollos* to Los Angeles.

The remainder goes to the coyote who had organized the entire operation. For trips further inland, the *mule* may collect more, and the *pollo* is charged more. The operation is fairly safe for the coyote. The big-time operator acts through yet another middleman so that neither *pollo*, drop house operator, *pasadore*, nor *mule* knows the coyote's true identity. Additionally, *mules*, *pasadores*, and others are often juveniles, recruited specifically because if they are caught, American authorities will not deal harshly with them. The big-time coyote may also collect twice for each *pollo*: once from the immigrant and once from the American employer who "buys" the *pollo* to work at his or her farm, company, or restaurant.

The well-run smuggling operation is a combination of an illicit travel agency, housing locator, and employment broker. As such, it can provide many needed services to the undocumented worker. Were the Border Patrol to suddenly suspend operation, the coyote might surface as a legal and above-ground multiservice agency for undocumented workers. Because smugglers operate underground, however, they become key figures in a deadly circle of exploitation. Aware that they will face fines and imprisonment if caught, they will abandon their own cargo—even to death—if their own safety is in danger. Because they are an unregulated trade, even beyond the controls of the free market, they can charge whatever they can extort—as much as $500 or more for a trip from Juárez to a Chicago suburb—perhaps the earnings of several years for the immigrant, perhaps the total amount a family has been able to raise by giving the local moneylender their plot of land, house, and all they own as collateral.

American Connections?

A few Chicano activists have argued that some coyotes must have connections with American border officials for some of their schemes to work. Several reports of undocumented aliens successfully passing through every piece of border technology designed to stop them suggest that this may be the case. But little has been documented that would substantiate these suspicions.

There have, however, been other American connections in the border crossing trade. In 1978, for example, a U.S. Customs inspector pled guilty to conspiracy and accepting bribes in connection with a smuggling operation working through the San Ysidro checkpoint.

In 1979, two more U.S. Customs inspectors were arrested on charges of bribery and conspiracy to smuggle aliens into the United States. The pair also worked at the San Ysidro checkpoint, and had apparently been accomplices of the inspector who pled guilty one year earlier. The arrests were made as the result of an investigation by the INS anti-smuggling squad working with the internal affairs section of U.S. Customs, and the use of an informant. An affidavit signed by one of the investigators alleges that smugglers were providing sexual favors as well as cash to the inspectors. The smugglers apparently operated both by verbal communication with the customs officers and by signals to determine which traffic lanes the inspectors were working, so the smugglers could enter the United States with their cargo. Five Tijuana residents were arrested with the two customs inspectors, including a Tijuana man charged with operating with the customs inspector who had pled guilty in 1978.

Lore of Los Coyotes

The folklore of Mexican smugglers is filled with colorful tales like that of El Abuelo, the grandfather, who was arrested in 1973 for smuggling Mexicans into the U.S., and escaped from a California jail after serving two months of his six-month sentence. El Abuelo was finally captured in 1978 in the small Oregon town of Springfield without putting up a fight. Meanwhile, warrants were outstanding against him in several cities, including a Mexican jurisdiction, which suspected him of heading a gang of bandits operating from the Sierra Nevada mountains near Durango, Mexico, that robbed tourists from the U.S. El Abuelo, it was said, made a habit of killing all of the witnesses to his crimes and was suspected of seventeen murders in Mexico. However, El Abuelo had never been accused of robbing or beating or cheating a *pollo*.

One of the largest smuggling rings on the West Coast was headed, for a time, by a Tijuana businessman known as El Indio, who, at his peak, employed an estimated 150 people in his ring. El Indio, according to an

INS investigator, finally ended up in a La Mesa, Mexico, prison cell because he became too big and too open about his work "for even Tijuana to tolerate." Recalls the investigator, "I have seen him on the street corner, openly passing money to police officers, *mordidas*, bribes . . . but he became too open. The Americans brought pressure on Mexico City and El Indio was put out of business."

In 1973 the U.S. government announced the breakup of one of the more ingenious rings to be recorded in recent smuggling lore. The operation, government attorneys estimated, netted $3 million per year and was believed to have smuggled as many as 15,000 Mexican nationals into the U.S. since 1970. The ring was known as Las Hueras, the blondes, because, of the twenty-five people involved, most were women, and two of the ring's organizers dyed their hair blond.

Las Hueras operated between Tijuana and Los Angeles and was organized, according to government attorneys, by Arcelia Robles, a Tijuana resident who maintained a home in Los Angeles, and Felicitas Gurrola, another Tijuana native living in Los Angeles. Assisting the pair was a bank vault teller at the Bank of America, Esperanza Dominguez, a naturalized U.S. citizen.

Las Hueras ran a very simple operation, so simple and straightforward that it escaped notice for three years. For a fee of $225, only a small part of which was paid in advance in Tijuana, the women loaned the immigrants real immigration documents that had been issued to other Mexican nationals and later sold to the ring. Then the *pollos* were simply driven, two or three at a time, through the San Ysidro port of entry from Tijuana to California. No attempt was made to hide the *pollos*, and they reportedly were rarely challenged by unsuspecting immigration officers at the border crossing. In this manner the ring drove from forty to fifty *pollos* per day through the checkpoint to a drop house in San Diego. When a lookout watching the border checkpoint near San Clemente called to say that the checkpoint had closed down, the *pollos* were driven to Los Angeles. In Los Angeles they were picked up by relatives or friends who paid Las Hueras the balance of their fee. Robles and Gurrola (Gurrola was still at large when the government announced its breakthrough) had opened bank accounts at Dominguez's branch of the Bank of America, listing their occupations as waitresses. During 1972, the government said, Robles deposited $260,000 in her account, and Gurrola $250,000 in hers. The bank teller, meanwhile, deposited $68,000 in her personal account.

Eleven members of the ring were brought into custody. The remaining fourteen, according to then Assistant U.S. Attorney Tom Coffen, were mostly Tijuana residents, and therefore not subject to extradition.

Much as Las Hueras must have laughed about the gringo biases that assumed women with blond hair could not be crooks, so laughed a smuggler still operating in late 1978. One of his activities, he told a reporter, was to "bring people here by commercial airplane, using three-day visitor passes. I buy the tickets here [Los Angeles] and meet them at the airport." Customs officials, he commented, "always make the mistake of thinking anyone with enough money to fly here must have a right to be here and don't ask questions."

Crackdown: Bilateral Cooperation

One of the difficulties facing U.S. officials trying to crack down on organized smuggling rings in earlier years had been lack of cooperation from Mexican officials. Smugglers were able to find relatively safe haven in Mexico, and U.S. officials were unable to pursue them. Most officials of the Mexican government viewed the regular migration of their nationals as a kind of safety valve for revolutionary tensions building in their own nation. Additionally, aiding the smugglers was a well-known way of life for Mexican public officials, *la mordida*, the bribe, being a supplement to token incomes. Few Mexican officials dared toy with *la mordida*, for the entire system of political stability was founded on it.

Cooperation between the governments of the U.S. and Mexico in ending smuggling apparently began taking root in 1977 when President José López Portillo visited President Jimmy Carter in Washington, D. C. Among President Portillo's concerns reportedly was the treatment of Mexican nationals in the U.S. Shortly after the visit, President Carter appointed Leonel J. Castillo to the post of commissioner of immigration and naturalization. Castillo was not only the first Mexican-American to hold the position, but was the first INS chief in decades whose career had not been built in the military—Castillo had been city controller for Houston, Texas.

Mexican officials, meanwhile, were also becoming increasingly concerned by the pressures of immigration to their own country from such nearby nations as El Salvador. Said Rodolfo Orozco, chief of Tijuana immigration, "We are picking up and deporting as many as one hundred foreign nationals a week who are working illegally here."

Two high-level conferences between Mexican and American immigration officials followed Castillo's appointment, capped by a day-long session in July 1978, when Castillo told a reporter that the governments had agreed to work together to topple "the top ringleaders" of smuggling operations. This was already several months after Castillo had announced a diversion of his own INS resources to support enhanced investigation of smuggling rings under a special new INS unit known as the National Anti-Smuggling Program (NASP). Such crackdowns had been tried before but, lacking cooperation from Mexico, their results were meager.

Mexican officials, it seemed, were serious about ending smuggling and its related abuses. In 1978 President Portillo appointed a special representative to study the border and return with recommendations. Explained Jorge del Rio, Portillo's appointee, "We are experiencing a tremendous drain of skilled workers and technicians. We are an emerging nation in the world and agriculture is our number one industry. We cannot afford to lose the technicians and skilled workers that are coming north to the United States." Del Rio also told reporters he had been assigned the task of heading up a pilot program to coordinate Mexican police relations with American immigration officials on the other side of the border. Additionally, he said, he would recommend that President Portillo create a national border patrol similar to the U.S. patrol as a means of eliminating Mexican police corruption and extortion surrounding border affairs. He had, he said, received "many complaints from Mexican citizens about robberies and mistreatment by Mexican police officers that have greatly concerned President Portillo." Asked if raising the Mexican police officers' wages—then ranging from $275 to $320 per month in Tijuana—would help curb corruption, del Rio responded firmly, "I think higher pay would help, but for the most part, the officers who are involved in the extortion of our citizens are crooked and need to be fired!"

NASP had its work cut out for itself. Mexican officials themselves estimated that about 1,200 people were successfully being smuggled across the border—an underestimate, according to U.S. investigators. "On any given day," said Robert F. Milton, deputy district director of INS, "we know we've got in excess of 2,000 smugglers operating somewhere out there. These are not one-vehicle mom and pop operations. . . . There are indications that alien smuggling may be the fourth or fifth largest industry in terms of dollars in the San Diego-Tijuana area."

(Pursuit of mom-and-pop operators was not stopped entirely during the NASP program. They are often the easiest to crack, and once cracked, it is presumed the operatives won't continue. One such operator was a forty-five-year-old Roman Catholic priest, originally from Colombia, who, he said, as an act of compassion flew three Mexican nationals from Tecate, Mexico, to Fullerton, California, for relatives of one of his parishioners. He had been followed by an INS plane from Tecate to Fullerton and was arrested when he landed. The flying cleric, upon promising not to undertake similar acts of compassion again, was given probation by a federal judge.)

During the first sixty days of the NASP program twenty-two arrests were made within Mexico. Meanwhile, American NASP operatives had targeted several smuggling rings for infiltration and destruction. Included on the NASP hit list was one organization that specialized in smuggling El Salvadorians and Guatemalans. It involved an estimated 150 employees, including recruiters in Central America, drop houses on both sides of the U.S.-Mexican border, and its own counterfeiting operation. Another target on the NASP hit list operated in the Laredo, Texas, and Nuevo Laredo, Mexico, region. According to an INS investigator, the ring was so large it continued to operate even when its drivers were frequently arrested. "They have an auto maintenance yard in Nuevo Laredo big enough for a small community," said INS investigator Edward Molina. "They probably have twenty-five autos. As soon as one driver is arrested, a new driver comes in. 'Mules' are a dime a dozen: many of them are illegal aliens themselves and expendable. They also use juveniles, fourteen to sixteen, who won't be tried as adults. Even the principals can be replaced because the organization can't afford to slow down—they have too much invested.

"And transport is only one phase of the operation," said Molina. "They have contact points as far as South America. They have 'rolling stops' along the route where they change autos and auto registrations. They probably smuggle 8,000 to 10,000 a year."

Also on the NASP hit list was a multimillion-dollar ring allegedly run by a man in Mexico in his early fifties. He reportedly had four lieutenants on the U.S. side of the border who employed drivers and made other arrangements. Typically, an INS agent said, "the lieutenant in a smuggling ring will approach a legitimate truck driver and offer him fifty dollars each to haul the aliens one hundred miles past the checkpoint. He is careful to select a driver without a criminal record, someone who will be placed on probation and not sentenced to prison if apprehended." The hundreds of produce trucks leaving the Rio Grande valley daily cannot be searched individually, according to the agent, and "smugglers often build secret compartments in the floors of the truck beds where aliens can hide, covered by loads of produce."

In 1978, NASP-generated convictions began coming in. By the end of fiscal year 1978 NASP reported bagging 1,143 felony convictions against smugglers, as compared with only 497 the previous, pre-NASP, year. Meanwhile, Mexico had arrested and prosecuted several hundred smugglers on her own. "The warden of La Mesa prison says we are filling his place too full," Rodolfo Orozco, the Tijuana immigration chief, commented wryly.

Convictions continued in 1979. In January three smugglers who were part of what the government described as the biggest San Diego-area smuggling ring were jailed. Twelve people were sentenced as members of the ring which, U.S. Assistant Attorney Sandra Wittman told the court, had involved the smuggling of about fifty people per week, for fees ranging from $150 to $500 per person, depending on whether their destination was Los Angeles or Chicago. A thirteenth man was indicted, but was still at large when the others were sentenced. He, unfortunately for NASP, was considered to be the local ringleader of the operation.

The case was concluded as a result of surveillance of drop houses in southern California. The ring, said Wittman, had been in operation for years, with some of the same principals continuously involved in the conspiracy. Other ringleaders had also escaped the NASP net, according to Wittman, including one in Mexico, one in Los Angeles, one in Chicago, and one in Fresno, California.

Early in 1979 INS agents raided another drop house where twenty-one Mexican nationals were found huddled in a shed. Four of them were juveniles. The INS also found a printing press, which they believe was used to produce counterfeit alien registration cards and social security cards, and two guns. Four men were arraigned as leaders of the ring, which was said to have smuggled "thousands" of people across the border from Mexico since 1977. The ring apparently specialized in transporting *pollos* to Chicago. At one time, sources close to the investigation said, at least forty vans were used by the ring. Three of four of the ring's alleged organizers were found guilty in federal court. All were believed to be Mexican nationals. Two of the trio also faced deportation orders after a 1977 arrest in Chicago.

The INS broke up another ring in a series of arrests beginning with eight alleged smugglers, including four Mexican nationals, who used the Flamingo Hotel on Border Village Road in San Ysidro, California, as their first U.S. drop house. The group was reportedly moving seventy-five to one hundred people per week to Los Angeles, Chicago, and New York. Three of the ringleaders eventually pled guilty in a plea bargain arrangement. Their testimony eventually led to the indictment of the wives of four Americans stationed at the Camp Pendleton Marine base near the San Clemente INS checkpoint. The women allegedly each made about ten van trips per year between San Diego and Los Angeles. They hauled twelve people per trip for a fee of $100 per person. Their military ID enabled the women to drive safely through the Marine base, thereby avoiding the San Clemente checkpoint.

In January 1979, NASP had a lucky break. Agents arrested a Guatemalan national in a routine traffic check and found thirty-seven Central Americans, aged six to fifty, hiding in his semi truck. According to Border Patrol agent Bill Glenn, "Initially, we had no idea of who he was until agents of the antismuggling unit managed to identify him." The man, one of five arrested, was José Dolores "Lolo" Mozz-Rodriguez, identified, according to Glenn, as "one of the top South [sic] American arrangers of illegal entries" and one of the key links in a well-known smuggling operation extending from Mexicali to Guatemala. "The surprise is," said Glenn, "we never expected to see him in this country." Others arrested with Mozz included a Mexicali native, two natives of Sonora, Mexico, and Mozz's seventeen-year-old wife, "who may have been the reason for his visit to the U.S.," according to Glenn. This ring brought its passengers across the border at night about thirty miles east of Calexico, California. The *pollos* paid $200 to $300 for crossing the border and an additional $600 to $750 each for transport between Guatemala and the border. The Mozzes reportedly were en route with their passengers to Los Angeles when they were stopped.

Another large-scale operation was broken up with Mexican cooperation. This one, according to the INS, used railroad boxcars to move large numbers of people from Laredo, Mexico, to San Antonio, Texas. The ring was headed by smugglers in Mexico. A previously convicted smuggler was allegedly the Mexicans' American lieutenant. He retrieved the *pollos* from the boxcars and arranged transportation for them from San Antonio to Houston and southern Florida.

The NASP program, with its cooperation from Mexico, has, according to at least one Border Patrol agent, Harold D. Mims, been successful in crimping smuggling operations. "We just about put some of the alien-smuggling operations out of business for a while," Mims bragged. Some rings, he added, "are having trouble recruiting aliens and drivers." And, with the crackdown on coyotes, more would-be immigrants are apparently being forced to cross on their own, through miles of U.S. desert, without guides. They often die there, lost and without water.

6: CROSSING THE BORDER

If one is not so fortunate, or so rich, as to be able to buy a well-forged alien registration card or commuter shopping card that will pass inspection at the legal ports of entry along the Mexican border, there are other ways to enter the United States. Occasionally, a gringo tourist will bring home one or two, perhaps three, people smuggled in his or her trunk. Sometimes it is for the extra money. Sometimes it is an act of compassion. Sometimes it is a simple way to find a maid and other household workers. In certain parts of Texas, a ranch foreman can cross to Mexico to find a work crew to break a strike, or to replace those the INS has taken, fill his pickup, and reenter the U.S. with impunity. At other times one can buy a ride across the border in one of the concealed holes under a truckload of vegetables. And during some seasons, near Laredo, a boatman will ferry passengers across the Rio Grande River. But for most people, there are only two ways to cross the boundary between the U.S. and Mexico—by walking or by swimming. Both are deadly.

The U. S.-Mexican border extends some 1,945 miles. Much of it lies in barren desert; the high desert of the mountains or the low desert of the great Sonora, where sand dunes shift and sandstorms bury anything in their way. Much of the border is marked by water; the Rio Grande, which cuts Texas off from Mexico, and the canals that bring water to U.S. fields. Dotting the border are a string of towns and cities. Some of the Mexican border towns seem to have only one reason for being where they are: to supply the U.S. with cheap temporary workers. They supply the maids from Juárez, who earn enough money in El Paso to support their families; the farm workers of Ojinaga, who for years harvested the crops of Presidio across the river; and the farm workers of Mexicali, who for years have been hired to pick the vegetables of California's Imperial Valley, a desert made to blossom from the water of the Colorado River.

Since 1965 there has been a second reason for the cities. American manufacturers, through special agreements between Mexico and the U.S., have been encouraged to locate the labor-intensive parts of their operations across the U.S. border. They use the cheap labor available there to assemble U.S. parts and then bring them back across the border for final preparation. The plants, owned by single companies with operations on both sides of the border, are called twin plants or *maquiladoras*. Some U.S. labor unions call them runaway shops. The plants have brought workers to the border towns. It is said, in some parts of Mexico, that the operators of *maquiladoras* recruited workers from central Mexico, and that they recruited more workers than they needed just to drive down wages further. In any case, they brought jobs to the towns, and the jobs brought people hungry for work, and the people swelled towns into big cities.

The arrival of the *maquiladoras* changed the demography of Mexico. Its northern border is now its most highly urbanized region, with more than 75 percent of the people living in cities of more than 100,000 residents. Tijuana's population increased from fewer than 400,000 in 1970 to more than 600,000 in 1978, and, some people estimate, up to 800,000 by 1979, making it the second most populous city on the West Coast of North America. Mexicali's population more than doubled, up to nearly 600,000 during the same period. Nogales, Mexico, saw an increase in population from 65,000 to 150,000, while Nogales, USA, increased from 8,946 to only 12,000. The fastest growing border town may be San Luis, which had only 63,000 people in 1976 and 135,000 three years later. Meanwhile, its U.S. neighbor, Yuma, Arizona, increased its population from 29,007 to a meager 35,204 during the same period.

The *maquiladoras* came and went as economic circumstances in the U.S. dictated. In mid-1978 they numbered 450 and provided jobs for only 83,000 people – not nearly enough jobs for all the people lured by new factories being built at the border. The economies of the Mexican cities were not sufficiently strong to provide for such population increases, and, just as people have done around Mexico City and the other capitals south of the U.S., the newcomers crowded the border with cardboard and wooden crate shanties. The economies of the cities suffered so greatly that one city, Mexicali, was not able to fix its sewage treatment plant. As a result, raw sewage was being dumped into the New River, which happens to flow north into the United States. It was perhaps appropriate in the scheme of things that the country which built the population of Mexicali beyond its limitations should be receiving its excrement.

For these people, many of whom came in hope of finding work at one of the *maquiladoras*, jobs on the other side of the border seem to be a final chance of a better future. The people of Juárez do not need a television set to see the wealth of the U.S. It is readily visible on any clear day.

The most frequently used crossing point into the U.S. is Tijuana. It is known throughout the hemisphere as a city where one can always find a coyote. One man left a town in southern Argentina, for example, with only his clothes and some money. He also carried with him the telephone number of a coyote in Tijuana. Tijuana would seem an unlikely crossing point into the U.S. It is hundreds of miles out of the way for those arriving from Mexico's interior who would find the trip shorter were the border crossed at some place along the way, at Juárez, Mexicali, San Luis, or Tecate. But north of Tijuana is the mainline into California's industrial and farming heart—Interstate 5—the road to Los Angeles where a Latin can find safety among his or her peers, and the road that links the state to other arteries leading to every state.

The border here, separating California from Mexico, ranges eighteen miles from the Pacific Ocean and into the Otay Mountain range. In the midst of the flatland between the ocean and the mountains is the San Ysidro checkpoint for the border crossers who have either white skins or proper documents, or who speak English well enough to pass a quick inspection. South of San Ysidro, draped like some fast-sprawling, creeping plant, is Tijuana and its poverty-ridden *colonias*. Between the two is a piece of fence extending several yards from the vast tarmac and turnstiles of the port of entry, a ten-foot fence reinforced by wire mesh. To the west, toward the ocean, the Tijuana River Flood Canal Project and its vast expanse of usually dry cement extend to the Pacific. On the south side of the flood canal slough are a few strands of barbed wire, a largely symbolic reminder that someone once drew a line there and created a border. To the east of the official border checkpoint the terrain becomes rough, and again the fence disappears into a few strands of barbed wire, more symbolic than significant. And further east, through the mountains, there is no fence at all. On both sides of the border checkpoint the terrain, which is peaceable in daylight, turns into a combat zone at night.

Tijuana War Zone

The foreign national crossing the border on foot here faces forces much more hostile than the Border Patrol. He or she faces bandits. On the east side the bandits are said to be mostly Mexican nationals, and on the west side they are most often American youths.

This war zone, as in any war, has its own character and legends, especially on the east where the terrain begins a tortuous geography that will eventually peak at Otay Mountain. Here are the canyons that are too steep for even the Border Patrol's four-wheel-drive vehicles to traverse: Spring Canyon, Smuggler's Gulch, and Dead Man's Canyon—so named because many bodies have been found at its rocky bottom scored deeply by the footpaths of tens of thousands of immigrants who have crossed, or tried to cross, through this natural gateway into the United States.

In 1975, 130 assaults were reported in the Tijuana border region, including 4 homicides. But the reported incidents represent only a small fraction of the assaults, for those who are still physically able to travel on do not report their injuries for fear of deportation. Evidence of armed robberies, assaults, and rapes lies randomly through the scrub brush both east and west of the border checkpoint, just yards away from the border line: old wallets rotting, bits of discarded clothing from rapes, and here and there an old shoe, which a bandit has taken in search of hidden money.

Border zone banditry finally received official attention in March of 1976 when Ruben Ochoa – sixteen years old, one of twelve children of a farm laborer in Michoacán State – crawled through a hole in the fence about two miles west of the checkpoint, walking with four companions up the sand of Imperial Beach. About seventy-five yards into the United States the five were attacked by seven teenagers armed with knives who took what little money the Mexicans had – eighty-five dollars – and left Ochoa writhing on the ground, with stab wounds that partially severed his spinal cord. Doctors said that if he were ever to walk again, it would only be on crutches with steel braces on both legs. Eventually, from police photos, Ochoa identified three of the youths and they were arrested. All were from the south San Diego community of Nestor.

That same night six Mexican adults attacked an eighteen-year-old Tijuana woman and her twenty-six-year-old Mexican male companion as they tried crossing into the United States from the east. The man managed to dissuade the robbers from raping the woman, but they took his shoes, his fifteen dollars, the woman's watch and rings, and her one dollar. When the Border Patrol reached them, four of the robbers had fled back to Mexico, leaving only two to be arrested for their crimes.

As one official commented at the time, "It's almost become a fad now to roll wetbacks for a few dollars, or for kicks."

Such human tragedies in the war zone had been known to officials in San Diego, in Mexico, and in the INS. Attention surrounding the Ochoa incident led to one coordinated attempt among ten agencies of both nations to stop such brutal incidents. On one weekend 407 Mexican nationals were arrested north of the border and 50 were arrested in Tijuana. Of these, 87 were charged with crimes against border crossers. The charges ranged from rape to robbery and assault. When the coordinated efforts stopped, border brutality returned to what it had been.

During the first five months of 1976, at least 5 would-be immigrants were killed and there were 93 other reported attacks in the war zone, including shootings, knifings, and beatings with clubs. The Border Patrol estimated that the reports represented only one in twenty of the real incidents of violence.

Border violence had become so brutal and apparently intractable that Mexico's newly elected president, López Portillo, urged the United Nations to intervene. Meanwhile, San Diego Mayor Pete Wilson asked the Justice Department for an emergency financial grant so San Diego police could intervene to curtail the violence. Mayor Wilson received his grant, and the San Diego Police Department, in cooperation with the INS, established a special Spanish-speaking task force, the Border Crime Task Force. Their work paid off. In the less than two years they were in operation, the dozen or so men made more than 350 arrests. Hand-to-hand fighting marked much of the undercover unit's work and every member suffered injuries. The task force was pulled off the job in March 1978 when the INS decided border crimes were a federal problem and not a local police matter.

Among the Border Crime Task Force's discoveries, kept secret until February 1977 in the interest of maintaining harmonious relations between the U.S. and Mexico, was that among the bandits were some Mexican law enforcement officers. The lid of secrecy was finally sprung after a Mexican immigration agent—whether out of duty or perhaps out to steal—ambushed the task force members who were posing as illegal aliens, pointing his .45 caliber revolver at them. The task force group fired on the man and arrested him, charging him with illegal entry into the U.S., assaulting an officer, and attempted robbery. The Mexican agent, meanwhile, claimed that he was trying to stop some Mexican nationals from leaving his country illegally and that he had not realized he had crossed the border. The matter was dropped and the Mexican immigration officer released, again in the name of harmonious U.S.-Mexican relations.

The incident, however, sparked San Diego Police Chief William B. Kolender to go public with his charge that tan-uniformed Mexican regular and auxiliary police officers from Tijuana were among the bandits crossing the border to rob their fellow countrymen at gunpoint. Chief Kolender's charges were confirmed by a man from Jalisco, Mexico, who reported that he had been robbed of sixty dollars on the U.S. side of the border by a Mexican wearing the tan uniform of the Tijuana police. Kolender's charges were confirmed by the Border Crime Task Force and also by U.S. Border Patrol agents who reported that several people they had arrested had complained of robberies in the U.S. perpetrated by Tijuana police.

Border violence was not limited to clandestine border crossers. In

January 1977, someone from the Mexican side shot at the Border Patrol helicopter. Although shots had earlier been aimed at the patrol's airplanes—which presumably could glide to a fairly safe landing if need be—the helicopter attack aroused concern because one well-aimed shot could bring chopper pilot and passenger crashing to the ground with no chance of survival.

California state officials, concerned that a remedy be found for what was a growing problem, pressed President Carter to come to some agreement with President López Portillo in their February meeting. Whether the meeting between the two presidents produced more than discussion is not known, but the following month the Border Crime Task Force was called off the job. During the same month one hundred extra Border Patrol agents were sent to the region in an effort to curb the violence.

Among the INS's tactics aimed at discouraging both bandit and clandestine border crosser alike was to order its Border Patrol agents to make themselves more visible along the border. Increased visibility, however, only inflamed some Mexican nationals. Not only did border violence increase, but agents found themselves the targets of rocks tossed at them from Mexico, especially on the west side of the border inspection point where the Tijuana flood control project was under construction. Border Patrol officers also reported being fired at with high-powered rifles from two houses on the Tijuana side of the border, from the slum areas near Colonia Libertad. Between May and September of 1978, twenty Border Patrol officers had been injured by rock throwers, and some thirty windows of patrol vehicles had been smashed apart by rocks. Seven shootings had been reported between July and September, but no one was injured. At one point in September of that year a group of about seventy Mexican nationals began a barrage of rock throwing at Border Patrol officers near the San Ysidro entry point. The officers put in a hurried call to Tijuana police who chased away the youths. It was speculated that these and other rock throwers might be working for the coyotes, trying to divert the patrol's attention from their smuggling efforts. After the mass rock throwing, a telephone "hot line" was installed between the U.S. station in San Ysidro directly to the Tijuana police department to quicken Mexican response time to attacks from the Mexican side of the border.

Violence against border crossers continued throughout the period. In August, a twenty-five-year-old Guadalajara man was shot in the neck and chest with a shotgun just after crossing into the U.S. from Colonia

Libertad. In October, three Mexican nationals were arrested following a series of robbings and stabbings along the border. Within the following week eight assaults against groups of border crossers had been reported, and, by the end of the month, two more undocumented immigrants had been wounded in shooting incidents on the U.S. side of the border. One was reported in critical condition after having been wounded in the neck just after crossing the border west of the point of entry. In November a twenty-nine-year-old Tijuana man was picked up and taken to a local hospital after six men had surrounded him, beaten him with a club and their fists, and finally kicked him as he lay on the ground. The assailants netted ten dollars for their efforts. Later that month the San Diego police arrested two American youths who had allegedly posed as police officers to rob a family of Guatemalans, and then turned them over to the Border Patrol. The pair were also suspected in the robbery of two men from Guadalajara. In January 1979, San Diego police reported that three Mexican men had been robbed by two unidentified people who held them at knifepoint. The robbers took twenty-seven dollars in cash and a watch and then left.

In March 1979, Mexican officials crossed the border in a series of nightly raids in U.S. territory aimed at breaking up some of the gangs from Tijuana preying on border crossers. In the first week they arrested fifteen men, aged fifteen to twenty. They promised to make further raids along the border until the Mexican gangs were put out of business.

The war zone had finally become a no man's land. Rock throwing and sniper fire finally forced the Border Patrol to concede part of the border west of the San Ysidro checkpoint in mid-1978. Until the summer of 1978 the Border Patrol had patrolled the American section of the Tijuana flood control project all the way up to the top of the south levee, which once had a reinforced chain link fence standing behind it to mark the border. The nightly barrage of rock throwing, however, began to push the agents further back into American territory. Finally, Mexican nationals began to lay out plywood planks with nails on the bottom of the flood control canal so that agents' vehicles became trapped there with flat tires. Thus crippled, the cars were barraged with more flurries of rocks. Despite the fact that the Border Patrol had armed its Dodge Ram Chargers with unbreakable glass and steel mesh to protect both windows and headlights, the last tactic was too much even for these "war wagons." By the end of the year, the agents patrolled only the north side of the levee, watching as Tijuana children and others ven-

tured down to the middle of the levee—several yards into U.S. territory—waiting to make apprehensions until after the levee had been
crossed.

Meanwhile, the Border Patrol began to report even more sinister attacks—threats on their lives and those of their families. It was rumored
that a professional killer contract was out against one of the agents.
Commenting on this, Richard L. Jones, assistant chief patrol agent for
the sector, said, "It has happened too often to discount."

The Tijuana region may be the most active border war zone, but it is
not the only area where violence has been reported against clandestine
border crossers. In American cities along the Rio Grande, reports of
Mexican drownings are frequent, and many people attribute some of
these not to natural causes, but to vigilantes and other groups terroriz-
ing the would-be immigrants.

An area somewhat similar to Tijuana in its youthful Mexican violence against border crossers is the desolate border region just outside
the city limits of Nogales, south of its American sister city in Arizona.
Both Mexican and American officials there agree that bandit gangs of
Mexican juveniles wait to ambush, rob, and even kill people trying to
cross into the United States. The juvenile marauders reportedly wait in
holes they have dug along the border for their unsuspecting victims
and, at gun or knifepoint, charge a fee—from fifty cents to one hundred
dollars (or all the victim has)—for allowing people to cross "safely" into
the U.S. In late 1978, two men and one woman apparently could not
afford the fee. They were found shot to death just outside of Nogales.
The three were believed to be either Guatemalans or El Salvadorians.

Incidents such as those described above are reported all along the
U.S.-Mexican border. Even as far east as Reynosa, Mexico, across from
McAllen, Texas, men and women who want to swim the Rio Grande to
America are warned of the dangers from thugs and rapists.

Natural Barriers

The border crosser, having survived whatever gangs may have had in
store, must now confront two further barriers to life in El Norte. One of
these will be with her or him everywhere in the United States—fear of
immigration officials. The second is the natural barrier of the terrain. It
is the more deadly of the two.

Border terrain is either desert or running water. Unknown thousands
of undocumented immigrants have crossed the Rio Grande, the best
known of the water barriers. Despite its often placid appearance and its

image as a successful crossing point, relayed by the word *wetback* to describe a Mexican national in the U.S.—*mojado* in Spanish—the river can be treacherous. At times its brown waters swell from a normal width of two hundred feet. The river can go wild when flash floods hit it. It is a river that heeds no boundaries between nations, is in fact so unpredictable and has shifted course so often that new agreements had to be made to determine the boundary between the U.S. and Mexico. Its currents can be swift. It can offer surprise eddies and undertows, all of which can kill. The discovery of bodies is so routine that local newspapers make little, if any, note of them. No one really knows how many men and women have started to cross the river and drowned before reaching the other side. In 1978, twenty-four bodies were washed ashore on the American side in Laredo, Texas. No one knows how many may have washed ashore on the Mexican side. Eight more drowned in January 1979. No one knows how many bodies have floated down the river and into the Gulf of Mexico, never to be found. In 1979, INS Commissioner Leonel Castillo ordered that a study be done on the number of deaths of those trying to cross the Mexican border. He estimated a total of "up to several hundred per year."

A second water barrier, even more deceptive than the river, faces those who would enter California's Imperial Valley—the All American Canal, built in 1939 to bring Colorado River water to the desert. Crossing the official border between the U.S. and Mexico is no problem here. It is just a line on paper. But within a few feet on the U.S. side, the two-hundred-foot-wide canal awaits. Nowhere is it less than twelve feet deep. Water travels through it at ten miles per hour, and it is dangerous not only because its depth provides no place for feet to grab hold for a rest from swimming, but because beneath its calm surface are deceptive currents. For every yard a person swims across the canal, the current drives the swimmer several yards down the canal.

In 1978 four men, three from one family and a friend, had survived the harsh walk through the Sonora Desert, crossed the border near the town of Algodones, and paused to look out over the lush, green Imperial Valley stretching before them. Then they began their swim. The youngest was about three-quarters of the way across when he turned back to see his father, his uncle, and the family friend disappear underwater. Several hours later the bodies were found by the Imperial County sheriff's office. Since the families could not afford to pay for the bodies to be sent back home for burial, the three Mexicans were buried in county plots.

Since 1970, at least sixty-four foreign nationals have drowned in the

All American, ten in 1978 alone. The sheriff says the number may well be an undercount because some who drown may never be found or reported.

Those who are not killed by the river may die in the deserts of California, Arizona, New Mexico, and Texas, deserts where daytime temperatures sometimes reach 130 degrees, deserts that are the domain of rattlesnakes and scorpions. It is said about the desert that everything in it will either scratch you, bite you, or poison you.

In 1977 an undocumented worker described to reporters his trek through the Arizona desert to a job on a Phoenix-area citrus ranch, a trek led by an experienced guide. "One young, short boy hurt his leg. Alberto [the guide] wouldn't let us carry him, saying, 'No, leave him.' The boy was left in the desert with one gallon of water and unable to walk, an entire night's walk from the U.S. border. . . . In the path of the desert were many human skeletons and loose bones, alongside empty water cans," the worker recalled. It was not an isolated experience. A fellow worker who also survived such a trek recalled that one of his companions was bitten by a rattlesnake and left behind to die.

Sometimes the person in search of work comes very close to his dream, El Norte. In February 1979, sixty miles east of El Paso, a man was found. He had first crossed the desert, and then the river. Next to his dead body were some cans of beans and sardines he had hammered against a rock in a futile effort to break them open. His hunger and the heat had killed him.

7: DESTINATION: POINTS NORTH

The undocumented immigrant who is poor and from a non-English-speaking country is handicapped by his or her absolute lack of English, lack of knowledge of even the most simple things American, and limited knowledge—and that usually second-hand—of U.S. geography. How does the immigrant get from the border (presuming a safe crossing has been managed) to a job, to relatives in some large city, to fellow villagers or friends who will help the newcomer begin a life in the U.S.? The immigrant knows only one thing for certain—fear of La Migra, the immigration authorities ready at any time and in any place to arrest, detain, and deport. La Migra and its ways are important topics of conversation in most Mexican border cities and in many towns in Mexico's interior as well. Knowledge of La Migra and its habits is necessary for the undocumented worker to stay in the U.S. long enough to earn a grubstake to take or send back home. It is this set of circumstances, this fear, and this knowledge, that has led the *pollo* in Mexico and Central and South America to the coyote from the beginning.

To be sure, he or she has picked up certain tips along the way; from the person who will help with the border crossing, from those already in the U.S., from fellow immigrants who are making a second, third, or fourth trip to El Norte and know its ways, or from someone at the motel or drop house in Mexico where the *pollo* waits before being taken across the border. He may even have been told to go to a nearby barbershop specializing in gringo-style haircuts.

The California-bound *pollo* may have also learned that a few yards inland, near San Ysidro, taxis will provide a no-questions-asked ride further north, or that, a few miles north in San Diego, freight trains can be jumped for a free ride to Los Angeles. Those coming from Juárez may similarly be told they can pick up a train headed for Chicago on the outskirts of El Paso.

At the San Ysidro border area across from Tijuana, taxis come down beginning at two or three in the morning, waiting for passengers to flag them down from the roadside. Cabbies have found a fortuitous loophole in the law: they are required to pick up any and all passengers, and therefore cannot be prosecuted for transporting undocumented aliens unless it can be proven that they know their passengers are illegal. Local cabbies, however, prefer to stay within San Diego County, not wishing to cross the inland checkpoint on the way to Los Angeles, and their trips are usually made to drop houses or other locations within the San Diego area. According to one cabbie, "You can make more money in town. If things are really moving, you can get fifty dollars for one trip from the border to downtown San Diego. Sometimes it's so busy you'll have to hide them [near the road] and keep coming back until they're all gone." A normal run from the border to San Diego costs only ten dollars.

One INS National Anti-Smuggling Program investigator thinks the cabbies also pick up fares for delivery to job sites where the foremen at north San Diego County ranches will "pay a considerable sum for the cheap labor aliens represent." Many passengers from San Ysidro, according to one cabbie, do ask to be taken to Escondido, a central point of north county agriculture. Such a run, says the cabbie, can net about eighty dollars per passenger, while registering only fifteen dollars on the meter. The NASP investigator notes that the cabbies are difficult to prosecute because, unlike coyotes, they wait to collect their money at the end of the trip. All that the INS has been able to do to restrict the cabbie trade is stop them en route and remove the suspected illegal entrants. "One week," recalls one cab driver, "they caught me three times. They figure if they catch you enough times and take away the aliens, the money will be gone." Such was not the case in mid-1978, when the underground cabbie traffic was at its peak.

According to the INS, 58,007 deportable aliens were located in checks of public transportation by the Border Patrol in fiscal year 1978, and 40,721 of these were found on freight trains.

Border Patrol officers frequently check freight trains for suspected deportable aliens, especially in El Paso and San Diego. In El Paso, the immigrant may attempt to board the Rock Island Line freight to Chicago from the railroad yards at the edge of town. INS searches at the El Paso train depot are sometimes futile. One Rock Island check, for example, found no passengers on board at the El Paso depot, but by the time it had reached Almagordo, New Mexico, about forty miles north, another check caught ten undocumented aliens aboard. By contrast, the train-busting business is a major job in San Diego, where Mexican nationals are apparently boarding the northbound freights out of the Santa Fe yard in increasing numbers for the ride to Los Angeles. According to some estimates, as many as one hundred people find passage each night on one of the two 30- to 100-car Santa Fe freights that run northward. Passengers, apparently, are those who don't have the money (perhaps after being robbed at the border) to pay a professional smuggler, or those who simply don't want to pay because they have used this mode of travel before.

The train jumpers cause problems not only for the INS, but for the railroad as well, according to a Santa Fe special agent. "For Santa Fe, we find sometimes there are so many aliens on a freight that we can't move the train—it's just too dangerous for both them and us. The concept of getting hurt is completely out of their minds. They go under, around, on top and alongside trains, even in places we won't go. I see my job as helping to prevent injuries as well as upholding the law which they violate. [For them it is] a desperation attempt to get north. They lie on top of the wheel truck two inches from wheels that when moving can cut their heads off . . . it's incredibly dangerous." Despite the fact that many freight riders are injured, according to another Santa Fe special agent, the line "will never learn about most injuries. Only on those where a foot gets cut off or something do we find out."

Davil Zaragoza, an unemployed laborer from Juárez, had a dream. He was among those the freight line learned about. His dream was to get to Muscatine, Iowa, where he knew a young woman he wanted to marry. He thought that perhaps they could settle down in Iowa or Mexico and make a life. His dream ended beneath the wheels of a freight train in Freemont, Nebraska. He lost the lower portion of his left leg. When news got out that he was in the hospital, his girl friend, Dawn Mentria, came from Iowa to visit him. Even then they could not marry, for Nebraska had just raised the age for marriage from sixteen to seventeen. Dawn Mentria was only sixteen. The people in Freemont took Davil into their hearts. They raised more than $850 to pay a Juárez doctor, who treated Davil and outfitted him with an artificial limb.

Not surprisingly, freight trains are also seen as a way to return home—especially for the worker who has come to El Norte to earn his fortune only to find that his meager earnings have done no more than buy his food. In 1978 five Mexicans, all without funds, were found in the Greensboro, North Carolina, Southern Railway station, hoping to catch a ride south and, eventually, to return to their homes in Santa de Aguilla. Similarly, seven Mexicans were taken into custody by the INS when railroad agents stopped a southbound Chicago and Northwestern Railroad train in Gillespie, Illinois, to toss the train jumpers off. They too had wanted to return to their homes in Mexico.

Cross-Country Traffic

The undocumented worker's first ride in the United States may be by train or cab, but these are only short-term measures. For cross-country transportation, the novice must rely on the coyote—an arrangement that sometimes can be more dangerous than a ride on the wheel truck under a speeding freight train.

Having been guided across the border by their *pasadore*, the flock of *pollos* is told to wait at a certain place where transportation will meet them to take them on. Near Yuma, Arizona, this can mean as far as twelve miles from the border through the desert. In smaller American towns, it might mean an all-night walk around Tecate or Calexico straight to outlying houses — drop houses that will hold the *pollos* until a load is made up for the trip north, or until the trip is deemed to be "safe."

Drop house operations are not difficult to distinguish from other neighborhood homes. What first comes to attention is the large number of people coming and going. Second is the occasional appearance of a van or semi truck. Careful observation will detect people furtively leaving the house for the back of the van or truck.

It is by surveillance of such drop house operations that the INS NASP team gets many of its leads. Only occasionally, however, are the smuggling-ring leaders at the drop houses. Management of drop houses is usually left to lieutenants. When the INS believes that a lieutenant or even his boss may be present, drop houses will be raided. In February 1979, a major raid of this type was tried. Fifty-seven men and women, aged sixteen to fifty, were taken into custody. Despite precautions, which included a police cordon around two drop houses, no coyotes were caught in this operation.

Drop houses are also often points of assembly for many groups of *pollos* arriving from the border, a sorting stop where those who are to be delivered to local families are segregated from those going on to Chicago, Oregon, Florida, or cities in the Northeast. Drop houses also serve as points of collection of fees in some rings, and nonpayment is punishable by threats of deportation or worse. In one 1979 case, twenty-seven people were arrested at two southern California drop houses after one *pollo* managed to escape and bring help from a local sheriff's office. According to the Border Patrol agents who made the arrests, the *pollos* had told their coyotes that they could not pay the $225 each they had been charged. The smugglers then said they wouldn't get any food. The group had not eaten for two days when two men tried to escape to find help. One was caught, beaten, and returned to the drop house, but the other managed to reach help. When the Border Patrol arrived at the drop houses, most of the people were found sitting on cardboard boxes on the floor of a room that had only a television set and a dining room table. "That's the situation usually," said Border Patrol officer Earl

Morgan. "I've hit two-bedroom drop houses with as many as sixty-five [aliens] in them." Among the twenty-seven were six children. The two youngest, aged one and four, were released to relatives who were legal U.S. residents. None of the *pollos* would identify the coyote. That is not unusual either, according to Morgan, because *pollos* are told that "if they say anything north of the border, then they will be taken care of when they get south of the border."

Earlier, in 1976, the INS reported that "aliens being held for ransom by smugglers when unable to pay the agreed price upon destination have been on the increase. In one case, officers at Los Angeles assisted the Mendocino County sheriff's office in locating and apprehending two kidnap suspects. The victim, whose father and two brothers were smuggled into the U.S. but ran away without paying, was abducted near Ukiah [northern California] and transported to Maywood [near Los Angeles]. He was held there while an attempt was made to extort $1,200 from his father. The kidnappers were tried on state charges and received life sentences upon conviction."

Generally, there are two types of drop houses on the U.S. side of the border. The first, like those described above, is located somewhere between the border and the checkpoints posted by the INS on major northbound freeways. The second, well past the checkpoint, is the staging ground for cross-country trips.

In California, for example, the INS checkpoint near San Clemente blocks all northbound traffic on the main freeway from San Diego to Los Angeles. It is virtually impossible to reach Los Angeles from San Diego without passing this checkpoint, where INS inspectors are on the lookout for smugglers. Therefore, the largest rings use drop houses south of the checkpoint where the *pollos* are held until the checkpoints close down. Such rings hire lookouts at a convenient place near the checkpoint to call the drop house when the checkpoint closes. "Two minutes after we close the checkpoint because of rain," says a California Border Patrol agent, "the vans and other vehicles waiting at the safe houses and assembly areas will be loaded with illegals and on their way. There is always somebody watching us from the viewpoint. We know they're there and they know that we know. We even know most of the lookouts by name. Lopez, for example, may be on day shift this week."

If anyone fears La Migra more than the *pollo*, it is his driver. The passengers, after all, usually face only deportation. The drivers can face criminal penalties and up to five years in prison for each charge of smuggling. The driver's fear of capture can be deadly for his or her passengers. One such driver, Johnny Ventura, apparently made a mistake and thought the California checkpoint was closed, or thought he could bluff his way through. It was a fatal mistake. Border Patrol agents suspected him and flagged him over to inspect his car. He tried to outrun them in a one-hundred-mile-per-hour chase up the freeway in which his car sped out of control. Ventura, who was on probation for a 1977 alien smuggling conviction, ended up confined to a wheelchair as a result of the accident. One of his passengers, Roberto Martinez, was killed. Three others were injured.

Other smugglers resort to different ways of avoiding the checkpoints. In Brownsville, Texas, twelve aliens were arrested on their way to the ship channel, where smugglers were going to lead them to a cabin cruiser for a quick run up the coast to Corpus Christi, past the inland checkpoints.

One California smuggler, a small-time operator who was never caught and is now out of the business, told a reporter that he had a contact at Camp Pendleton, a Marine base that surrounds a checkpoint area. "I paid one of the Marine guards on the gate twenty-five dollars a head to drive through the base. This was a sure way to get around the checkpoints." This cozy arrangement collapsed when the Marine recruit was transferred.

Another smuggler, also retired from the business, explained that he and his partner arranged to meet groups of twelve Mexicans at a time about a dozen miles from the border near Yuma, Arizona. The people were loaded into a van which was outfitted with typical tourist equipment in an attempt to disguise it. One of the partners in this enterprise drove the van and the other drove a car several miles ahead of it. The two communicated with CB radios. When the driver of the car noticed something suspicious, the lime-green cars of La Migra for example, he warned the van, leaving plenty of time for the passengers to get out and begin to walk a few miles up the desert, to be picked up again later after the trouble had passed.

Were a map of the U.S. stretched out on a wall, it would be crisscrossed with the various routes taken by smugglers with their passengers. Fundamentally, according to several INS investigators, there are four cities that act as staging areas for transport throughout the U.S. These are Los Angeles, which draws immigrants from Tijuana and other border towns generally no farther east than Yuma; Phoenix, which draws from border towns along the Arizona border as well as from Tijuana; El Paso, which draws from Juárez; and Dallas, which draws from Del Rio, Laredo, and other Mexican border towns. There are also subsidiary staging areas; for example, Douglas, Arizona, which is a mainstay of the trade to Colorado.

From Los Angeles, aliens are shipped primarily to Chicago and to San Francisco.

Phoenix, meanwhile, is a major transit point. Some *pollos* are sent to Nevada, where smugglers can take their crews up back roads to jobs in Idaho, or over other back roads to the Las Vegas airport, where they are loaded onto planes destined for Newark and other eastern cities. Phoenix also sends workers to California's Imperial Valley, to Oregon and Washington, to Idaho and Utah, to Montana and Wyoming, and to Chicago and New York.

From El Paso, workers are sent primarily to Chicago.

Dallas ships workers to Orlando, Florida, Houston, Virginia, North Carolina, and to New York, the District of Columbia, and other East Coast cities.

To combat this traffic, the Border Patrol also uses roving checkpoints and makes occasional aircraft checks. During fiscal year 1978, the Border Patrol apprehended 70,711 deportable aliens in traffic checks and 5,657 in aircraft checks.

Meanwhile, as smugglers find one route becoming too "hot," they switch to another. Interstate 80 to Chicago became perilous for smugglers in 1978, so many began using back roads through Montana, Wyoming, and North Dakota.

The routes described above are only the major ones. Each staging area also has subsidiary cities and towns where workers are shipped.

Once picked up at the border, safely taken past checkpoints, and sorted out in various drop houses, the *pollos* are taken to their final destinations, crossing the U.S. in cars, station wagons, vans, and trucks. And this, perhaps, is the most dangerous part of their journey.

T. L. Giorgetti, who in 1978 was assistant director of investigations for the Chicago-area INS, briefly explained the conditions of cross-country travel: "We have found instances where people have died on the trip due to dehydration. They are crammed into the vans and sometimes abandoned if the smuggler feels any heat."

A few reports illustrate Giorgetti's account:

• February 1974: a routine check of a large truck in the Los Angeles area led to the arrest of twenty-four aliens who had been huddled together without food or water in the bay of the truck for two days. The driver was located and charged with suspicion of smuggling aliens.

• November 1976: twenty-seven Central Americans were driven

from Los Angeles to Washington, D. C., in a metal cabin atop a pickup. They were jammed together on benches and had eaten only oranges and sandwiches on the sixty-hour cross-country trip. Officers reported that similar trips had been made from California to Boston and New York.

• July 1978: a Californian was arrested in Duel County, Nebraska, after twenty-six Mexicans were found jammed into his motor home—nineteen men, five women, and two children. They were en route from Los Angeles to Chicago when they were stopped.

• November 1978: a Californian was arrested in New Jersey after thirteen aliens were found in his Chevy van—ten men and three women. They were en route from California to New York. Arresting officer Michael Trupkiewicz, a state trooper, recalled one case where twenty-five aliens had been crowded into a single van. "They transport them like cattle," he said.

• January 1979: a Houston resident alien was charged in connection with the smuggling of twenty-seven undocumented Mexicans in one van.

• February 1979: one man was arrested at a California rest stop when seven undocumented aliens were found in his car. Three were crammed in the trunk.

• March 1979: after a tip from a Greyhound bus driver, the Border Patrol apprehended forty-three suspected undocumented aliens in a truck. The truck was driven by a seventeen-year-old:

In October 1978, the California Highway Patrol found two dead El Salvadorians sprawled near a one-ton U-Haul truck in the middle of the desert just south of the Palm Springs resort area. The two were among more than twenty El Salvadorians who had been crowded into the six-by-ten truck on the U.S. side of the border near Calexico and hauled in the daytime desert heat. The doors of the closed truck had rubber seals admitting little air, and the people began to have trouble breathing. They beat on the truck cab for several hours, even, as they grew desperate, threatening to kill the driver. Finally, the driver stopped. As the men and women crawled out of the truck they saw the driver leave in a small sedan with a man and a woman. It was too late for two of the passengers. One of the men stumbled out, walked a short distance from the truck, and died. The other had to be lifted out. He was already dead.

Three people were indicted later that month on nine counts of smuggling aliens, conspiracy, and transporting aliens. No explanation was made of why charges of negligent homicide, manslaughter, or perhaps murder, were not also brought. One woman, Maria Aurora Sandoval-Oros, a twenty-five-year-old resident alien, was located and arrested. A man, reported to be a resident alien who had lived in Calexico, was still at large. Also still at large was a Mexican national who was identified only as El Gordito. The El Salvadorians, according to testimony, had each paid 1,700 colones—about $700—to be smuggled to Los Angeles. Three of the El Salvadorian women, Assistant U.S. Attorney Barton C. Sheela said, had been singled out to provide sexual favors for the driver and two guides.

The woman was tried and found guilty. In January she was sentenced to five years in prison and five years' probation. The two men were still at large when she was sentenced.

In February 1979, a convoy of eight cars picked up fifty Mexican nationals who, according to the sheriff's office of Webb County, Texas, had agreed to pay $400 each for transportation away from the border. A 1973 Pontiac in the convoy caught fire east of Laredo. Six passengers escaped the flames, as did their driver. Two people who were locked in the trunk burned to death. The Mexicans said they didn't know there was anyone in the trunk when they abandoned the car, and were unable to provide much help in attempts to identify the driver.

In November 1978, sixteen Spanish-speaking foreign nationals were found by a highway patrol officer alongside Interstate 90 in South Dakota. They were standing, on a 25 degree morning, where the van they were riding in flipped over on an icy patch of road near Sioux Falls. The driver walked away from the wreck and, without so much as a word to his passengers, climbed into a mobile home and disappeared down the road. The aliens, aged fourteen to fifty-four, had been picked up near the Mexican border and driven to Los Angeles, where they waited for two days in a warehouse before they were packed into the van. Tossed into the van with them were two packages of luncheon meat and one loaf of bread. They were given nothing to drink. They were not allowed out of the van.

As their story unfolded, more aspects of America's grim slave trade were exposed. They said that they had been on their way to Chicago, and that those with money had paid $50 in advance for the trip. In Chicago, they were told, someone would help them get jobs. In return, they were to turn over about 10 percent of their salaries for seven to eight months until the cost of the trip was paid. They were also told that they would have to give another 45 percent of their salaries to the people who would give them a place to stay.

No one thought to ask when they would be free.

8: ALIENS ON ORDER

Four men walked through the departure line of an American Airlines flight from San Antonio to Chicago's O'Hare International Airport on Monday afternoon, January 29, 1979. They pretended not to be nervous and avoided looking anyone in the eye as they tried to blend in with the airport crowd. They were conspicuous to no one but themselves. They went out into the bitter Chicago winter, where they were met by a van that would take them into the city. The four were Mexican nationals. Each carried a bogus six-month work permit. They were here with two American brothers who were taking them to meet their new boss, a man who had ordered some wetbacks to work in a small welding firm.

The owner of the firm had arranged with one of the Americans to buy eleven "wets" from Reynosa, Mexico, and had agreed to pay $3,000 for the first shipment and $600 each for the seven other wets who were to follow in a second shipment.

The American brothers had just fallen into an INS trap. When they reached the intersection of Jackson and Dearborn outside the Dirksen Federal Building they and the Mexican nationals were arrested. The employer who had ordered the wets was an INS agent. The welding firm was a cover.

The Mexican nationals reportedly had paid not only for their bogus work permits, but also a fee for their jobs. Eleven of the Reynosa men who had been ordered had tried to swim the Rio Grande as the first stage of reaching their jobs in Chicago. Reportedly, one of them drowned in the crossing.

Such was the story pieced together by Chicago *Sun-Times* reporter Betty Washington from federal sources and court documents. It is a story repeated many times in America's underground slave trade, and would probably not have made news had not one of the brothers been the head of a federally funded job placement center in McAllen, Texas, and claimed to be a friend of INS Commissioner Leonel J. Castillo.

The director of the job placement agency, his brother, and a third man were indicted by a federal grand jury in Chicago on charges of conspiring to smuggle illegal aliens from Mexico to Chicago. The indictment charged that they had used the Texas job placement agency as the base of their operations. The grand jury additionally charged that the head of the agency had arranged with the "owner" of the welding firm to supply the Mexican laborers for a fee. Court records, meanwhile, showed that the agency's director, a notary public, allegedly prepared false work permits at the job center.

The focus of the INS investigation then moved on to Brownsville, Texas, where investigators were trying to determine the extent of the smuggling operation. Reporter Betty Washington's sources told her that evidence being developed suggested the group may have shipped hundreds of Mexican nationals.

Of the stories of America's slave trade, the fact that aliens can be purchased through smuggling operations to work at whatever jobs their employers wish is one of the least often told and one of the most difficult to tell. Employers seldom discuss it, and although in most states it is not illegal to employ undocumented workers (and in those states where it is illegal, the law is not enforced), no employer wants to be indicted as a co-conspirator in the transport of his illegal workers. And, since employer sanctions are nonexistent, testimony about this aspect of the slave trade is seldom brought into a courtroom, or even sought. And so, while experienced members of the Border Patrol and the INS Investigations Division say, as does INS Commissioner Leonel Castillo, that the darker side of alien smuggling is aliens on order—slavery—evidence to support such charges (and they are made frequently) are difficult to document. Despite these difficulties, some evidence is on record.

Some of it is circumstantial, as is, for example, evidence surrounding a ring operating from Texas to North Carolina and Virginia and points in between. South Virginia tobacco growers, in 1978, had a shortage of harvesters. The INS annually sweeps area ranches and farms for undocumented workers, but in 1978 two of its sweeps, resulting in seventy-five apprehensions, were special. They were related to an investigation of a smuggling operation.

One of the Virginia tobacco farmers whose ranch was raided was found to have employed two undocumented Mexican workers. Robert L. Reese of Skipwith said that the two Mexicans were brought to him by a truck driver "who said they were from Texas. I didn't know they were illegal. If I had known they were illegal I sure would not have given him [the driver] a certified check." (Virginia is among the states with a law banning the employment of undocumented aliens.) Reese paid the driver $150 for the Mexicans' transportation, which he deducted from their wages—the minimum, $2.65 per hour.

Neither Virginia authorities nor federal authorities claimed that Reese had knowingly hired the illegals, or that he had "ordered" them. But a federal grand jury in San Antonio investigating an interstate smuggling ring subpoenaed six Virginia tobacco farmers, including Reese. As it turned out, the certified check Reese had given the truck driver who delivered the two "Texas" Mexicans was made out to Durwood Walker Woosley of Meridian, Texas. Woosley was indicted by the

San Antonio grand jury on three counts of conspiring to transport illegal aliens. He pled innocent and was held in jail in lieu of $100,000 bail. The grand jury had subpoenaed Woosley's records from banks in Texas, Oklahoma, and Clarksville, Virginia. It also had interviewed 150 undocumented workers and spread its investigation from Texas to Arkansas, Oklahoma, Louisiana, North Carolina, Virginia, and Tennessee. A Memphis INS agent was said to be the source of the tip that a large smuggling ring was operating from Texas.

Woosley pled guilty to reduced charges of conspiring to transport ten undocumented workers from Leakey, Texas—about seventy miles inland from the border—to his home in Meridian, near Waco, about two hundred miles northeast. The plea bargain, according to Assistant U.S. Attorney Dan Maeso, was made in exchange for Woosley's cooperation in the investigation.

Pleading guilty with Woosley was Crescenciano Garduna Falcon of Leakey, who entered guilty pleas on two counts of aiding and abetting illegal entry into the United States, and Jack D. Sweeney of Hermitage, Arkansas (apparently the next stop on the smugglers' route), who pled guilty to misprison—failure to report a felony. Two others pled guilty to conspiracy.

A few months later R. Hart Hudson, head of the Virginia-Carolina Agricultural Producers Association, was indicted by a federal grand jury on one count of conspiracy to transport two Mexican nationals from Texas to his farm in South Hill, Virginia, and two counts of aiding and abetting the illegal transportation of the pair. Hudson, according to the INS, was among farmers in as many as ten states who were allegedly supplied with smuggled aliens by Woosley.

Evidence of a similar operation surfaced a year earlier in California when a man was convicted on federal charges of harboring "illegal aliens." His business, according to authorities, was recruiting Mexican nationals and delivering them to his brother, a labor contractor in the fertile San Joaquin farming valley of the state. When he was apprehended, according to Border Patrol agents, his workers, who were living in the orchards, said they were told to go and "hide" from La Migra.

According to Glenn Smith, of the Stockton Border Patrol, in the heart of the San Joaquin valley, contractors and growers have been known to hire undocumented aliens and then turn them in to the patrol to avoid paying them. Pointing out that most contractors run "clean" businesses, he described it as a middleman's business that invites exploitation. More than half the undocumented worker's wages may go to the contractor or smuggler, who provides them with their work, transportation, and low quality food. "I've seen them charge these people a dollar for cigarettes or fifty cents for a soda," said Smith. "We have rounded them up in labor camps where there was not one legal in the whole camp."

Mexican nationals on order for farm work is an old story, a system dating back to the 1920s. It is a system that, while slowed by the deportations of the 1930s, the farm owners' acceptance of the Bracero Program between 1942 and 1964, and the unprecedented roundup of "wetbacks" during 1954, has never really stopped.

Farm owners always seem hungry to employ undocumented workers. It saves them a great deal of money in wages, housing costs, and sanitary facility costs they would have to invest in for workers who are free to complain if laws for their protection go unenforced. In the early 1970s, recalled one retired smuggler, if the Mexicans he picked up near the Yuma border for the trip to Los Angeles had no friends or relatives to take them in, "We could always take them up to a farm in northern California which would always take all our illegals off our hands. We sold them for fifty dollars a head, as many as we could get." On occasion, recalled this smuggler, undocumented workers were shipped to ranches in California's Merced and Kings counties, where "they were housed in a barn. They were charged for the housing, charged high prices for rotten food, and were charged fifty dollars for getting the job — and all of that was at fifty percent interest, taken out of their wages. I don't think they ended up earning any money at all." Two or three times the group serviced orders from ranches as far away as Idaho. "Basically," he explained, "we had three types of passengers — those who were on order to work on some business, those who wanted to join relatives, and those who were just poor and without any contacts looking for jobs." The three groups were just about equal in size, he recalled.

In 1973, according to a sworn statement made by an undocumented farm worker on behalf of Investigative Reporters and Editors, Inc. (IRE), who assembled in 1976 to begin an investigation to learn who had murdered Dan Bolles, a reporter from the Arizona *Republic* who was investigating organized crime in the state, the worker and a group of fellow Mexican nationals were taken directly across the Arizona desert border to their jobs at the Arrowhead Ranch complex. The ranch was owned, in part, by Senator Barry Goldwater's brother, Robert. They worked, said the citrus picker, six days a week for salaries that ranged from nothing to forty dollars. The payments were kept low by deductions for food brought to the workers by their foremen and by allegedly phony social security deductions. "For a bag of flour, two dozen eggs, salt, and three cans of beans, we were charged up to twenty dollars, which was taken out of our checks," the worker told IRE reporters. IRE reporters also found evidence of what they believed to be phony social security deductions on paycheck stubs found on the ground at the Arrowhead Ranch. "The social security number on one check, for instance, was 000-00-4394, a phony number. There were other stubs with equally invalid numbers," IRE reported. Despite tales of high wages migrant workers can earn harvesting citrus fruit in such Phoenix-area ranches as Arrowhead, even the best workers, in 1976, they told IRE, could make only ten dollars a day. (Conditions had not changed two years later. After a frost had ruined part of the crop, workers told reporters the most they could make was six dollars a day at some of these ranches.)

The story of conditions at Arrowhead was only a sidelight to IRE's main report, focusing on organized crime in the state, but it bolsters evidence of the reality of aliens on order in the U.S. One of Arrowhead's labor supervisors was Francisco Sanchez, hired around 1965. According to the IRE report:

> In the spring of 1976, Raymond Feld, head of the Phoenix Border Patrol Office, got an informer to infiltrate the Arrowhead operation. At Sanchez's direction, the informer took two loads of aliens to Idaho, one load in the back of a loaded truck and the other in a large U-Haul van. The informer witnessed payments by aliens to Sanchez, and received money himself from aliens and from one Idaho rancher. Aliens not needed in Idaho were turned in to be deported, Feld said.

Similarly, an enterprising investigative reporter of the Elgin (Illinois) *Courier-News*, Vic Caleca, developed evidence that Hispanic nationals were available on order not only as farm laborers, but as service workers as well.

Caleca's first interview was with the wife of a convicted smuggler, who told him that during the five years before her husband's arrest in 1978, they had placed hundreds of undocumented aliens in local jobs. She told Caleca that they regularly placed workers at jobs at the Milk Pail restaurant, two hospitals, a local foundry, and a local hotel. When the aliens were unable to pay for their transportation north, she told Caleca, she arranged with one of the employers to have the money deducted from the workers' pay and turned over to her. She refused to disclose which of the businesses made this arrangement with her and her husband, but said they did a lot of business with the Milk Pail and the foundry.

Caleca followed up on the Milk Pail lead. He reported in February 1979 that "a man who until two weeks ago was an employee of Centro De Informacion Y Progresso [a local service agency] has told the *Courier-News* that 'eighty percent of the people who walked through our door were illegal. We knew it. We all knew what was going on, but we had mixed feelings about it.' ".

One of the former Centro employee's jobs involved helping find work for those who came to the agency for help. The reporter continued, "He said he met regularly in a local pizza parlor with a representative of the Milk Pail, José Rodriguez, to discuss sending illegals over to work at the restaurant."

At a meeting between the former Centro employee and Rodriguez that was observed by the *Courier-News*, Rodriguez disclosed that he was not an employee of the Milk Pail itself, "but works for a Des Plaines-based firm called Economics Laboratory Inc., which manages, hires, and fires the restaurant's dishwashing and cleanup crews." Economics Lab, according to Rodriguez, provided the same service on a contract basis to "many large Chicago-area restaurants." Rodriguez's job was to manage the day shift dishwashers at the Milk Pail. As the *Courier-News* listened, Rodriguez told the former Centro employee that "he is interested in hiring illegals because they make the best dishwashers and cleanup people.

" 'Most of them work real hard, I would say. They work real hard. That's why they're here. Besides, no one else would do this work,' he said."

The former Centro employee offered "to send a 24-year-old legal American resident to apply for a dishwashing job, but Rodriguez turned him down flat. 'He wouldn't fit in, I'm telling you. He wouldn't last a week. He just wouldn't be comfortable. All we have is Latins back there and he wouldn't fit in,' Rodriguez said."

When confronted with the story by the *Courier-News* reporter, Milk Pail owner Jerry Reagan said that the story didn't surprise him, and praised the hard-working and honest nature of the employees Rodriguez had recruited.

One of the National Anti-Smuggling Program's earliest breakthroughs into the slave trade was made during its first sixty days of operation, in February 1978. Sixteen immigrants, fourteen men and two women, were followed across the border into Laredo, Texas, where they were packed into a U-Haul truck and the doors sealed tight after them. The U-Haul drove through Dallas, then Memphis, then to Chicago—a thirty-hour drive in the pitch dark of the one degree above zero February air. No food, water, or toilet facilities were provided for the human cargo. Two of the people in the U-Haul were later hospitalized with frostbitten fingers and toes.

At the wheel of the U-Haul was a Chicago resident, Eraclio Dominguez-Mendez, who, according to federal agents, was a long-time smuggler. The INS made its arrest at Dominguez-Mendez's Chicago home. According to the INS agents, his home was used as a dormitory for undocumented workers. After finding jobs for his passengers, the INS charged, Dominguez-Mendez would collect a $300 to $400 fee by having his workers' wages garnisheed. In addition to this, Dominguez-Mendez also reportedly charged his workers rent, which left them, according to the INS, with little money for other needs. They were, one INS agent said, like modern day indentured servants or slaves, since they could hardly complain about conditions unless they wanted to be deported.

Another NASP investigation, in early 1979, broke up yet one more aliens-on-order operation, described by the INS as the largest known North Texas smuggling ring, and in the process nabbed its alleged ringleader.

This story began in Del Rio, Texas, across the Rio Grande from the Mexican border town of Ciudad Acuña, where a group of border jumpers went in search of jobs after having crossed the river. Accused smuggler Jerry Dwayne Pettijohn found ten of them and promised them safe passage to North Texas and a guaranteed job, in return for which they allegedly agreed to pay Pettijohn several hundred dollars from their wages. The ten men were loaded onto the back of Pettijohn's pickup and driven to a secluded spot near Rock Springs, about seventy-five miles north of the border. Here, according to investigators, Pettijohn's alleged accomplice joined them and they made their way from Rock Springs to a small farm near Cleburne—about fifty miles southwest of Dallas and a center of the local dairy industry—where, the men were promised, they would be turned over to a farmer who would give them a good job and a nice place to live.

The Cleburne farmer, however, turned out to be an undercover INS agent with whom Pettijohn had allegedly earlier made a deal to deliver the men. After final arrangements were made at the Cleburne ranch for the "farmer" to buy the ten men for $150 each, Pettijohn and his alleged accomplice were arrested and taken to Dallas, where they were charged with transporting illegal aliens.

INS assistant director for the region, Rick Norton, told reporters that agents had gathered enough evidence to prove that Pettijohn had made similar deals for one hundred to three hundred undocumented aliens per month over the last five years.

Local dairy owners in the area, having been told about the arrest by reporters, admitted that the local industry relied heavily on undocumented workers from Mexico. Intriguingly, few of the dairy owners admitted that they themselves hired such workers. Most agreed with Gary Adams, a local dairy operator, who said, "I have never used them, but the only reason that I have not is that I cannot talk to them. It would be a total disaster if they were no longer available to work. The reason being that they are the only ones the dairy farmer can get."

Pay for area dairy hands reaches up to $600 per month. From this is deducted the cost of room and board. The work is long and hard, and because cows must be milked every day, twice a day, there is no pause for weekends or holidays. Some area farmers start their first milking as early as four in the morning. The last milking is done before sunset. In between milkings barns must be cleaned of manure, fences have to be mended, food is spread for the cows, cows are herded into the milking barn, and, more often than anyone would wish, a cow that has managed to escape through the hole in a fence must be chased down. Breech births have to be attended to and sick heifers must be cared for—bottle feeding them back to health.

One farmer who admitted he relied on the work of undocumented aliens, but did not want his name used for publication, explained that the elimination of the "wetbacks" would probably "double labor costs," and might cause the price of milk to "jump thirty or forty cents a gallon." He termed INS enforcement activities a waste of time and money, and harmful to U.S. consumers. "These people feel like God put them here on this earth to work and that's all they want to do. They're not here collecting welfare; they're here trying to make a living," the farmer said. "The wetbacks are going to get here some way or another whether there are smugglers or not. The smugglers just make it easier for them because they give them a ride," the man concluded.

The dairy-operator was probably correct, Pettijohn or no Pettijohn, the "wetbacks" will be back. Once a pattern of alien migration is set, knowledge of where jobs are to be found is spread to friends and family members and the employer no longer has to order a shipment of "wets" from smugglers. Where migration patterns are the most firmly established, the coyote is no longer a trader in human flesh, but an illicit travel agent operating in an underground labor market where the worker is exploited because of his undocumented status.

9: JOBS IN THE UNITED STATES

Workers from Las Animas—a small town in the Mexican state of Zacatecas, about eighty miles north of Guadalajara—began a tradition of migrating to El Norte generations ago. The older men of Las Animas recall working in the early 1900s in the mines and on the railroads of the West. In the 1920s they picked up agricultural work in California and Texas, and then, in the 1940s, the Bracero Program turned what had been a migrant trickle into a stream, often leaving Las Animas and other villages of Zacatecas virtually empty except for its old men, women, and children. Young men make their first trip north between the ages of eighteen and twenty, heading toward places where others from their town work, where the old-timers will help the newcomers get jobs and places to stay.

Periodically, the young migrant returns to his home. Eventually he chooses a wife and then spends a couple of years establishing his family and working as a sharecropper on land owned by a big ranchero. Once his family is established he heads to El Norte again, to earn the money to support his children, and perhaps his parents and other relatives as well. He returns once a year, or more frequently if he can afford it, to visit his family, especially for the Christmas celebrations. He will spend the next ten or twelve years mostly working in the United States, sending money back to his family and hoping to earn enough money perhaps to buy a small farm of his own. The Las Animas post office, as evidence of this migration, reports receiving an average of six hundred money orders from the U.S. arriving by certified mail each month. The total population of the town, when all its residents are home, is 2,100.

Today the men of Las Animas no longer work in the fields as their fathers and grandfathers did. They now make their way to San Jose, California, a city sitting at the end of the San Francisco Bay, where they work at a variety of jobs in the city's "secondary labor market" as janitors, restaurant workers, laborers for subcontractors in the construction industry, or in other small businesses and firms that support the industry. Most of them work for small employers whom they come to know quite well.

The men of Las Animas form a small subculture within the larger Hispanic community of San Jose. Additionally, there are people from other towns and villages in Zacatecas, who also comprise a miniature subculture within the whole. When one member of the tiny community is deported, his friends are likely to make sure he receives money to return from Tijuana. Often, his boss will hold his job open for him. When a new man from Las Animas arrives, he comes prepared with the addresses of his fellow townspeople, who will help him find a job and housing.

Similarly, villagers from the town of Intipuca, on the southern tip of El Salvador amid high volcanic peaks, have begun a tradition of migration to Washington, D. C., where they work primarily as dishwashers in local restaurants. No one is precise about the date the Intipucans began their migration, but it is said that one villager went to Washington in 1966 and saved enough money to buy a used car. When he sent his family at home a photo of himself and the car, the migration began. According to Intipuca's residents, about one thousand of the town's five thousand people are at work in the District at any given time. As with the men from Las Animas, the Intipucans help their fellow villagers. When they have worked long enough in Washington to help their families build new homes, they save money to help their relatives make the long journey to El Norte and then return home themselves. Today, according to reporters, "there are jobs in the kitchens of certain Washington restaurants that have been held—traded back and forth for years—by the men of Intipuca." When one decides to return home, he passes on his job to a relative or friend. Similarly, apartments are passed on from one Intipucan to another.

The immigrants from Las Animas and Intipuca are in one way fortunate: they have help from friends in the United States, making them much less vulnerable to the depredations of the coyotes once they reach their destinations safely. There are similar pockets of tiny subcultures representing one or another town or village in many parts of the United States, but still there are many newcomers from towns and villages and cities that have never sent anyone to El Norte. They are less fortunate until they also develop patterns of migration over many years that can serve to protect them in some of their worst difficulties.

In 1975, in an effort to develop more reliable information upon which to base United States policy on immigration, the U.S. Department of Labor commissioned David S. North and Marion F. Houston, two prominent social scientists, to study "the role and characteristics of illegal aliens in the labor market." Their study was based on a sample of 793 foreign nationals who had worked in the U.S. for at least two weeks before they were apprehended by the INS. The North-Houston sample included foreign nationals from fifty-three countries, most of them in the Western Hemisphere (which, in INS terminology, means North, Central, and South America, as well as the Caribbean; the so-called Eastern Hemisphere includes everyone else). The sample had some biases of its own that parallel INS apprehension statistics: more than half their foreign nationals had been apprehended in only three states—California, Texas, and Arizona—and fewer than 10 percent came from Eastern Hemisphere countries.

About 5 percent of the sample had been employed in white collar jobs, 55 percent in blue collar jobs (15 percent in crafts, 25 percent as operatives, and 15 percent as nonfarm laborers), 21 percent employed as service workers, and only 19 percent employed as farm workers—a much lower percentage of farm workers than INS apprehension data present. By contrast to their total sample, Mexicans surveyed had a 27 percent employment rate as farm workers, and only slightly more than 1 percent in white collar jobs.

Average wages in the underground market, the researchers found, were highest in the construction industry, where the average was $2.98 per hour. Ranking second was manufacturing at $2.92 per hour. Coming in last were private household workers—domestics—who earned an average of $1.63 per hour. Second to last were agriculture, forestry, and fishery workers, who made $2.07 per hour. Average unemployment for undocumented workers during the five preceding years, North and Houston estimated, was 10.2 percent.

There were, however, sharp differences among three groups—Mexicans, other Western Hemisphere, and Eastern Hemisphere—in both numbers of years of education and in English comprehension levels. Mexicans, they reported, averaged only 4.9 years of education, and 76.4 percent spoke no English; other Western Hemisphere nationals averaged 8.7 years of education, and 53.2 percent spoke no English; while the seventy-five Eastern Hemishphere nationals averaged 11.9 years of education (close to the U.S. average), and only 16.2 percent spoke no English. Not surprisingly, they found that the Eastern Hemisphere natives tended to earn higher wages than the others. In general, the researchers found a direct correlation between the number of years of education and wages, placing the Mexicans at the low end of the wage scale.

The statistical picture drawn by North and Houston was one of a group of workers limited to the secondary labor market (where wages are low and jobs dead-end) earning substantially less than native Americans working at similar jobs.

Missing from both INS and the North-Houston profiles is the large presence—estimated by the U.S. House Select Committee on Population to account for 40 percent of the U.S. illegal population—of foreign nationals who overstay their tourist visas, people such as those described by Los Angeles *Herald-Examiner* writer Denis Hamill as "vast pockets of white illegal aliens who go unchecked by public outrage, political rhetoric, newspaper investigations or INS raids. In Santa Monica there are thousands of visitors from the British Isles who arrive here on visitor visas and never decide to go home. . . . They take more jobs away from American citizens than the Mexican workers ever will. They can do this because they are white. And if you're white and speak English in America the only other thing you need for successful assimilation is to add the words nigger and beaner to your vocabulary when speaking about what is wrong with the country." Of the more than one million deportable aliens located by the INS during fiscal year 1978, fewer than 5 percent were visitors in violation of their visa status.

Despite the fact that neither North-Houston nor overall INS apprehension data reflect the total resident "illegal," or "out of status," population, they do paint a clear picture of those in America's underground labor market most likely to be victims of her slave trade.

David North reported in 1976 that 23 percent of the foreign nationals interviewed had been paid less than the minimum wage, and that 18 percent of the workers interviewed felt they had been hired *because* they were undocumented workers. Another study, this one commissioned by the Mexican government in 1972, revealed that although 80 percent of former illegal immigrants were willing to go back to the U.S., 67 percent complained they were not paid regularly and/or were still owed wages when they were apprehended.

Farm Workers

There is little doubt that the worst employment conditions in the undocumented sector of the economy are in farm labor, and that most of these jobs are held by Mexican nationals, although the percentage of farm workers from other Hispanic nations appears to be increasing. In fiscal year 1978 the INS reported that Border Patrol agents found 90,847 deportable aliens in its routine farm and ranch checks. Of all foreign nationals apprehended by all INS departments, 98.5 percent of the farm workers were Mexicans. In other employment, by contrast, they accounted for only 78 percent. Figures such as these have led some observers to describe illegal Mexican immigration as only the old Bracero Program gone underground. Tending to support this contention was a study conducted in Mexico in 1977 that found that half of the respondents who had migrated to the U.S. illegally also had fathers who worked in the U.S.—many of them during the Bracero Program.

Some farms and ranches are known to be places that rely almost entirely on undocumented Mexican migrant labor. These places, located primarily in Texas, Arizona, and California, are the most exploitative of all. Of the 185 undocumented workers surveyed by University of Arizona student Manuel De Jesus Alvarado and his associate, Theresa Medina, at such ranches in these states, 69 percent reported that they worked from fifty to sixty hours per week for an average wage of $1.14 per hour. Twenty-two percent had never attended school, and only 4 percent could speak or understand English.

California, in late 1978, began a special program to study agricultural working conditions in one county with a reportedly high percentage of undocumented farm workers—San Diego County. Forty growers had been contacted by state labor department officials as the study entered its fiftieth day. Only one of those forty, according to Barry Carmody, senior deputy in charge of the investigation, was in compliance with state labor laws. The team had already collected $15,000 in back wages for undocumented workers from just two employers, and expected the total to exceed $120,000 before their inquiry ended.

Under the special trial program, teams of three investigators went into the fields to talk with workers about how much they were paid. They also audited the growers' payroll records. The state minimum wage at the time of the audit was $2.90 per hour, but investigators found workers who were paid as little as $1.10 per hour. One grower, according to Carmody, was charging his workers forty cents for each hour worked for housing which Carmody described delicately as "substandard." Most workers, meanwhile, had to be content with cardboard and plastic "dwellings," which, Carmody said, "were literally collapsing in the wind and rain." Carmody estimated that 95 percent of the farm workers were undocumented aliens.

A few weeks before the state investigation began, an area grower, who admitted that at least 60 percent of his workers were undocumented aliens, told a reporter that "agriculture would cease to exist as we know it today in San Diego County if the illegal alien labor force were not available to us." The same employer admitted that his workers did not have housing up to even the poorest of American standards, commenting, "For those who are living in the brush or in groves, they live in conditions just as good, probably better than their homes in Mexico. True, they don't have electricity or toilets in the brush, but they don't in Mexico either."

Such conditions are not limited to southern California, according to the mayor of an agricultural community in the northern part of the

state. Healdsburg Mayor Abel De Luna, commenting that undocumented workers were being taken advantage of, explained, "When
I first came here I picked pears up in Ukiah. That was almost ten years
ago and I was getting five dollars a basket. Well, they are still paying
five dollars a basket and this is ten years later."

Meanwhile, a local vineyard owner said that "it is not a pleasant
thing to consider what would happen if the [illegal] work force were not
available." Agriculture in the county, he said, "might survive, but the
price to the American public would be phenomenal."

Neither are these conditions in farm labor limited to California
groves and fields. A greenbelt of citrus trees surrounds the "Valley of
the Sun"–Phoenix, Arizona. Hidden from view of those traveling on
Phoenix-area roads and highways during harvest time, when the citrus
trees yield their oranges and lemons in this irrigated desert, are some
two to three thousand undocumented workers, who, like their California brothers and sisters, live among the trees in cardboard and plastic
"dwellings" which also collapse in the occasional rain. One large
supplier of workers for the area's farms is Blue Goose Growers, which
runs its own citrus grove as well as a subsidiary, Clark Packers, and
supplies workers not only for the Blue Goose grove, but to about eighteen citrus ranches that contract with the packing company. Blue
Goose, ironically, is a subsidiary of the California-based Pacific Lighting Corp.—an energy conglomerate hoping to make a deal for Mexican
natural gas. George M. Babbe, vice president of Blue Goose, admitted
that undocumented workers "are an important part of the picking
force," but denied knowledge of substandard treatment of any of its
workers. Just one month earlier, in December 1978, workers at Clark
Packers testified in an Arizona court that they were being paid $1.65 an
hour.

Texas grapefruit growers also admit to using undocumented laborers.
American workers, they say, "move on" when the weather gets too hot.
It is not the weather that moves them on, for the citrus harvest occupies
the cooler months of the year. Pay for harvesting the fruit at most area
farms was, in late 1978, twenty-nine cents for each sixty-pound sack of
grapefruit picked–less than half a cent per pound. Domestic harvesters
move on, if any are indeed hired at all, because other crops in other
parts of the country pay more money. Raising payments to harvesters,
growers say, as do most farm owners, would drastically increase the
price of their produce to the consumer.

The fact is that the cost of harvesting labor is a very small fraction of
the total price Americans pay for their food. Using the Texas grapefruit

as an example, if the harvesters' pay were doubled, and all other things held constant except the increased payroll taxes that would accompany such a raise, the consumer price of these grapefruits would rise less than one and a half cents per pound.

C. H. Fields, the American Farm Bureau's assistant director for national affairs, attempted to explain American farm owners' need for foreign labor at U.S. Senate hearings on immigration in 1978:

> The production of such crops as fruits, vegetables, ornamentals, and certain field crops such as sugar creates substantial seasonal demands for hand labor that often cannot be recruited from the domestic workforce. This is not to say that there are not Americans who are in need of jobs, but we know from many years of experience that only a few of these people are willing, able, and qualified for work on farms; only a few are located in the areas where such jobs are available; and most are unwilling to travel hundreds of miles to take a temporary seasonal job or have little incentive to take on the kind of hard work involved in agriculture, when public programs [i.e., welfare] offer a more attractive alternative.

American migrant workers, of whom more than 12 percent are unemployed, cannot go to jobs paying less than a penny per pound, or $1.10 an hour, or even $1.65 per hour. These wages are not enough to pay for the gas to reach the farms, much less for food to eat once there, and for gas to go on to the next ranch and job.

Fields would have been more accurate had he simply said that some farm owners prefer foreign workers and make no bones about it in some regions of the country. Foreign workers, whether documented or undocumented, cannot complain about conditions, cannot demand the legal wage, and are always deportable if they do complain too much.

Fields might also have been more accurate had he said that some farm owners are trapped in an institution that is gradually squeezing them out of business. Prices for their produce must now in many cases compete with prices of produce imported by multinational agribusinesses, which have located some of their crops in Mexico, Central America, and even South America, where wages are lower and tax and other conditions are favorable to them. Louisiana, for example, once had a small, but thriving strawberry industry. Agribusiness moved the strawberries to Mexico. Some farm industries are now so capital-intensive that small farmers are being pushed out of business by the large owners who can afford to absorb the costs of expensive machinery. And many small farm owners are at the mercy of what the packing plants will pay for their produce. The only cost the small holder has any control over, as other costs—for fertilizer, tractor fuel, and taxes—rise, is the cost of labor. So the small farmer, squeezed by the big farmer or the packing plant owner, or pushed by the multinational corporation that can take its crops abroad, squeezes the worker. Both worker and small farmer are choked by the same institution.

Yet it is often the largest producers, who are best equipped to handle higher labor costs, who resist the hardest in raising wages to even minimum standards.

Unionization was bitterly resisted in the 1960s as the issue re-emerged in California fields for the first time since the Great Depression. Field workers earned a dollar an hour or less for harvesting table and wine grapes. Yet when the large grape growers were eventually forced to sign contracts with farm workers' unions, raising wages first to three and then to more than five dollars an hour, the companies did not go belly up, and neither did the prices of their wines go up any faster than competing brands made from grapes harvested by nonunion labor. Still, farm owners continue to resist both unions and higher wages. Their most frequent resistance tactic has been to import un-documented workers to break the strikes. As testimony presented to the U.S. Senate's 1978 hearings on immigration by the American Friends Service Committee noted: "On more than one occasion AFSC staff have observed that workers have been brought across the border to work in fields where U.S. labor organizations were negotiating for a collective bargaining agreement were on strike. In most of these instances, every effort was made to prevent the imported worker from finding out about the labor dispute."

The story of multinational firms choking both farmer and laborer repeated itself in early 1979 when unionized lettuce harvesters in the Imperial and Salinas valleys of California went on strike for higher wages. One of the large lettuce producers was Sun Harvest, a subsidiary of United Brands, a multinational conglomerate including not only a multitude of food processing and packing companies, but A & W International, the root beer and hamburger chain. (United Brands has made a substantial contribution to the development of migration patterns of undocumented workers from the Caribbean, Central America, and some South American nations to the U.S. It went to these countries in search of cheap labor and tax havens, and, like the *maquiladoras*, returned little to the countries themselves, but increased the division between wealthy and poor, which has driven the poor to make their futures in the U.S.) Rather than raise wages, the lettuce producers imported other workers, including undocumented workers. Concurrent with the lettuce strikes, the INS reported that California had broken all its previous records in the apprehension of deportable aliens, despite a decrease of one hundred Border Patrol agents from the prior year. The INS, in an intriguing piece of doubletalk, attributed the increase in arrests to the increased flow of border crossers allegedly because of worsening economic conditions in Mexico. Mexico's economy, however, had taken an appreciable turn for the better in the previous months. The INS made no mention of the California strikes as a contributing factor in the increased number of attempts to cross the border.

Rural to Urban Transition

According to officials at the Colorado State Employment Service, who have watched the undocumented labor market in both farm and nonfarm jobs, it takes about three years before the undocumented agricultural worker locates urban employment. As undocumented workers shift from the fields to the cities, so have underground immigration patterns. Undocumented workers in increasing numbers appear to be heading directly for major U.S. cities including Chicago, Washington, Los Angeles, and Houston.

There are many rungs on the ladder of urban employment for the undocumented worker. The lowest is the domestic worker, or live-in maid, which has become an institution in twin border cities like El Paso and Juárez, and is apparently also rapidly becoming an indispensable fixture in such cities as Los Angeles and Washington. Domingo Gonzales of the American Friends Service Committee spoke about the institutionalization of this underground labor sector in testimony at the Senate's 1978 immigration hearings. "Along the border on the U.S. side, some workers—mostly women—would not be able to work were it not for the presence of live-in maids. The jobs held by these American women are mostly minimum wage, dead-end jobs, which do not provide sufficient income to pay for day care, so the only alternative is the use of $10 to $25 a week Mexican maids. It is," noted Gonzales, "indeed a pattern and practice with a long history which has become quite acceptable." Unknown hundreds of families in Juárez depend on the earnings of the women they send to El Paso to work as maids. When the INS rounded up and deported some 140 maids from El Paso in March 1979, Mexican nationals were so outraged that they successfully blockaded the bridges between the two countries for about two days in protest, tearing down American flags and tossing them into the Rio Grande River. It was the strongest border protest against the U.S. in recent memory. While Gonzales observed that "Both Mexican women and the women on this side are exploited, working at the bottom of their respective economic systems," the symbiosis of exploitation had at least provided some kind of earnings for women on both sides of the border.

Further removed from the border, the exploitation ceases to be symbiotic and is reduced literally to slavery. Silverio Coy, community coordinator for the Washington, D. C. Catholic Center, explained, "The way it's done is that an agency in a Central American country will hire a woman, give her a contract, promise her a salary that would be very good in her country and not very good here, and also promises her certain privileges. When they come to this country, they find there is no way to enforce the contract." As a result, INS spokesman Verne Jervis commented, "The people are forced to remain in almost literal bondage." It is only after living in the United States for a while that the undocumented domestic worker is confident enough to escape and seek out work for herself.

One maid escaped in Alexandria, Virginia, only to be apprehended by the INS. But her testimony to the grand jury resulted in the indictment of a former U.S. ambassador to Costa Rica and his wife. The grand jury charged that not only had the ambassador transported the maid to the U.S. illegally, but then paid her only $12 to $25 a week when, according to the law at that time, she should have been paid $2.50 per hour, plus room and board. Ironically, the man had served as a commissioner on the Equal Opportunity Commission until a month before his indictment. After leaving his ambassadorship, he chaired the U.S.-Mexico Border Commission for two years.

Another woman, Celestina, a thin, intense nineteen-year-old Mexican national, had come to the U.S. at seventeen, alone, five months pregnant, and desperate. She was hired by a domestic service which shuttled her to cleaning jobs in station wagons, hiring her and others like her at $18 to $20 a day, but returning only $5 to $7 a day to them. Celestina worked in such an arrangement in Orange County, California, and received $5 a day for her housecleaning (the minimum wage in some Mexican cities is $6.50 per day). She was one of the lucky ones. She broke out of this scheme without being deported by her bosses or apprehended by the INS. Celestina now gets her own work at $16 a day.

One step up the urban employment ladder are jobs in the garment sweatshops of New York, New Jersey, and Los Angeles for women; and for men, work as dishwashers and busboys in most U.S. cities.

As with agribusiness, employers in both industries complain that they simply cannot find American workers to fill their employment needs. And, as with agribusiness, questions arise over the conditions of the jobs employers offer. In an exploratory study similar to the audits of San Diego County farm employers, the California Department of Labor undertook, in late 1978, a survey of Los Angeles garment factories and restaurants. By the end of the year, the fifty-nine member task force turned up violations that resulted in employers paying one million dollars in back wages and unpaid overtime to workers. Fines totaling $576,000 for violations of workers' compensation laws and $122,600 for violations of child labor laws were also levied. Although only a portion of the garment industry employers and some local restaurants were checked, according to task force director Joe Razo, of the 3,800 businesses visited by investigators, nearly 90 percent were found to be in violation of at least one of eleven protective labor laws.

Said Razo, who estimated that 65 percent of California garment industry workers were undocumented, "The issue becomes whether people who have legal status are simply unwilling to accept these jobs [in preferance for welfare], or whether they are unwilling to accept jobs at these pay levels"—levels just at, or below the minimum wage or without overtime compensation. Union-organized garment workers, meanwhile, were earning about $4.50 per hour.

The International Ladies' Garment Workers Union (ILGWU) has learned a lesson similar to the farm workers' unions about the recruitment of undocumented workers as strikebreakers. When it began organizing the increasing number of nonunionized garment sweatshops in 1975, undocumented workers were often brought in to break up organizing efforts. Employers replaced those who were thought to be pro-union with new workers. In 1975 one garment industry employer was finally caught red-handed and was indicted by a Los Angeles grand jury for harboring and transporting undocumented workers. Bernard Cowan and his son Roger were indicted after local police, tipped off by a union organizer, stopped Roger with a truckload of twenty-three undocumented workers from his father's plant, Bernie Cowan Inc., where a strike was in progress. Bernard Cowan later pled guilty to charges of harboring aliens.

This incident and others like it have led the ILGWU and a few other unions to break ranks with some of their compatriots in the AFL-CIO and include both documented and undocumented workers among its members and in its organizing drives.

(The importation of undocumented workers in strike situations is apparently not limited to only the garment and agriculture industries. In 1979 twenty-five undocumented Mexican workers were arrested at the

Louisiana-Pacific Corporation's lumber mills in Urania, Winnfield, and Alexandria, Louisiana. The International Association of Machinists and Aerospace Workers, at the time, was in the process of negotiating a contract for workers at the Urania plant. Meanwhile, those arrested at the Urania plant told authorities they had been "brought" to work there. The company provided some of them with housing – a company-owned house trailer for which four undocumented workers paid the company $320 a month rent. Joining the ILGWU in organizing undocumented workers have been the United Auto Workers, United Electrical Workers, International Longshoremen and Warehousemen's Union, the Amalgamated Meat Cutters, United Mine Workers, and the National Maritime Union.)

Food We Eat Out

Most Americans who make a habit of eating out – whether at the Sans Souci in Washington, D. C., or the local Milk Pail in Elgin, Illinois, or certain ethnic restaurants from cities as far off the beaten track as Corvalis, Oregon, or those famed for their cuisines in New York and San Francisco – have probably at one time or another benefited from the services of the undocumented workforce. In an argument that by now seems repetitive, restaurant owners, too, say that their businesses would fold without their wetbacks.

• A San Antonio restaurant owner said: "In fact, the illegals make damn good workers. They come to this country with the idea of working. I wish I could get a few American citizens to work like they do. They would rather take welfare. But not the illegal worker. If they could ever round up all the illegals in this city, I'd have to close my doors. No one else wants to work."

• Milk Pail owner Jerry Reagan said: "They fill a need. Restaurant owners couldn't fill these jobs without these people. Our experience has been very good with them. And I'll tell you something else, they never steal. You know, if a box of rib steaks, for instance, is sitting out, someone like you or me might take them. But they won't even touch them. Because they're afraid, I think. The consequences are a lot worse for them if they're caught. If we had to go and replace these people with higher-priced help, menu prices would skyrocket. You wouldn't be able to eat out."

In Washington, D. C., which during the early 1960s relied on black Americans to fill its low-paying jobs as dishwashers, busboys, salad makers, and assistant cooks, Executive Secretary Ron Richardson of the Hotel and Restaurant Employees Union, Local 25, estimates that about 20 percent of his membership consists of workers from foreign countries.

Some restaurant owners make little secret of the fact that they hire, and even prefer, undocumented workers. One, Giulio Santillo, owner of the popular Tiberio Ristorante in Washington D. C., proudly mentions that he himself was an illegal alien when he came to the U.S. and opened the restaurant.

In New York, the owner of five Japanese steak houses in Long Island, New Jersey, and Connecticut was indicted by a federal grand jury on charges of importing and harboring Japanese workers (who got, and overstayed, their visitor visas). The workers, estimated at nearly one hundred by INS investigators, had allegedly been recruited in Japan through newspaper ads promising to pay their way to America. The employer, it was charged, imported these workers, who then went to work at his restaurants to pay back the cost of their transportation.

One Step Up

Another step up the ladder for undocumented workers is employment in small manufacturing plants where wages, while lower than those prevailing in the industry at large, are sometimes higher than minimum. Such was the case for sixty people arrested on the suspicion that they were undocumented aliens on their way to work at a mobile home manufacturing plant in Fort Worth. Their wages, they said, ranged from $2.75 to $3.75 per hour. Most earned $3.25.

While for many, light industry might be a step up from washing dishes, for others it is no better than any other work in the underground labor market, as a Newark *Star-Ledger* account, published in August of 1978, reveals:

A Passaic plastics firm where three Mexican juveniles were found working by the U.S. Immigration and Naturalization Service (INS) has been fined $360 for violating the state's child labor laws.

The three boys, all 14 years old, were arrested last May with 13 other workers when immigration investigators obtained a warrant to search Milco Plastics Corp. for illegal aliens.

In July, the New Jersey Department of Labor and Industry filed charges against the company for 19 violations of the child labor law in connection with the three teenagers, citing the factory for such infractions as employing minors under the age of 16, employing them in excess of eight hours a day and working without certificates.

William Clark, assistant state commissioner for labor standards, said it had been found that one of the youngsters worked more than 71 hours one week.

Out of the 19 counts, all but six were dropped by the state. Milco Corp. pleaded guilty to those in municipal court Monday.

Summarizing the employment picture in the underground labor market in 1978 was F. Ray Marshall, U.S. secretary of labor: "Undocumented workers are employed most often in low wage jobs. Some employers claim they can get only undocumented workers to do these jobs. Accordingly, they argue that the influx of undocumented workers has little impact on our domestic unemployment problems. I believe these claims are, in many cases, a self-fulfilling prophecy which can and should be undone. There have been instances where employers have structured jobs that are so demeaning that only the frightened and desperately poor undocumented worker will take them."

"In a nutshell," according to the American Friends Service Committee, "U.S. jobs [are] degraded to below survival level, and 'illegal' immigrants [are] forced by fear of deportation to work under inhuman conditions."

10: LA MIGRA

A man from Ecuador works in a Brooklyn restaurant washing dishes. He works twelve hours each day except Monday and earns about two dollars per hour, from which are deducted his meals and his rent for the restaurant basement space he shares with two other men. His boss, for a 5 percent fee, sees to it that his letters and his money are sent home to his wife. He considers himself lucky because he has been able to work at the same restaurant for three years. His boss has helped him, and once, when there was a raid by immigration inspectors, the boss found him a place to hide until they were gone. If he can hold out for two more years, he says, his family will have enough money for a decent house and to start a small business. He misses his family very much, and from the damp walls of the basement droop a few precious photographs of his wife and four children.

Aside from his boss and the two others who share his cement-walled basement, he has spoken to no one for three years except a Catholic priest. Even though he was grateful to see the priest, he asked that the priest not come back.

The man has not left the restaurant and its basement even once for the entire three years he has worked there. He has not seen daylight for those three years. The lack of daylight has taken its toll even on his deep brown skin, giving it a yellow pallor like a soil once rich and dark but overplanted and drained of life.

The Ecuadorian dishwasher chooses to stay inside, in what has become a kind of prison, because he fears La Migra, the immigration authorities. If they found him, they would return him home before he could finish accumulating the grubstake that might make his family's life a bit better than it was. His fear of La Migra is so great that when he needs medicines, rather than telling his boss and asking him to go, for fear his boss will fire him, he waits until his wife can send them. This way, he says, he can be more secure for the two more years it will take until he has made the money he thinks he needs and can return home from exile.

Not all undocumented workers go to such extremes as the dishwasher, but they live with the same fear. It is a fear that builds so much tension, community workers say, that it often brings illness. And the fear keeps them in hiding, going out only to their jobs, to buy food, and perhaps to attend an occasional mass. They trust no one they do not know. For no one knows who will call La Migra. If they are beaten or robbed, they will not complain to the police for fear of La Migra. If they are sick, they will not go to the hospital for fear of La Migra. If they need help, they get it from friends they can trust, and not from public agencies set up to help the poor. They are a people in hiding, and, as such, invisible to most Americans. They hide because no matter how difficult their life in the U.S., their poverty at home is much worse. At home, as they watched their children go hungry, their meager earnings never quite enough to fill a belly, there was no hope. In America, even in fear and hiding, at least there is hope.

The Immigration and Naturalization Service is improperly named. It was designed, built, and strengthened for the primary purpose of keeping "undesirable aliens" out of the U.S., and for deporting such "undesirables" as find their way in. It is an agency of the U.S. Department of Justice, the government's law enforcement arm. Its territory often overlaps with the FBI, another agency of the Justice Department, and the two occasionally cooperate. Its Intelligence Unit is designed to ferret out information about foreign born people who may be criminals or subversives, and therefore subject to deportation. Its Investigations Division not only conducts investigations of domestic immigration fraud, but cooperates with other government agencies in developing information on subversives, criminals, and terrorists, especially in the Caribbean and Latin-American nations. By the end of fiscal year 1976, the division had indexed a total of 221,335 names of such foreign nationals and made the information available to other government agencies on request. During the McCarthy era the INS provided eighty-three undercover operatives who made their testimony available at deportation and other hearings. The Investigations Division also assists with activities of other Justice Department agencies in investigating organized crime, and, having established a liaison with Israeli intelligence, investigates charges against alleged Nazi war criminals. In addition to these activities it performs what is called "area control," a term for locating undocumented workers in major metropolitan regions.

The Border Patrol is the second arm of the INS that apprehends aliens. Its character has been militaristic since its founding early in the century, when its men wore cavalry-type uniforms and patrolled the border on horses. Reminiscent of fugitive slave hunters of an earlier century, the patrol also made use of tracking dogs in their search for unauthorized border crossers. The tracking dogs were eliminated in 1958, and the horse patrol in 1962. All that remains that would remind contemporaries of its early origins are its cavalry-style, dress campaign hats. The Border Patrol's primary responsibility is to prevent the unlawful entry of aliens into the U.S. It also searches public and private transportation for "deportable aliens," and performs regular farm and ranch checks for undocumented workers. On occasion, members of the patrol are deputized as federal marshals to assist other government agencies in policing riots and civil disturbances. Its most recent intervention as an adjunct to other federal police activities reportedly was at the 1973 American Indian occupation of Wounded Knee, South Dakota. During World War II the Border Patrol assisted in locating alleged enemy agents, and during the anticommunist postwar era, cooperated with the FBI in rooting out "subversives." More recently, it has been active in helping local police search and rescue parties because of its extensive skills in tracking, or "sign cutting."

The Investigations and Border Patrol groups are augmented by a Detention and Deportation Division responsible for returning "deportable aliens" either to their home countries or across the Mexican border. During the last few decades, Detention and Deportation has tried a variety of tactics to ensure that unlawful border crossers from Mexico do not return. In the early 1950s, this division flew Mexican nationals to the Yucatán Peninsula, a place that, at the beginning of the century, was a deadly forced-labor penal colony. In the early 1970s, it was charged, if a person admitted coming from Tijuana, he or she would be deported to a border point at some other location in an attempt to frustrate re-entry. During fiscal year 1976, an experimental program was tried that deported some Mexican nationals to their home states. The program was dropped, however, because it did not appear to stop these people from re-entering the U.S.

Additionally, the INS is supposed to provide services to those who are legally entitled to and wish to become U.S. citizens. This effort, however, has taken a back seat to enforcement, and few undocumented workers who think they may be entitled to adjust their status and become legal, permanent residents go to the feared INS for assistance. Such fears are not unjustified. In 1976 the Border Patrol raided, without a search warrant, Arizona's Manzo Area Council, which had earlier received federal funds for its program of assisting people wanting to learn about, or adjust, their immigration status. Four of the Manzo workers were arrested and charged with harboring illegal aliens, despite the fact that when it received its federal grant, authorities were fully aware that some of those they would be helping would be undocumented workers. The Border Patrol also seized some of the council's records and used them to round up 150 undocumented workers who had come to the council for assistance. The charges against the Manzo council workers were later dropped.

Over the last decade the INS has also developed a reputation for racism. Its practices by their very nature are racist. Because more apprehensions per hour can be made along the Mexican border, in the name of fiscal efficiency most Border Patrol resources are channeled there. Virtually none are channeled to the much more time consuming and difficult task of tracking down Canadians working in the U.S. in violation of law, or the great number of visa abusers who are also illegally present in the U.S. Because of a presumption that most undocumented immigrants are either black people from the Caribbean or Hispanic people, street sweeps have been concentrated in Spanish-speaking barrios. When the INS occasionally checked New York City subway riders, only blacks and Hispanics were questioned—a practice that was stopped after vociferous complaints from Congress. In New York City discrimination by the INS was believed to be so bad that the Puerto Rican government offered to give its workers there special identification cards to prove their status as U.S. citizens. Based on the same premise, raids on places of employment were also concentrated on those companies hiring predominantly minority workers. In 1977, much to the later embarrassment of the INS, it raided a clothing manufacturing plant in Harlington, Texas, that employed mostly Spanish-speaking workers. The Border Patrol questioned all 930 employees and arrested 14 as illegal aliens. All 14 were U.S. citizens.

In an ongoing battle between the INS and a District of Columbia restaurant owner who employs undocumented workers, the owner, Ulysses S. Auger II, filed suit against the INS in 1978 charging that the warrant it used to search his restaurant was invalid because the affidavits on which the warrant was based were discriminatory. Auger's attorney cited some of the reasons given by INS investigators for obtaining their search warrant. They included observations that "several people there spoke Spanish, appeared to be of Hispanic descent, had dark hair and dark complexions, had foreign-style haircuts, and wore ill-fitting and inexpensive clothing and foreign-style, inexpensive shoes." Auger's suit was similar to one brought by the International Ladies' Garment Workers Union in Los Angeles the same year.

As with any police agency, the INS has come up against charges that it is corrupt and that it has been excessively brutal in its handling of those people it has arrested. In the early 1970s charges that INS officers had taken bribes, run prostitution rings, and otherwise abused their powers led the U.S. Department of Justice to announce that it would launch an investigation into these charges. The two-year probe was called Operation Clean Sweep. If there was any sweeping during the two-year probe, most observers agreed, little ended in the dustpan.

INS higher-ups had been charged, in 1972, with practices such as releasing apprehended aliens to ranchers for four dollars a day, about one-third of the then going rate; keeping some border-area ranches off limits to Border Patrol searches; hiring Mexican nationals as informants and then sending them on to favored Texas ranchers as cheap laborers. In exchange for favors to ranchers, patrol officers in the lower ranks alleged, ranchers gave INS chiefs special privileges, including hunting rights on their extensive land holdings.

Finally, under pressure from Congress, the Department of Justice disclosed its findings in 1974. It had investigated 321 cases of possible corruption, mostly on the southwest border. Of those, 224 were closed. Fifty-eight cases were still under investigation. Decisions on whether to prosecute the remaining 39 cases had yet to be made by U.S. attorneys. Most of the charges involved bribery, the Justice Department reported, stemming from the smuggling of both drugs and undocumented workers. According to statistics later released after further pressure from Congress, the Justice Department reported that 59 people had been indicted as a result of the probe and that 42 of those had been convicted of various criminal charges. Among those indicted were many civilians. Only a small number of indictments had been brought against U.S. border officials, and the few INS officers indicted were low-ranking men. These statistics led some members of Congress and others to cry cover-up, and a Congressional probe into the "clean sweep" was launched.

Members of Congress heard testimony from a former assistant attorney general that he had been offered prostitutes three times—and rejected them—when spending an evening with five or six INS officials on a border inspection trip in Texas. The attorney told congressional investigators that at first he felt the offers of prostitutes were just "misguided hospitality," but began to have questions about the offers a year later when one of the officers was accused of helping to operate a border prostitution ring. The officer, it turned out, had been one of a total of only seven INS officials indicted under Operation Clean Sweep. Despite further cries of cover-up, little more was forthcoming from Clean Sweep and the subsequent congressional investigation.

Complaints against the INS have never really stopped, and the shooting of two Mexican nationals by a Border Patrol agent in 1979 sparked demands by Hispanic and other civil rights groups that a complete investigation of the INS be undertaken by Congress. The two Mexican nationals had been handcuffed together when shot. One was killed.

The shooting was an open invitation for Hispanics and others to demand an investigation because, for once, the Border Patrol had done something that could be proven. The activist groups had amassed a long list of charges against the INS, including excessive brutality against those it arrested and collusion between INS agents and employers trying to break strikes. In cases of brutality, few victims or uninvolved witnesses are usually left to testify for grand jury or other investigations because they have been deported. Other evidence is often either circumstantial or second-hand, coming from volunteers who have worked with undocumented aliens and have heard their complaints.

San Diego police homicide investigators cleared the Border Patrol agent of the fatal shooting, saying that the surviving wounded Mexican national had confirmed the agent's story that he had shot only after having been attacked by the two men. Police officers in Baja, Mexico, however, said that witnesses had come forward to testify that the two men had been shot while trying to run back to the border. Police on both sides of the border denied the credibility of these witnesses, saying that they were probably from among the crowd of forty or so who had gathered after the shooting. One remaining witness, the border jumper who was arrested with the two shot Mexican nationals, did successfully get back across the border and had not been located by Mexican officials. Homicide police, meanwhile, told reporters that evidence indicated the shots had been fired at close range.

An earlier shooting incident along the border near Calexico, California, appeared less complicated. There, the Border Patrol officer involved apparently did not report it to his superiors. The incident came to light only after the victim had been sent back across the border to Mexicali, told there were no facilities to treat him there, and eventually went to border officials in order to get treatment for his wounds in the U.S.

According to the victim, Rodriguez Gomez, a Border Patrol agent had apprehended him and six or seven other men about one hundred yards from the border and ordered the men to stand up. Gomez said he had lifted himself about halfway from the ground when he heard the shot. "I didn't know it was a bullet. I thought it might be a rock. I could walk, so I tried to return to the fence like the others." The Border Patrol agent, according to Gomez, caught up with him and tried to stop the bleeding from his wounded leg with a towel. Then a man on the Mexicali side told him to stay in the U.S. for treatment, and asked that the agent take Gomez to a U.S. hospital. According to Gomez, the agent replied: "There are no doctors at this time." The agent apparently escorted Gomez back to the border where he was unsuccessful in finding treatment. The agent claimed he had shot Gomez because he thought he was armed. The INS promised to investigate the case, but no published reports on its investigations were made.

The most common complaints made by civil rights activists are that the INS discriminates against Hispanic people. Such charges are fairly well documented. It is part of the INS policy game: attempting to protect civil rights while trying to prevent the entry of Mexican nationals who are not entitled to entry, and also trying to deport Hispanic foreign nationals. As long as the INS believes that its most effective policy is to apprehend people at or near the Mexican border, and as long as INS data continue to lead to the conclusion that those now illegally present in the U.S. are either Hispanic or black people, it is undoubtedly a policy that will be continued. This runs into the fact that it infringes on the rights of minority groups who are legally present in the U.S. and who, in many cases, are citizens of the U.S. entitled to equal protection of the law. The INS walks a very thin tightrope and doubtlessly errs on both sides. Meanwhile, to protect minorities from the type of discrimination such policies engender, several groups have brought lawsuits to prevent not only "street sweeps," but sweeps of factories and searches of residences (performed without a warrant) where undocumented workers are believed to live.

Charges of collusion between the Border Patrol or the INS Investigations Division with employers trying to break strikes are ample, but equally difficult to prove because neither employer nor the INS is likely to admit to such practices.

In 1975, for example, leaders of the International Ladies' Garment Workers Union charged that immigration officers had actively helped the owner of a strikebound plant. After an ILGWU walkout, new workers came to replace the old, and the union, suspecting that they were undocumented workers, asked that the INS raid the plant. The INS finally did inspect the plant, after giving the owner several days' notice. When the INS arrived, half the workforce was absent. Of the 293 employees listed as workers, only 146 were present for work on the day of the raid. After interviewing all the workers present, the INS arrested 17 workers. All were union members.

Douglas, Arizona, City Councilman Francisco Barraza testified before the U.S. Senate's 1978 hearings on immigration law: "Let me say this: Before the farm workers—undocumented workers—began organizing, there was not the problem of INS coming in, or immigration authorities coming in, and arresting the people in the numbers that they were being arrested. There was not that problem. As soon as they became organized, and started demanding better working conditions–especially better working conditions–then you would see the problem of the immigration authorities coming in in force and arresting these people in large numbers. . . . Obviously, it is very good and fine to have undocumented people picking their crops, while they were living under the trees, while they were unorganized. As soon as they become organized, then, obviously, they encourage the immigration authorities to come in."

An undocumented worker testified about INS practices at Arizona ranches where attempts at organization were being made: "You must know that we not only have problems with work, but also with immigration. It is chasing us day after day, and, after chasing us, and not catching some of us, they destroy the food that we have accumulated for the week, and destroy our houses [in this instance, tents that the workers had forced the growers to provide them with]."

The INS, like some other police forces, also has an internal investigations unit. It generally does not make its findings public. The Chicago *Tribune* reported, however, that as of early 1979, seven of the INS's thirty-four district directors had been investigated during the past year for alleged mismanagement, waste, and corruption. The newspaper also reported that during 1978 there were 358 internal investigations of charges that Border Patrol officers and other INS employees had engaged in drug smuggling, bribery, brutality, and sexual abuse of deportable aliens. This, the *Tribune* reported, was a 70 percent increase in investigations over the previous year. A few INS officials have been charged with criminal acts. During a one-year period, these reports surfaced:

• A federal grand jury in Miami accused an immigration inspector of selling tourist visas to Argentinian prostitutes so they could work in the U.S. Under the alleged arrangement, each woman was issued a form allowing her to remain in the U.S. on tourist status for two weeks. The women, according to the indictment, were then required to pay $3,000 for six-month visas.

• In Chicago an INS district director was quietly demoted one civil service grade and transferred to Vermont after an internal investigation. The investigation reportedly involved allegations that gifts were accepted from people suspected of employing undocumented workers.

• In Los Angeles, an INS criminal investigator was indicted for accepting more than $7,000 in bribes between March 1974 and November

1977. The indictment was not brought until 1979. A U.S. attorney said the officer had reportedly accepted kickbacks for releasing undocumented workers caught by both the INS and local authorities.

• A Dallas County grand jury indicted an INS agent on charges that he stole $540 from a Mexican national he had arrested.

• Witnesses in a San Antonio federal court hearing testified that a Border Patrol agent shot an undocumented alien in the hand and knee, hit him on the head with the butt of his pistol, and dunked him several times in the Rio Grande. The hearing ended when the undocumented alien was found guilty of assaulting the Border Patrol agent.

Incidents such as the above may inflame both minorities and human rights activists, but they are not the incidents that bring fear of La Migra to the undocumented worker. They are afraid of being arrested on the street, being turned in to the INS by their bosses, or of being arrested on the job. While few undocumented workers come forward to testify about INS tactics, U.S. citizens occasionally do.

As part of a class action lawsuit to test the Border Patrol's constitutional right to make warrantless searches and sweeps of farm workers' camps, several witnesses testified about their experiences with the INS for a federal court proceeding in Washington State:

• Sally Wilson, an American citizen, swore in an affidavit that she was asleep in her farm labor cabin in the predawn hours one day in 1978 when an INS agent entered her bedroom and told her to pull down her bedcovers because he wanted to see if the two shapes beside her in bed were undocumented workers. They were her two children. "After he asked me my name several times, he left my bedroom. He did not ask my permission before entering my bedroom and did not excuse himself or apologize for his conduct. I was frightened by this incident and I felt angry that I should be subjected to such treatment."

• Charles LaDuke, also a seasonal farm worker and a U.S. citizen, said immigration agents searched his living quarters without a warrant or his permission while looking for undocumented Mexican workers. "I was awakened when a flashlight was shined in my eyes and someone said, '*Buenos días, señor*.' After I responded and the intruder discovered I was an Anglo, he questioned me as to whether Mexicans lived in the area and whether anyone else lived in the tent with me. The entire interior of my tent was also flashlight searched by the intruder, who shined his flashlight through the tent window. At no time did the intruder identify himself as a Border Patrol agent or anything else. And at no time did I give permission to anyone to make a flashlight search of my tent."

A month later LaDuke had moved from the tent to a cabin. A few hours after dark, he was awakened by the "rattling of the chain latch on my door. I looked up and saw a hand inside my door. The hand passed through a crack in the door and an agent was apparently attempting to unlatch the chain." LaDuke said the door opened wide enough for someone to shine a flashlight in his face. He was questioned about his identity and whether there were any Mexicans in the area. "My entire cabin was also flashlight searched without my permission. Meanwhile, another agent went to the side of the cabin and inspected the side window to my cabin with his flashlight."

• Carlos Garcia, an American citizen as is his wife, Consuelo, are also migrant workers. They were staying in a motel when Garcia saw "official-looking vehicles" in the motel parking lot at about five in the morning. "After watching the activity in the parking lot for several minutes, I heard a noise that sounded like a radio from the back of the house. I then walked to the back of the house and saw a man in a uniform with a Border Patrol patch standing in the middle of my kitchen. The man questioned me regarding my place of birth and the identity of other occupants of the apartment. I responded, and he left. The immigration agent who entered my house did not ask for or receive permission to enter my house."

Consuelo Garcia filed an affidavit supporting her husband's statements.

The Garcias, LaDuke, and Wilson were joined by others who claimed a pattern and practice by the INS that violated their Fourth Amendment right to be protected from unreasonable searches, as well as their right to privacy under federal and state laws.

A section of the United States code provides that "Any officer or employe of the [Immigration and Naturalization] Service authorized under regulations prescribed by the attorney general shall have power without warrant to interrogate any alien or person believed to be an alien as to his right to be or to remain in the United States."

It is this law and the enforcement tactics that accompany it that put fear into the undocumented worker's heart, causing him or her to always be on watch for, and to always hide from La Migra, or anyone else who might turn him in. La Migra, it is said, can strike anywhere and at any time.

11: SLAVE TRADE THUGS AND RACKETEERS

A twenty-eight-year-old El Salvadorian woman, an undocumented worker employed as a maid in Virginia, left an Arlington store carrying a bag of groceries and was enjoying an unusually pleasant winter day in 1978 as she walked. A man approached her and said in Spanish – the only language that she speaks or fully understands – that he had been following her from another store. He showed her a fake ID card and said he was an immigration agent. He ordered her to come with him for a physical examination. She obeyed and got into the man's car. He drove her to an apartment, and the woman knew that something was wrong. She tried to run away but was beaten and taken into a room where two men were waiting. Someone drew a gun and told the woman to undress. Another told her that if she did not cooperate with them she would be taken to La Migra in the nude. Terrified, she undressed. The men raped her. Then one of the men drove her back to the shopping center and took the groceries and all her money – four quarters – "for gas." Before she was released she was told, "If you report this to the police you'll be deported."

The woman, like many unknown hundreds like her, did not call the police.

Distinguishing her case from others like it was a chain of events that allowed her to talk to the police, almost one year after the crime. The maid eventually told a friend of hers, a naturalized El Salvadorian who was an American citizen, about the rape. The friend, outraged, told local police about it without using any names. The police then talked to the INS, and they agreed not to deport the maid if she helped them in their case. The maid's friend relayed this information to her, and the woman decided to talk to the police and even to testify against the criminals if they were caught. With the maid's help, one of them was identified and a warrant was put out for his arrest.

Virginia criminal investigators, meanwhile, had developed evidence for what they believed was a five-man ring involved in crimes against undocumented aliens. Their problem, until the maid decided to help, was that they could find no one who would press charges against, or testify against, the suspected criminals.

According to Roger Hensley, head of the Alexandria police's intelligence and organized crime section, "These people [undocumented foreigners] are scared of two things: they're scared of the men who are committing these crimes, and they're scared that if they report the crimes they will be deported."

A District of Columbia police officer cited another example, what he described as a typical incident. Police, responding to a report of a domestic quarrel, arrived to find a woman bruised and bloodied, her boyfriend gone. She refused to press charges and rejected offers of medical help. Finally, as the police questioned her further, they learned that both she and her boyfriend were undocumented aliens. She begged the police to leave her alone, telling them that the man's family had threatened to kill her if she said anything that resulted in his arrest or deportation. Commenting on the case, a District police officer said, "The situation here is probably typical of big cities around the country with large alien populations. Illegal aliens, if they even come in contact with the police, are extremely hesitant about giving out any information.

"Criminals who operate in this community have a haughty disdain. They taunt their victims because they are so sure their crimes will never be reported."

Others also rely on their victims' fear of La Migra to profit from their undocumented status. An unknown number of landlords find riches from the slave trade as well.

A young worker from Guanajuato, Mexico, arrested by the INS as he was going to work at a mobile-home factory in Texas, said he and his fellow workers earned $3.25 an hour. However, he paid $30 a week to a woman for room and board, and another $25 a week to the same woman for transportation to his job. Apparently this arrangement was also made with the second undocumented worker found in her car that morning. Despite his earnings at the factory, said Sergio Rangel, eighteen years old, these payments made it impossible for him to send any money home to his parents and brothers and sisters during the four months he had worked at the plant.

Early in 1978, Texas INS agents found more than twenty Mexican nationals working in an insulation factory. They worked sixty hours a week and were paid $70. They lived in an old wooden barracks near the factory. Out of their $70 came $20 to $30 a week for their housing.

In Tyler, Texas, forty-five Mexican nationals were found living in a three-bedroom, one-bath farm house that was described by INS agents in 1978 as derelict and run down. Each man was paying the American owner $20 a week rent—a total of $900 a *week* for a single dilapidated dwelling.

A fancy Mexican restaurant in the Los Angeles area reportedly has a crew of twenty Mexican nationals. They are housed by the owner of the restaurant in a small house nearby. They sleep there in shifts. Rent is deducted from their wages.

The stories of rent profiteering are endless and range from coast to coast, wherever there are undocumented workers. Some INS officials observe that it is harder for the foreigners to get housing than it is for them to find work. They therefore are easy prey for landlords who can crowd them into substandard housing at rents much higher than they can extort even in urban slums. Their tenants, after all, cannot complain.

Some landlords have come up with an even more brutal scheme to increase their earnings. Richard E. Norton, an assistant director of the immigration service, explains: "They get a full month's rent from the alien and then they call us. That way they can rent the apartment – and get the full month's rent – several times every month, and what they're doing is not illegal." (Actually, such landlords who knowingly rent to undocumented workers are violating federal statutes against harboring undocumented aliens.)

Rackets of All Kinds

One Los Angeles employer, according to city council member Arthur K. Snyder, adapted this rent-and-eviction scheme to his own purpose. A local laundry plant, said Snyder, charged undocumented workers $200 each for their jobs. Within a couple of months the workers were fired, and another group of *pollos* were charged $200 each to replace them, Snyder added.

Outright abuse is not all that plagues the undocumented immigrant. Hundreds of people have devised a variety of ways to make a dollar or two from the misery of those whose choice is hope in the U.S. or hunger at home. Rackets and schemes to bilk money from misery include promises of jobs that don't exist, high-priced forged documents that won't pass any but the most cursory inspection, marriage arrangements that don't withstand INS probes, and phony advice from alleged immigration "consultants" who either charge for work that could be done for nothing or collect fees on false promises of hope of a legalized life in the U.S. If their fees aren't paid on time, there is always the threat of La Migra.

Indicating the variety of such schemes were 1975 indictments by a Newark grand jury charging eleven people for fraudulent schemes involving thirty undocumented immigrants. Charges included impersonating immigration officers, performing sham marriages, and luring foreign crewmen off ships docked in Philadelphia and New York with promises of American jobs. U.S. Attorney Jonathan L. Goldstein explained that the defendants named in the five indictments were not part of a conspiracy, "but rather a subculture of people who exploit illegal aliens." The defendants allegedly received from $200 to $2,000 from those who engaged their services.

One of the men charged in the New Jersey indictments was a sheet-metal worker who allegedly posed as an immigration officer and threatened undocumented immigrants that he would turn them in to the authorities if they did not pay him "bribes" of from $200 to $300. Another of the indictments charged that a mother-daughter team boarded a merchant vessel docked in New York and lured a Chinese crewman ashore with the promise of a job. After the crewman jumped ship and went to work illegally as a dishwasher, the pair demanded $200 from him. The remaining indictments were for sham marriage ceremonies costing between $1,000 and $2,000 each.

The fake marriage racket, according to INS officials, began to accelerate in 1968 when the first quotas were placed on Western Hemisphere immigrants to the U.S. The waiting time for legitimate immigration—in those cases where it is possible—ranges from two to three years in many countries, both because of quota backlogs and because the INS is slow in processing applications. Marriage to an American citizen can reduce that time, and brings the newlywed outside the quota system entirely.

In some cases, would-be immigrants are so desperate that they promise to pay their "spouses" a monthly fee for years. According to the INS, fraudulent marriage rackets are broken up every month—like the one involving a Miami woman and her two daughters who had petitioned for entry into this country for thirteen "husbands," all Haitian nationals. In a District of Columbia racket, one U.S. citizen was found to have "married" fifteen aliens from African nations.

American citizens who agree to participate as phony husbands or wives are often poor people themselves, badly in need of the $300 to $500 that is their usual cut from the deal. But would-be immigrants are even more desperate. A District of Columbia priest recalled a domestic worker from Central America who had purchased a fake marriage and was then investigated by the INS. "Immigration visited the house where she was living with friends," said the priest, "and they told her that if she was married she should live with her husband. So she went to her husband's apartment. I don't know what happened to her there, but she committed suicide." The priest suggested that perhaps the "husband" had insisted on consummating the "marriage," and, "she felt so bad she jumped off the Sixteenth Street Bridge."

José Leon, a Mexican national in his twenties, was told by an immigration "consultant" in Los Angeles that all he had to do to get his immigration papers was to go through a sham marriage. The fake wedding cost him $1,300. When Leon learned that the deal was a fraud, he tried to get his money back – unsuccessfully.

In Baltimore, after a grand jury indicted five people in a fraudulent marriage scheme in late 1978, Robert Short, assistant director of investigations for the INS, said about 40 percent of the fraud cases his office handled involved marriage fraud.

Fraudulent documents are also a big business in the underground population. They are sometimes sufficiently well made to fool employers (when employers choose to ask to see them), but seldom pass muster with local police, or with La Migra. In the early 1970s Los Angeles police found 60,000 fake immigration documents in a public locker. Their estimated street value was $3 million. Charges and arrests in the illicit document trade were also made in 1977. In 1978, police again found a load of forged alien registration cards in California. The cards bore the same numbers as cards confiscated in Tucson earlier that year. The haul in California was only forty blank cards ready for speedy preparation, but the police also found laminating machines, drills, and typewriters at the scene, suggesting that the forty cards were only part of the operation. INS investigators called in on the case said the central printing operation was in Mexico, where blank cards were run off by the thousands and then smuggled into the U.S. These were then sold to individuals in the U.S. who offered to make up the cards for fees ranging from $50 to $1,000, depending on the distance of the "applicant" from the Mexican border.

In early 1979 two Brooklyn police officers arrested a Trinidad native who, it was estimated, made $100,00 a month selling phony alien registration cards. The Brooklyn officer had acted on a tip from an acquaintance, the superintendent of an apartment building, who said he had given the Trinidad man $25,000 in behalf of thirty-six people – his friends and fellow church members. In some instances, the purchasers, mostly Dominicans, were paying for their cards in installments. In cooperation with the police, the building superintendent took $500 in marked money to the salesman. Accompanying the superintendent was a police officer who posed as a Panamanian also wanting to buy a card. The document salesman, apparently unaware that he was being set up, accepted the marked money. Two officers arrested him and he was charged with grand larceny.

Another common racket is the fraudulent immigration "consultant" operation. These men and women often operate under cover of a travel agency or as notaries public (in Mexico, the *notario publico* has many of the powers of an attorney, unlike his American counterpart). By one means or another, the travel agent, the notary, or the consultant convinces the undocumented immigrant that he or she can, almost as if working miracles, get the INS to provide legal documents for the client. One such client, a busboy working in Los Angeles, had paid $1,000 to one of these immigration consultants in return for paperwork that a volunteer worker could have done for free in just a few minutes. The consultant, however, "virtually promised" the busboy that he would receive legal status in the U.S., according to one official, even though the state labor commission almost never extends immigration permits to those who work as busboys.

One of the better-known consulting rackets was broken up in 1975 when its head, Arnold Kligerman, received a ten-year prison sentence. Kligerman worked with an outfit called Universal Visa Services, and then, at the time of his apprehension, at Mundial Visa Services. Kligerman was charged with nine counts of taking money from would-be immigrants and promising to help them legalize their status, when he knew his clients did not meet the eligibility requirements for legal immigration. Mundial Visa Services, meanwhile, was barred from doing business in Nevada after state authorities there accused it of misleading advertising.

A year later, Green Card Information Service, which collected up to $1,000 for immigration advice, was charged with fraud. Despite promises of a free initial consultation, according to authorities, the company persuaded its clients to put up at least $50 as a down payment and to sign an installment-payment contract for its poorly rendered services.

Two years later, police announced they had broken up yet another allegedly phony consulting group, this one stretching throughout the state of California, with offices in Los Angeles, San Francisco, and San Jose. The story was a rerun of the old tale: allegations of phony advice, phony papers, and phony marriages. "In short," prosecuting San Francisco District Attorney Joseph Freitas, Jr., told reporters, the firm "tells its customers what they want to hear—that their case will not be a problem and that it can be resolved within six to eight months." In fact, Freitas said, some of the firm's clients had been waiting for more than three years and their cases still were not resolved.

Thugs and Killers

A special breed of criminal preys on undocumented farm workers. Occasionally, these are small-time coyotes, who well know where they have taken their clients. Most coyotes (usually retired) who give interviews tell of the empathy they have for the people they help come to the United States to get work they cannot get back home. One has even bragged that he has made a trip to Michoacán State in Mexico where many of his customers have originated, and that they greeted him like a hero. Even, he said, the *rurales* (local police) left him unmolested because he had provided trips to El Norte for them as well. "After all," explained one coyote, "it is a word-of-mouth business. If you do these terrible things, you have no more business."

Perhaps there are "clean" smuggling operations – groups who have delivered what they have promised without abandoning, robbing, or killing any *pollos* on the way. Perhaps.

One retired smuggler in northern San Diego County revealed that some coyotes, small-time operators like himself, have specially rigged trunks in their cars that can be filled with carbon monoxide exhaust, killing unsuspecting passengers as they are being transported. This is used, said the coyote, only when the passenger is known to be carrying a large amount of money with him. The *pollo* is lured into the trunk where, he is told, he will be safer because he will be out of La Migra's sight. "I know an illegal who wanted to go into town to buy a new car," the smuggler recalled. "He had $5,000 on him and one of his supposed coyote friends told him he'd take the guy into town. He was talked into getting in the trunk so he wouldn't be seen by the Border Patrol. He was left for dead alongside a country road – minus the five thousand bucks."

A true story? Or just a fabrication to make a journalist think his or her source is more important than he really is? No one, perhaps, will ever know. But there are other stories, stories of a similarly gruesome nature, that say much about a defenseless group of people who, it would seem, can be beaten, robbed, and killed with impunity.

In 1978, police reported, three armed men staged an early morning holdup of seven undocumented workers in an Oceanside, California, tomato field. The armed robbers moved in on a compound of makeshift huts, firing into the ground as they approached. The workers were rounded up and forced to hand over an undisclosed amount of cash. A police officer said the workers had been saving their money for Christmas visits to their home towns in Mexico.

Fort Worth police announced in early 1979 that they were looking for a couple who allegedly were part of a crew of four armed robbers preying on undocumented aliens in the area. The gang was suspected of committing two dozen or more robberies in Tarrant County. Sheriff Lon Evans and Fort Worth police Lieutenant L. O. Fowler said the group posed as INS officers, or, on other occasions, had one of their members pose as a prostitute to gain entry into aliens' homes. After gaining entry, they pulled out their pistols and robbed the defenseless victims. In some instances, according to the sheriff, the victims were beaten so severely with pistols that they had to return to Mexico to recuperate. The robbers, said Sheriff Evans, averaged from $400 to $500 per robbery.

Smugglers regularly bring prostitutes into farm labor camps, usually on the evening of payday. A retired smuggler described how one such prostitution operation worked. The smuggler reported making a trip once with a fellow coyote who regularly brought prostitutes into the farm labor camps of southern California. "He gets the girls from Tijuana and splits the take with them fifty-fifty. They supply the entertainment, and he supplies the transportation and booze. They take the booze into the camps and sell it to the workers and the women go to work."

Some of the reported killings of undocumented farm workers in the area, the retired smuggler suggested, were the result of fights over these women. Explained the smuggler, "When these women come into a camp, the men get the booze and stand around and drink while waiting. Someone will get a little drunk and announce he's going to be next and maybe it isn't his turn—tempers will rise and fights begin—someone usually gets stabbed, maybe even killed, and dumped in the bushes." Thirteen Mexican nationals were reported killed in farm labor camps in San Diego County during 1978.

Not all undocumented farm workers take such outrages quietly, however. In 1978, one Mexican national walked out of the vast tomato fields near Oceanside, California, to summon help. He reported to police that armed robberies of the hidden labor camps in the area were frequent and that he had been the victim of such a robbery. He was able to assist police in their investigation of the robberies by revealing to them the locations of camps and the routes in and out of them. As a result of his efforts, police were able to arrest eight people, including two fifteen-year-old girls, believed to have been responsible for some twenty-three armed robberies. The others charged in the case were five U.S. Marines and one ex-Marine. A search of one of the suspected robber's homes revealed a cache of stolen items, including clothing, radios, watches, rings, Mexican money, and a .22 caliber rifle. "Those people went right up to the camps and shacks where the aliens were living and robbed them at gunpoint. They beat the people and sometimes even fired shots at them," said one of the arresting officers. With the cooperation of the INS, robbery victims were allowed to remain in the country on special work permits to testify against the gang.

Operaciones Estafadores

Los Angeles police, in the early 1970s, began a program to combat crimes against undocumented city residents that could serve as a model for other urban centers. They opened a center in the heart of an East Los Angeles barrio in a storefront near what was sometimes called Junk Yard Row. There, as part of Operaciones Estafadores (Operation Swindlers), Spanish-speaking police officers offer a "no questions asked" clearing-house where residents, documented and undocumented alike, are able to report allegations of criminal conduct and consumer fraud. More than 60,000 complaints had been received by the office in about five years. Although undocumented residents were still reluctant to appear in court as witnesses, police were at least able to compile a list of charges against swindling outfits in the area, some of which led to prosecutions by city and state attorneys.

By March 1975, the unit had already produced some convictions. Encouraged by this success, police in Pasadena, California, and Venice – a Los Angeles suburb then a poverty area – established similar operations. In 1978, U.S. Representative Hamilton Fish, Jr. commended the program as one that police in other urban areas should contemplate instituting to combat crimes against undocumented aliens.

12: BUILDING A LIFE IN THE UNITED STATES

British journalist Henry Fairlie, it was reported in 1979, had lived in the U.S. as an "illegal alien" for more than ten years. During those years he had built a reputation as the author of several books, including *The Kennedy Promise, The Spoiled Child of the Western World*, and *The Seven Deadly Sins*. Additionally, the fifty-five-year-old Fairlie had written regularly about the American scene for such prestigious publications as the *Washington Post,* and the *New Republic*. While he was living "overground-underground" as an out-of-status alien, he said, he never acquired a social security number, nor even opened a checking account because of all the questions asked on the application forms. "It's very difficult to live out of status," said Fairlie. "I used to look at those figures [estimates of the number of illegal aliens in the U.S.]–twelve million–and think, 'Who are the other 11,999,999?' "

Even though Fairlie finally decided to apply for U.S. citizenship, deportation to England would pose no severe hardship for him. His life in the U.S. went well, as, doubtlessly, would his life in England. In the paradox that marks U.S. immigration procedures today, it is he who is more likely to get the American citizenship he wants than those others he used to wonder about, the other foreigners, those in America's underground slave trade. For them, building a life in the U.S. is a much more difficult prospect–whether it is just long enough to earn a grubstake to ensure a better life for a family back home, or a permanent home in the U.S. Fairlie noted, "As everyone points out, I've hardly been hiding myself." Nor had the INS been searching for him very strenuously. His one-year journalist's visa expired in 1967. It wasn't until 1976 that he was first officially ordered to leave the United States, and it wasn't until three years later that the INS finally acted on the order, giving him thirty days' notice to leave the U.S. voluntarily.

Most of the others who make up the INS apprehension statistics are unlike Fairlie in almost every respect. They are actively pursued by La Migra. They are often caught as soon as they find a job, and, more often, before. And their deportation notice is carried out overnight. So they do not live "overground-underground." They hide. They hide where they can blend in best–with the poverty of their ethnic brothers and sisters in ghettos, barrios, and run-down Anglo neighborhoods, the poorest even of the poor among whom they live. They are afraid, because for them deportation would mean a return to a life worse than that they live here. Deportation might mean not only the slow, gnawing hunger of malnutrition, but, as they try helplessly to scratch out some kind of living, might mean watching their children starve.

For these exploited peoples, even a few days, or even weeks without

114

decent food or shelter is better than La Migra. Because in the U.S., at least, they have hope of work.

Hunger in the Fields

In stark contrast to journalist Fairlie is the story of a band of "illegal aliens" who eventually sought help – because they had no food – from a San Dieguito, California, Catholic priest. The priest, Frank Sierra, went with an illegal Mexican national who had come from the hills seeking his help to see things for himself. It was January 1978, one of the wettest seasons in the state's history, breaking a two-year drought. The Volkswagen van driving Padre Sierra to the illegals' camp where he was to say mass plowed through six to twelve inches of mud in the canyons of the Encinitas foothills where there once were firm dirt roads. After a long and difficult ride, the van stopped to meet a group of men who escorted the priest two miles in the rain across fields and over fences to a place near their camp where they had put together an altar made from some old and water-logged crates. The priest celebrated mass and promised to return with food and clothes. What he had seen touched him: "As large a group as fifty men had not eaten in three or four days [except for] some vegetables found in fields, mostly discard. As far as he was able to provide for himself, that was his day's allowance. Some were so weak they couldn't get off the ground."

The priest returned every five days or so to that camp and to others like it with sacks of flour and beans, and clothing donated by his parish. The trips continued until the rains let up in March. "It hardly mattered which road I took," he told a local reporter, "places [of need] opened up daily."

Why didn't the men, in their hunger, return to their homes in Mexico? The border was less than one hundred miles south. They stayed on in the rain and the mud and, later, the floods because when the rains ended, they could return to their work in the fields. And besides, their lives on the other side of the border would hardly be different – except there would be no hope of work when the rains ended.

In New York City

In 1970 Francisco Rodriguez (not his real name) arrived in New York City. He had come from the Dominican Republic with a forged Puerto Rican birth certificate. After three months of looking, Rodriguez finally found a job in New Jersey where he mixed metallic dyes. He brought home $85 a week and was able to send from $35 to $50 home to his mother. After five months, the plant moved to another part of the state and Rodriguez decided it was better for him to stay behind in New York City, where few people noticed him and no one wondered where he came from.

With a friend, another illegal immigrant from the Dominican Republic, he started a business doing odd jobs. The pair made at most $12 a day, and after four months they gave up the enterprise.

Luck changed for Rodriguez when he and some friends moved to Paterson, New Jersey, where they found jobs at an electronics assembly plant, putting together teletype machines. For this he earned $2.44 an hour and brought home as much as $100 a week, most of which he sent to his mother. Six months later, the plant's workers went on strike. Rodriguez was afraid to apply for strike benefits because someone might learn he was not legally entitled to live in the United States.

He moved back to Manhattan and, in 1971, found his best job, at a Ford assembly plant across the river in New Jersey. He was underweight for Ford's requirements, but some of his friends convinced the boss that he could do the work. Here he earned $3.40 an hour plus overtime. He rented a large apartment and subleased parts of it to fellow countrymen for $15 a week. Rodriguez was becoming rich and was able to send so much money home to his family, he said, that he was finally able to buy a house for his mother. While at Ford he began to understand that he would never voluntarily go back to live in the Dominican Republic. Things had been so bad for him there that he had once or twice thought of killing himself. He tried to find a way to legalize his status in the U.S., offering money to Puerto Rican friends in his neighborhood if they would find him a woman to marry who was a U.S. citizen. Later in the year he had finally found a U.S. citizen to marry—not through a scheme, but through love. They married. But as the boss at Ford had predicted, the work became too much for him. He lost too much weight and his health gave out. Rodriguez finally had to quit. He went back to the street, hustling odd jobs while his wife earned a little money assembling jewelry at a local plant.

Despite his American wife, his life was not secure, for he was still a deportable alien. Citizenship could come later. Now he feared even asking the immigration officials how he might apply. Maybe sometime later someone would explain how to become a citizen, how to become a "legal."

Finally, he found work for a Cuban landlord who, sensing his fear, hired him. He was on call twenty-four hours a day. The landlord used

Rodriguez as a chauffeur, made him help at the restaurant he owned, sometimes made him work at a flower shop he owned, and always had odd jobs for him to do at the two apartment houses he owned. At night Rodriguez tended the boilers in the apartment houses. For all this he was paid $130 a week. But he knew better than to complain. Between what he and his wife earned he was still able to send some money back home to his family. And the job here, he said, was much better than anything a person like him—with only a year or so of school— could find in the Dominican Republic.

INS Stumbling Blocks

Marriage to a U.S. citizen is not alone sufficient to guarantee legal status, not sufficient to prevent deportation, as a San Antonio Catholic nun who works with immigrants explains. Sister Adela Arroyo tells of a man who left his home in Coahuila, Mexico, in 1972 and found a job in San Antonio for $25 a week. He also met a woman in San Antonio. They fell in love.

La Migra, however, apprehended the man and returned him to Mexico. But he came back to be with his loved one. The INS deported him again. Again he returned. The last time he was picked up by La Migra he had been married to the woman for three months. This time, however, he was not deported. He was sent to La Tuna federal prison in El Paso for repeated violation of the immigration laws of the U.S.—a felony.

Sister Adela Arroyo interceded in the case, working with the regional INS director to have the man processed for permanent resident status. After he served his sentence, the man was declared eligible to rejoin his wife.

"The most amazing thing about this story," said the nun, "is that now, everywhere the man and his wife go, they take her two small cousins. For all the years the couple went together while he was still an illegal, the parents of the little girls wouldn't let them be with the man. They feared if he was picked up for deportation, the little girls would be sent away too."

Margo Cowan, head of the Manzo Area Council, a Tucson service center for undocumented workers, explains the paradox of American immigration law that makes a man like Rodriguez an "illegal alien" despite the fact that the intent of the immigration law—that he should be a legal resident—is clear: "I think what is important to understand is that the INS system, as it is organized right today, doesn't push. If I take someone down who is a spouse of a U.S. citizen, and we file a petition, and we say, 'Here is my husband. I would like to immigrate him. I am a U.S. citizen. How can we do this?' The petition will be taken but it probably won't be acted on for sixty or ninety days. Then it will be acted on one way or another; either accepted or rejected.

"Then it is forwarded to an American consulate. They may or may not be seen within a year. . . . We are looking at someone who will have to be on, quote unquote, house arrest probably for a year before his petition can even be adjudicated by the State Department. So, we are talking about a time that this person, who has a legitimate right to be with his family . . . that is the whole underlying theme of the [immigration] legislation, since they began to enact legislation, was that U.S. citizens had a right to have their family with them, and we ought to process these things in a speedy manner, and there shouldn't be any roadblocks."

Margo Cowan notes that a very small percentage of the people she sees at the Manzo council are economic refugees. "Overwhelmingly, the undocumented people that I see, that are having contact with the INS, and that are having contact with the Border Patrol, are people who have a [moral] right to be here, who are in the process of legalizing their status. A quarter of our caseload are American citizens with no documentation; no birth certificate, no derivative petition, no naturalization petition. But they are people who have a [legal but undocumented] claim to citizenship."

Luis Gómez (not his real name) says "I've been lucky." He first crossed the border in 1972. He, unlike most others, crossed with his wife and family. His first stay in the U.S. ended in 1973 after their two-year-old daughter died of cystic fibrosis in DeKalb, Illinois, and their sadness was too hard to bear so far from home. After a time the family returned to the U.S., this time to New Orleans. And again they returned home, after Gómez's working hours were cut so short they could no longer make their way. This time Gómez tried to apply for an immigrant visa at an American consular office in Mexico. He was not eligible because he could not prove that he would not become a "public charge" in the U.S. So the family returned to the U.S. illegally again. After being settled in Houston for two years, the INS finally found the family and deported them. As before, Gómez came back to the U.S. But this time he came alone. And this time he was able to find a job that paid $200 a week in the construction business, enough to pay for his own needs in the mobile home he never leaves for fear of La Migra, and for the needs of his family in Mexico. His wife and three sons live in Nuevo

Laredo in a tiny, single-walled wooden house not a third as large as Gómez's mobile home in Houston. The house has electricity and gas, but Maria Gómez must do the laundry by hand. Despite the insulation installed by Luis, it seems that it never gets warm in winter and his children continually have colds and bronchitis.

Once, while at his job, the INS picked up and deported a worker at the same job site as Gómez, but he was inside and escaped notice. So, he explains to a reporter, he has been lucky.

Not all are so lucky as Luis Gómez.

Pedro (not his real name) came to the U.S. from the Yucatán Peninsula of Mexico. "Where I lived in the Yucatán there are not many jobs. Those who have jobs are exploited by the employers. The government knows the employers exploit the workers, but the government doesn't care. In Mexico the government is a combination of the employer and the government. Mexico does not have a government of the people. It will never get better in Mexico. In the Yucatán the rich are very rich and the poor are very poor."

Pedro, one of the poor lucky enough to have a good paying job, earned $43 a week as a chauffeur in Yucatán. He and his wife and son lived in a house without plumbing. They did not see how they could ever make their lives any better in Yucatán. In 1977 they sold their household belongings, left their ten-year-old son in the care of relatives, and began the long journey to El Norte. After a trip of nearly four thousand miles, Pedro and his wife ended up in a San Francisco suburb, where they live in a rented house with another Mexican couple. Their trip from Mexico had used up most of their money. The only work Pedro could find in the Golden State was as a janitor where he works part time, sometimes earning $75 a week. "My boss says he has to deduct taxes," says Pedro, but "he takes away tax money and puts the money in his pocket. We make enough here only to live and there is nothing to put away. But life is still better here. At least we have good food and a balanced diet. The house we rent has plumbing.

"My dream would be to bring my son to the United States. I would like to go to night school and learn English. If I could pick up papers, I would like to stay here. But now, I do not have any hope. I live in constant fear of deportation. It is a very sad life. You expect nothing from nobody. My hope now is to make enough money so we can go back to Mexico."

Consuelo is a Mexican national who has made a small life for herself and her six children in a Tucson barrio. She has worked in the United States as a maid for five years. One of her children was born in Tucson.

Consuelo is not rich; she only brings home $320 a month, enough to pay the rent and buy food and clothes for her children and pay for her transportation to work. But she is wealthy in another way. She has friends in the barrio, friends who, when she was deported to Nogales two years ago with all her children, went to Nogales and started crossing the children back over the border as part of their own families. One by one the children crossed, and when they were all safe, Consuelo did the same.

"We didn't have any relatives in Nogales," she said. "We had to sleep in a cave in a small hill. We were not allowed to take anything with us [when we were deported]. My children got bitten by bugs all over." La Migra had come to her Tucson home at noon and told her she was being deported. By 6 P.M. she and her family were in Nogales. "But they [the neighbors] found us the following day."

Consuelo wishes only to stay in the United States. "My children have grown used to it, and I have grown used to my neighbors. I like it here." Despite the fact that one of her sons is an American citizen, there is no way that she can legalize her status here. So she lives in fear of La Migra, but also knows she has friends who will help her.

Into a Third Generation

Not all undocumented immigrants are the first in their families to come to the United States. Nor do all spend only a few years in the U.S. – time to make enough money to improve their lives at home. Some are successful in building lives for themselves. One such family lives in Sonoma County, California, where the grandparents have lived, illegally, for almost thirty years. Several years ago their married son came to join them from his home in a small Michoacán village – one of those civilization has left behind – a village without electricity, without plumbing, and without roads or cars. After working five years the son had saved enough money to send for his wife and children. On receiving word from her husband, Anna (not her real name) left her village and traveled to Morelia, the capital of Michoacán. There she boarded the bus to Tijuana. "I was scared to leave my home," she recalled, "but I was coming to my husband, and to work. This is where there are jobs." In Tijuana she contacted a coyote who brought Anna and her children to El Norte.

Working together, Anna and her husband bought their own house, where their teen-age children and her husband's parents live with them.

They are not a rich family and would be eligible for some forms of public assistance if they were citizens, and even for available private assistance if they were not afraid of deportation nor too proud to seek it. So they work. Everyone who can works at whatever jobs they can find. Both Anna and her husband work at a local manufacturing plant for the minimum wage, her husband taking the night shift so he can work days in the apple orchards. Anna herself sometimes works two shifts for the extra money. "The kids go to school all day," Anna explains, "and then go to pick apples [during the season] until it is night and they have to come home. I have a daughter who is twelve, but she is tall, so she says she is sixteen so she can work."

Being a working mother and working so many double shifts have taken their toll on Anna, whose health was already weakened from the poverty of the Michoacán village. She has been in the hospital three times for exhaustion in the last five years. But she does not complain. "When you have money you can pay for your own medical expenses. It is beautiful to spend your own money knowing that you have worked for it."

Only once has the family had trouble with La Migra, when Anna's mother-in-law was deported several years ago. She was bused to the other side of the border with only a little money. She had no friends in Tijuana, and all her family was in Sonoma County. Without money to pay a coyote, she crossed the border herself, striking out into the mountains and trying to move north. She was lost in the hills for almost a month and lived only on what she could gather. Finally, her hunger forced her down to a farm house where she offered to work for some food. There she learned she was in the United States, and from there she made her way back to Sonoma County, about six hundred miles north.

Anna's family includes three generations. None are American citizens. All can be deported at any time with little legal recourse—even the grandparents, who have been settled in the same region for more than a quarter of a century: even the teen-agers, who after five years of American education are more American than they are Mexican.

13: BREAKING OUT OF BONDAGE

> Those who profess to favor freedom, and yet deprecate
> agitation, are men who want crops without plowing the
> ground. They want rain without thunder and lightning.
> They want the ocean without the awful roar of its waters.
> This struggle may be a moral one; or it may be a physical
> one; or it may be both moral and physical; but it must be
> struggle. Power concedes nothing without a demand. It
> never did, and it never will. Find out just what people
> will submit to, and you have found out the exact amount
> of injustice and wrong which will be imposed upon them;
> and these will continue until they are resisted with
> either words or blows or with both. The limits of tyrants
> are prescribed by the endurance of those whom they
> oppress.
>
> —*Frederick Douglass, August 4, 1857*

If American stereotypes of Mexicans were analyzed, two conflicting images would probably surface. One might be summarized by the single word *mañana*, tomorrow—the Mexican is lazy. The other could be taken from the mouths of their farm and factory and restaurant employers: hard working. These images strangely parallel the way many southern slave holders characterized their human chattel more than a century ago: the black slave was basically lazy and would not work without the overseer's bullwhip at his back. But, by God, they were the only people he could find who could do the hard work of picking cotton. Indians died from it and white men couldn't do the work; only the black slave could be made to work hard enough to sustain the southern plantation.

When slaves rebelled, either singly or in groups, these acts were written off to slaves "gone bad," not to the nature of the peculiar institution that held them in bondage, nor to the fact that the lazy human property were also a people who could rise up and say "no more" with all of the dignity—and power—of the early slave holding colonists declaring their independence from King George III.

The U.S. House Select Committee on Population projected, in 1978, that the undocumented immigrant may "become wedged into an inferior status, part of a substratum in American society that is outside the education and social service systems. Although illegal aliens, because of their self-perception as natives of another country who expect to earn money here and return to their country of origin—may be willing to accept these circumstances, comparing them favorably to the far worse conditions from which they came, their children are unlikely to

122

accept the same exploitative conditions and low-paying, 'dead-end' jobs.

"The children that illegal aliens bring to the United States, although lacking U.S. citizenship, will think of themselves as Americans with rising expectations and dreams of upward mobility. . . . Continued illegal immigration under such conditions may in time produce a second generation of alienated, frustrated young people in our society, capable of producing hostilities, disturbances, and protests like those of the 1960s."

In other words, if the slaves are not revolting now, their sons and daughters surely will. But the rebellion has already begun. The Mexican immigrants of today *are* the sons and daughters of first and even second generation "illegals."

The rebellion is not so simple as a mere protest here and there against certain facets of life in underground America. It has the portents of a much greater rebellion, a rebellion against basic institutions that have seldom been questioned in the U.S.

On one front, it is a rebellion against archaic and absurd notions. The notion of citizenship itself, for example. In feudal times, citizenship derived from fealty, loyalty and willingness to fight for a feudal lord. What today defines who is and who is not a citizen? Place of birth is almost universally accepted. But how is the term used when a person born in one place wishes to change his or her loyalty to another? This is determined by laws that are periodically changed. If the foreign-born would-be citizen fits into one of the limited categories of persons eligible to become citizens, then he or she may apply. After five years, and following lessons on U.S. government and history, and lessons in English, and, after swearing before a U.S. judge and flag, right hand raised, "that I absolutely and entirely renounce and abjure all allegiance and fidelity to any foreign prince, potentate, state or sovereignty . . . that I will support and defend the Constitution and laws of the United States of America against all enemies, foreign and domestic; that I will bear true faith and allegiance to the same; that I will bear arms on behalf of the United States when required by the law . . . and that I take this obligation freely without any mental reservation or purpose of evasion; so help me God," then the one-time "alien" becomes a naturalized U.S. citizen. Why five years? Why lessons in English? Why not a citizenship determined by place of primary residence? Why are the native-born considered more likely to be good citizens than the foreign-born? In past wars it has been seen over and over again that the foreign-born are often more patriotic than their native-born neighbors and comrades at arms. What is the reasoning that says the native-born child is a citizen, but his foreign-born parents are "illegal aliens," eligible to apply for citizenship only when their child has reached twenty-one? What is the reasoning that says the American-born child, as a citizen, is eligible for free health treatment if his or her mother is poor, but the foreign-born brother or sister is not eligible?

On another front of the rebellion is a mass protest against an entire set of circumstances that destines those on one side of an invisible line to be poor, ill, homeless, and starving while those on the other side of the line—who can be watched on television or seen just by looking across the line—have jobs, food, health, and money. It is a protest against the fact that those who work for the same company are paid different wages, depending upon which side of the line they live. And it is a protest against something greater than all of that, a protest against the institution of inequity itself.

Peter Schey, a Los Angeles attorney originally from South Africa, who specializes in immigration law and has been active in the struggle for expanding the rights of the foreign-born, explains:

> This country saw massive anti-war movements. This country saw a massive movement, a grass roots movement, to support the rights of Black persons. I do not think that North America has ever seen the kind of civil disobedience that is going on with the mass of undocumented persons that are here today. It is the biggest single act of civil disobedience in the history of North America.

Within the last few years, as Schey's "biggest act of civil disobedience" grew, those undocumented immigrants and workers in the U.S. also began to rebel. Once silent for fear of La Migra, more and more undocumented workers began to stand up and speak out for their rights as human beings. And they began to fight for those rights.

Joining their fight have been a variety of domestic groups with a voice in the American political system. Among these have been individual priests and bishops of the Catholic church and groups from other faiths known for their concern with human rights, such as the Society of Friends (Quakers). Hispanic-American groups, finding their constituents increasingly affected by INS enforcement policies which tend to single out brown- and black-skinned people, have supported the cause as have some Urban League members. Civil rights groups such as the American Civil Liberties Union have also increased their support for the rights of the foreign-born, noting that those who are apprehended by the INS are only *suspected* law violators, and as such are entitled to certain constitutional guarantees. As noted in earlier chapters, some labor unions, most notably the International Ladies' Garment Workers Union, have also fought for the rights of documented as well as undocumented workers—both trapped together in the same sweatshops. Also coming to the aid of Mexican nationals in the U.S., since López Portillo became president of Mexico, has been the Mexican government itself, perhaps as much concerned by the increasing use of its own territory as a pipeline for foreign nationals from other countries as for its own citizens in the U.S. Nonetheless, it has begun efforts to at least protect the rights of Mexican nationals in the U.S.

The result of this influx of support has been increased agitation for the protection of the human rights of undocumented immigrants and workers, increased pressure on the INS to speed up its service to legal immigrants and to those claiming the right to legal immigration, and an increased awareness on the part of many American opinion molders that there is an interdependence between the U.S. and Mexico of which undocumented workers are only one aspect in a much greater pattern of economic relations and difficulties.

In August 1976, three men from Mexico were walking through ranch lands in the parched Arizona desert owned by George Hanigan on their way to a nearby ranch, where they had worked the previous year and had again been promised work. On the way, they were discovered by Hanigan's two sons, both former high school football stars. The sons allegedly collared the men and returned to the ranch house for their father. From there, the Mexicans say, they were driven off into the desert, robbed, beaten, threatened with castration, stripped of their clothes and shoes, then filled with buckshot and told to return to Mexico. It was not a very unusual story in the annals of Cochise County.

The Mexicans made it back to the border, barefoot and naked, and did something to change that history: they reported the entire incident to Mexican authorities. As a result of pressure from the Mexican government, then Arizona Governor Raul Castro appointed a special prosecutor to try the three Hanigans on the charges brought by the Mexicans.

The father died before the trial began, so in late 1977 the two sons were tried by an all-white Cochise County jury on charges of kidnapping, assault, and robbery. Cochise County returned to its typical, historic pattern: the Hanigan boys were acquitted on all counts.

The complaints and the trial were themselves unprecedented. Even more unusual was the fact that Hispanic organizations decided—believing that the prosecution was prejudiced and the judge's tactics dilatory–to pursue the matter. Their only recourse was prosecution of the Hanigan boys in federal court for violating the workers' rights under federal law. The U.S. Department of Justice took the case "under review." After one year of review and no action, the Hispanic alliance took the Department of Justice to court to force the issue. Response was immediate once a lawsuit had been filed. The U.S. attorney for Arizona announced that there was nothing for the federal authorities to prosecute, because, "under the present statutes, since the three men weren't citizens, there was simply no criminal activity" justifying federal action. The Mexican nationals had no "protected civil right" comparable to that which a U.S. citizen would have in the same situation, a "defect in the law" that Congress could remedy.

The Hispanic alliance again threatened to sue for justice, noting that there were in fact several federal laws involving criminal activity that had allegedly been violated by the Hanigans. "First of all," said Antonio Bustamante, secretary of the national coalition on the Hanigan case, "the aliens were clearly on their way to work–which is protected activity. Second, there were violations of the interstate commerce statutes, since the Mexicans were on their way to pick crops to be shipped interstate. Third–ironically–their abductors are guilty of concealment and harboring illegal aliens, and last, transportation of illegal aliens–violations the Justice Department comes down hard on when some of our people are involved." The Justice Department's position, said Bustamante, would be "a hunting license" for anti-alien groups.

As concern over illegal immigration has grown, local police have become increasingly active in attempting to enforce immigration laws by arresting "suspected illegal aliens." Minority spokespeople have charged that these arrests are just part of a pattern and practice of police discrimination against them, especially when they have found minority citizens arrested on suspicion of being illegal immigrants. These police practices, most notably in Texas, have created such a degree of distrust in some communities that when undocumented aliens are victimized by crime they are doubly hesitant to report it to authorities.

In a piecemeal fashion, the police practice of arresting people as "suspected illegals" and putting them on "immigration hold" has been gradually changing.

An early breakthrough against this practice was made by David Rubio, a Mexican national with a valid U.S. alien registration card.

Rubio was arrested by Wheatland, Wyoming, police in 1977 as a suspected illegal. Rubio sued the city for damages, charging that he was
held in jail illegally for sixty-two hours without formal charges made
against him nor bail set. In a consent decree signed a year later by a
U.S. District Court judge in Cheyenne, Rubio was not only awarded a
token sum in damages, but the police of Wheatland were ordered to stop
trying to enforce immigration laws, to stop interrogating people for the
sole purpose of ascertaining their immigration status, and to stop asking people arrested for misdemeanor or traffic violations about their
immigration status, unless the officer has reason to believe, on articul-
able facts—other than physical appearance of Latin-American ancestry
or a Spanish surname—that the detained or arrested person is unlawfully present in the U.S.

In August 1978, U.S. Attorney General Griffin Bell, after pressure
from minority members of Congress, requested, through a memoran-
dum signed by INS Commissioner Leonel J. Castillo, that local law enforcement agencies "not stop and question, detain, arrest, or place an
'immigration hold' on any persons not suspected of a crime, solely on
the ground that they are deportable aliens."

This apparently finally moved at least some law enforcement agencies in California to act on a 1977 policy ruling by the state attorney
general along the same lines. In March 1979, the Los Angeles Police
Department, one of the nation's largest, was ordered by its governing
police commission to instruct its officers to ignore the immigration
status of all persons—suspects or victims of crimes—except those
charged with the most serious crimes. The policy statement had been
recommended by the police chief, Daryl F. Gates. Gates noted significant changes in the department's policy toward foreign nationals during
the course of his career, "going back to the time when our officers engaged in wholesale arrests of illegals, merely for their immigration
status."

During the same month the Illinois Department of Law Enforcement
announced policies similar to the new Los Angeles policies. The department's director cited three factors that would no longer constitute
"probable cause" for his officers to "stop, question or detain persons for
suspected violation of the Immigration Act." Those factors, alone or in
combination, were: lack of fluency in English, a Hispanic or other
foreign surname, and color of skin. Officers were also instructed not to
inquire about the citizenship status of people who report they are crime
victims.

Two unions launched court suits against the INS that could result in greater protection for undocumented and documented workers alike. The International Ladies' Garment Workers Union (ILGWU), in a suit that would probably please many of the employers who hire undocumented workers, said that INS searches of plants where undocumented aliens are suspected of working violate the workers' rights of due process and privacy and protection against unreasonable search and seizure and self-incrimination. The ILGWU was joined in its August 1978 suit by four of its members, all citizens or legal residents of the U.S., who claim to have been interrogated during INS raids at the garment factories where they work. The suit asked for an injunction against the INS that would order it to stop interrogations of workers without first informing employees of their rights. The union also asked that the INS be prevented from arresting or questioning workers because of their Latin appearance unless they had a valid search warrant. It also demanded that the search warrant name the specific individual being sought. "The only basis employed by the defendants for determining which employees to question," the suit charged, "was whether they appeared to be, from their features, facial characteristics and their clothing, of Latin origin."

Earlier in the year, attorneys for the American Civil Liberties Union and several Los Angeles Hispanic organizations succeeded in getting a temporary restraining order preventing the INS from deporting some 120 suspected illegals it had picked up from the Sbicca shoe factory, then being organized by the Retail Clerks Union, because they had not been informed of their right to counsel and the right to remain silent. This suit led to an apparent victory in late December when a U.S. District Court judge ordered the INS to inform the people they arrested or detained of their rights to counsel, to remain silent, and other Miranda rights before it began interrogations of suspected illegals.

In March 1979, to draw attention to the unionization effort of about 800 allegedly undocumented workers at the Sbicca factory, a rally was held. Although the rally drew about 150 workers, union officials, and community leaders, most of the factory workers stayed away, said Jorge Espinoza, a factory worker and organizer of the rally, because they were "scared of losing their jobs or getting deported if they showed up. To be an undocumented worker in this country is a terrible thing," Espinoza said. "I have seen that it is not the fear at work, but it is the psychological sickness, like cancer, that if not checked in time would be pretty hard to correct." Another factory worker told the gathering, "We are forced to work below minimum wages and we do not get paid for our overtime." One undocumented worker said that although deportation is a risk, unionization "is the only way we can be assured of some rights."

Los Angeles legal aid attorney Linda Wong noted that the rally was "the beginning of drawing attention to a much larger problem. There are thousands of working illegal aliens . . . something has to be done to protect them. Hopefully by unionizing they won't be taken advantage of by their employers."

Mexican federal officials stepped in to help their own citizens in August of 1978 by setting up a consular office near the San Ysidro, California, Border Patrol station. The job of the office, said Consul Jesus Rodriguez Navarro, would be to file claims for unpaid wages, file claims or indemnifications for accidents or injuries, investigate claims of unjust treatment or violations of human rights, and, at the request of deportees, notify families, employers, and landlords. Consul Navarro said the Mexican government hoped to extend the program to other border cities.

Speaking for Themselves

All of the activities described above—lawsuits, administrative rulings, government intervention, and union organizing—have one thing in common: they deal solely with the problems of the undocumented worker while he or she is in the U.S. If, for example, the ILGWU were to succeed in getting a living wage—four or five, or even six dollars an hour—and decent working conditions—free from cockroaches and unrepaired toilets—for workers at garment center sweatshops, who would benefit in the end? Doubtlessly, legal American workers would fill the jobs, replacing those who are now putting their futures on the line to build the union.

While it is certainly a benefit for the undocumented immigrant to be able to call the police without being deported, the change in policy of local police departments inheres primarily to the benefit of the legally resident, minority populations who will no longer be harassed as "suspected illegal aliens."

The undocumented worker is no longer silent. At the behest of unions, social service, and government agencies, and minority groups, the border jumper will come forward to speak. But who will be the ultimate beneficiary of such good deeds, of such struggles won? When grievous inequities are gone from the U.S., the deportable alien will still be deportable, the jobs she or he has held will be filled by others, and he or she will return home and find it little changed from the way it was.

No, this is not a revolt. The true revolt lies in the heart of the exploited alien, and this has only begun to find its own voice. Of the programs encouraging foreign nationals working in the U.S. without legal sanction to speak with their own voice and for their own needs is a singular group in Arizona called the Maricopa County Organizing Project (MCOP).

MCOP got its start in 1976 and is headquartered in El Mirage, a small farm worker community northwest of Phoenix. Here, in a nondescript one-story house on a quiet residential street, the moving force of the project, Lupe Sanchez, describes his background and the goals of the project. The house is sparsely decorated. Its interior is dominated by an MCOP flag with its crossed black shovel and hoe on a red background hanging over the fireplace. On another wall hangs a poster with the words *La Huelga-Que Viva*! (Long live the strike!)

MCOP began work in the Phoenix area to help farm workers improve their condition. It was a region of the state neglected by the better known United Farm Workers union led by Cesar Chavez. Three of MCOP's founders were former UFW organizers. Sanchez himself was born into the migrant life, and, he says, ended up in El Mirage when he was fourteen years old because his family ran out of money "and we couldn't get back to our home in Texas."

MCOP, says Sanchez, is not a union because "any agreement reached is not between us, but between the growers and the workers." Governing the project is a central committee of seven farm workers, three of whom are undocumented Mexican nationals.

"We try to organize workers at each ranch and get them to organize ranch committees to improve conditions," Sanchez explained to a reporter. "We have ranch committees at most of the citrus ranches in the Phoenix area." At these ranches, according to Sanchez, MCOP had organized some 2,000 to 3,000 workers by the beginning of 1979, most of whom were in the U.S. illegally.

MCOP has also organized in Mexico, concentrating its work in the five states that are the largest source of migrants for the Phoenix-area citrus industry: Sinaloa, Nayarit, Guerrero, Guanajuato, and Querétaro. Sanchez explained, "It is our central committee's opinion that the solution" to the Mexican nationals' problems are "in Mexico." And, in two years, MCOP says it has met with about 10,000 Mexican peasants. "We are not recruiting illegal aliens," he said. "What we are doing is offering the services of our organization once they're up here. We also teach them what their rights are in the United States."

MCOP's first target was the Arrowhead Ranch, owned by Robert Goldwater, Sr. and by members of the family of Phoenix-area attorney Joseph P. Martori. At this and other area ranches, said Sister Hilaria Pagazaurtundua, a Basque member of the Sisters of Charity who works with MCOP, the living conditions are worse than those of the illegal Portuguese of her native Spain. Workers at Arrowhead earned, at the time MCOP first became involved, sixty cents per bag of citrus—reportedly twenty cents less than that being paid by other ranches. At this rate of pay, during a good harvest, salaries ranged from about $1 to $1.75 per hour. The groves where workers not only harvested but also lived had neither sanitation facilities nor fresh water, and workers relied on the spigots behind company stores miles away for clean water. Most often they used the irrigation ditches running along the rows of citrus trees for both drinking and bathing. For shelter the workers had only what they could put together from orange crates and polyethylene sheets. Despite tales of wonderful Arizona weather, temperatures have been known to fall below freezing and rain has often turned camping grounds into mud flats.

Perhaps as a result of the investigation conducted by Investigative Reporters and Editors, Inc. into Arizona corruption, or perhaps as a general practice, supervisors had been known to patrol the groves armed, and several workers who had talked to outsiders about conditions had reportedly either been beaten or turned over to the INS.

Among the workers at Arrowhead—mostly Mexican nationals—were boys as young as eleven, women, and "veteran" migrants in their late thirties. According to one report, the incident apparently triggering the illegals into action at Arrowhead concerned Jesus Barrios, a father of four from Querétaro, who had made his way north to Arrowhead every year since 1972 for the late September through March harvest period. During his 1977 trip north, Jesus was assaulted by two Anglos who demanded his money. He had little money, which apparently made his attackers mad. One of them fired at Jesus with a shotgun, tearing his left arm to pieces. Friends transported Jesus to a hospital in Sun City, where he was refused treatment because he could not pay and was not a legal U.S. resident. Bleeding freely, he was taken another two dozen miles to the Maricopa County Hospital in Phoenix. By then it was too late to save his arm. It was amputated.

On October 3, 1977, 90 percent of the ranch's two hundred workers refused to pick up their canvas bags and gloves to harvest the fruit. It was a strike, perhaps the first strike in the U.S. by an illegal workforce. Instead of climbing the ladders to bring down the ripening citrus, the workers presented their demands to Arrowhead. The workers demanded advance notice of pesticide spraying so they could avoid inhaling the toxic poison, advance notice of irrigation, so they could move their camps from areas that would be flooded, and blankets.

At first the workers set up picket lines at the ranch, but, recalled Sanchez, "we lost half the committee when the Border Patrol arrived. So we had to change tactics. We've been having strikes where there have been no pickets. Everyone just stays in the field and doesn't work."

The workers fought throughout the 1977 season and continued to fight in 1978. As they fought, they raised their demands. In 1978 Arrowhead bosses quietly began negotiating with their workers.

During the next harvest season, beginning in the fall of 1978, a farm worker contacted MCOP's Sister Pagazaurtundua to tell her about "a small ranch in the middle of the desert. He said there were several ill persons there," said the Basque nun. She went to the ranch with the worker. "I pulled out quite a few ill workers. One elderly man had fallen off a ladder and hurt his back. He could only make $8 a day. His supervisor brought him Ben-Gay." She identified the fifty-acre ranch as the H. C. McGarity Ranch. "They didn't have any way to get to a doctor. They were living beneath the trees," she said. "I brought a medic there, but later they closed the gates to me." In November, at the request of about thirty workers, Lupe Sanchez went to the ranch to help the workers organize a strike. Sanchez was arrested. At first he thought it was simply another arrest for trespassing—he had been arrested eleven times in the previous thirteen months. Instead, the sheriff served Sanchez with a restraining order barring him or any other MCOP representative from going onto any properties owned by Blue Goose Growers or any ranches, including the McGarity Ranch, with which it had contracts.

It was then that MCOP learned that it was dealing with the giant of the local citrus business. "The first time we realized we were dealing with Blue Goose was when we got the court papers," said Sanchez.

"We started doing some homework and found out that Blue Goose was a subsidiary of Pacific Lighting," a Los Angeles-based energy conglomerate, said another MCOP spokesperson. "They came after us with such passion that we decided to make them one of our main targets."

Among the ranches owned by Blue Goose was Chandler Mesa Ranches, south of Phoenix. This Blue Goose outlet came to the attention of Father Henry Wasielewski, director of the special ministry to farm workers established by the Catholic Diocese of Phoenix, when workers there told him of their needs. Father Wasielewski visited the ranch himself and found that "they seemed to have almost nothing. There was a carton on the ground. Under one tree a guy indicated that he just piled up some leaves to make his bed."

In December, a parishioner, Paul Fernandez, visited some illegal Mexican workers at the ranch who had accepted a previous offer of food and clothing. As Fernandez testified in a sworn deposition for the hearing regarding the Blue Goose injunction against MCOP, "Juan Torres [a foreman at Chandler Mesa Ranches] was there in his truck and called me over and asked what I wanted. I said that I didn't want anything, but was bringing the promised food and clothing. He said it wasn't needed because he would provide whatever they needed. I asked what he had been providing. He said that a few days before he had given them twelve dollars or so worth of food. I told him that wasn't sufficient for the number of workers there. After a little discussion he reached down and pulled up a rifle and waved it back and forth in an upright position. He said he would straighten the matter out. . . . I then talked for a few minutes to the workers. They said Juan had been intimidating them by threatening to fire them if they were to associate with me or take any of the food or clothing."

Father Wasielewski told reporters that he himself had been forced off the property twice when he attempted to offer mass in the citrus groves.

Meanwhile, at the hearing, workers from H. C. McGarity Ranch testified that, when they were sick or injured on the job, they were unable to get medical attention. Lupe Sanchez was invited to the ranch, according to their testimony, after one of the workers was fired for asking for his pay at the end of the working day because he didn't have enough money to buy food.

The judge allowed the restraining order against MCOP to stand. MCOP realized it would have to expand its tactics. Having learned that the Blue Goose parent company, Pacific Lighting, was, through another subsidiary (Southern California Gas), one of the prime negotiators for natural gas from Mexico, it threatened the company with taking its complaints about its treatment of Mexican nationals directly to President López Portillo.

On January 25, 1979, the president of Blue Goose Growers, Robert Essick, flew from Los Angeles to Phoenix to meet with MCOP organizers.

Organizing at Arrowhead had not stopped. As the harvesting season began in 1978, the work of the previous season was built upon. Demands were refined, worker morale built up, and occasional strikes still remained a tool of protest.

By the last week of January 1979, at about the same time that Blue Goose was talking with MCOP, the project's work at Arrowhead finally paid off. Arrowhead signed an unprecedented contract with its workers. Typical of labor contracts were increased pay—$1.13 per sack of citrus to be raised to $1.35 at the start of the next harvest—health insurance to cover workers, and grievance and arbitration procedures. What distinguished the Arrowhead contract from all that had preceded it was the stipulation that for each hour worked the company would, in addition to the worker's pay, contribute ten cents to a trust to be used by the workers to finance projects in their Mexican home states.

"The workers realize that at some point or another they were going to work themselves out of a job. When the pay is up to a certain level, local workers will take over the jobs," explained MCOP's Lupe Sanchez. "Most of these undocumented workers come from farms of fifteen or twenty acres in Mexico and what we are trying to do with this fund is to provide money to improve the conditions at these farms, giving them money so that they can buy a tractor or something like that down the line."

Arthur Martori, co-owner of Arrowhead, in the face of heated criticism for signing an agreement with "illegal aliens," said, "Everyone in the Southwest has undocumented workers. This contract covers all of my workers at the ranch. We don't check to see if they are undocumented or not. We set up this contract with our workers in the ranch community so we can have rules and regulations that we can both live by.

"We recognize that these people are pretty much poverty stricken. What we are trying to do here is to try to set up a fund so that they can help their families both in the United States and in Mexico."

The trust fund will be controlled by the MCOP central committee, and, Sanchez said, "Any of our local committees in Mexico could then apply to us for money to buy things like farming equipment or whatever they need for their *ejidos* (common farms). If the peasants have sufficient work on their *ejidos*, they don't have to come to the United States to look for work." Other area growers, according to Sanchez, have approved the idea, although one expressed fear that the fund would be used by MCOP for strikes. "We wouldn't be against a grower's representative sitting on the committee that controls the trust fund," Sanchez noted.

During the press conference announcing the contract a question was raised as to how a contract could be enforced if the workers were in the country illegally, since a grower could get rid of a troublesome alien by calling the Border Patrol. Sanchez replied that undocumented workers have every right that an American citizen has in respect to working conditions. And with a signed contract, they can also obtain remedies in court if the terms of the contract are broken. "Besides," he asked, "would you rather be chased by the Border Patrol while making one dollar an hour or chased by the Border Patrol while making three dollars an hour?"

Said Sister Pagazaurtundua to a reporter, "The day you lose your fear you have taken an important step." The illegals working at Arrowhead took that step in October 1977. "Once the people, any people, are on the march toward freedom, they won't go back."

14: RENDING THE SOCIAL FABRIC

Racism rests chained in a back corner of the white American psyche, ready to be unleashed like hounds at the first scent of danger. In periods of economic distress the white man has sniffed the air and smelled danger, and the dogs were let loose for their deadly chores, blinding their masters to all else but the prey and the chase. A collapsed gold rush in California drove Chinese into ghettos; men who had been broken in the mines came down to the valleys and robbed and cheated brown peoples, pushing Mexicans from their lands in the Southwest. Economic chaos after the Civil War brought out the Ku Klux Klan to steal black people's freedom in the South. As racism shaped domestic policies, so it later forged immigration laws.

As the Great Depression moved through the land, President Herbert Hoover's secretary of labor soon found a new political scapegoat for a populace and a government looking for someone on whom to blame their economic woes—nearly half a million aliens who could be deported. It was a convenient finding for a white majority still reveling in its racism. Among the "illegals" were people who had brown skin, people whom most white Americans placed somewhere above blacks, but still far below the innate superiority of a white skin and heritage. Hundreds of local laws and practices already discriminated against the brown American. In the Southwest were both white schools and Mexican schools, white churches and Mexican churches, white public hospital wards and Mexican wards. Brown-skinned people were barred from certain public parks and pools, restaurants, and residential districts, as effectively as were black-skinned people. The difference between anti-black and anti-brown discrimination during this century was only that discrimination against black-skinned people was legal, while the brown-skinned people were white under the law. Yet the brown-skinned people counted their numbers murdered by the police just as their black-skinned brothers and sisters counted theirs lynched by roving bands of men blinded by the chase and the kill.

So when states began to follow in the footsteps of Hoover's program to locate and deport all "illegal aliens," the hungry hounds were unchained to roam free in the Southwest, and the first places they went looking for illegals were the brown barrios. And there they found them: people who had entered the U.S. before there were official procedures set up to document their legal emigration from Mexico, and who were unable to prove their legal right to exist in the U.S.; people whom farmers had recruited to work in their fields, cast off into cities when they were no longer needed; people born in barrio homes in San Antonio and Los Angeles to mothers who, because of their poverty, had not gone to hospitals to give birth and had no hospital birth certificates to prove their citizenship; and people who felt it was time to leave this land that hated them so. And the brown people were "repatriated" on trains traveling tracks they had helped build.

Pre-existing racial prejudice along with the need for a new scapegoat had poisoned the hearts of people with the wetback syndrome. Illegal alien, during the Great Depression, meant only one thing in nearly half the country: wetback.

When the economic panic ended, the syndrome receded like a feverous disease, waiting only for the next economic plague to inflame it. Meanwhile, East Coast journalists had discovered the brown-skinned people, the "pachucos," and the wetback syndrome spread to the rest of the nation. And in the 1954 recession the "wets" were again rounded up and shipped south. The syndrome was so prevalent that House Judiciary Committee Chairman Peter W. Rodino observed in 1972 with obvious surprise, after testimony in New York about illegal immigrants, "When we first commenced these hearings it seemed that the problem was focused on the Mexicans and the illegal alien was the Mexican. It was the judgment of this member, as chairman of this committee, that as we went on it wasn't just the Mexican; that illegal aliens came from every area. We must remember that the visitor who overstays is also an illegal alien."

Representative Rodino's observation went unheeded in the blindness brought on by the wetback syndrome, and the INS continued its usual practice of rounding up the wets (throwing in occasional black people for good measure).

By the time INS head General Leonard F. Chapman, Jr. announced in the midst of the economic crisis of 1975 that there were twelve million "illegal aliens" in the U.S. who were stealing jobs from Americans and costing millions of dollars in tax-supported welfare programs, America immediately thought race, and race meant wetback. And the INS went out to hunt the wetback and the numbers of Mexicans caught mounted, making a kind of evidence to sustain the syndrome. In the name of saving jobs and welfare money, General Chapman's INS troops moved once again through the barrios where brown people lived, into the fields where brown people worked, and ripped the meaning from the words "equal justice for all," trampling on the concepts of civil liberties, pitting a syndrome against a nation, turning white people against brown, black against brown, and even brown against brown. Meanwhile, as the general's troops were rending the social fabric that held a nation of diversity together, few thought to look for facts. Some were so blinded they did not even want the facts. They demanded a wall be built along the Mexican-American border, stationed with as many troops as necessary to ensure that no one crossed it—a simple solution formed in fear and blindness that would cure nothing.

General Chapman was replaced by Leonel J. Castillo, and Chapman's troops became Castillo's cavalry, and as late as 1978 the INS continued its barrio searches, euphemistically called city patrols, hauling in more than 53,000 deportable aliens from such patrols.

Local police and sheriff's offices were not immune from the wetback syndrome and also helped catch "suspected illegal aliens," locking them up in their jails until the INS could pick them up and take them away.

The trained eyes of both local and federal police could recognize the foreign nationals not lawfully present in the U.S.: they were brown-skinned and had black hair. Their ears were also trained: the illegals spoke Spanish. They had a finely tuned sense of social justice: only the poor could be illegal. And so the rich and the white continued to hold their jobs, and the fabric of law and justice was torn a bit more.

• In July 1978, a Texas-born American of Mexican descent filed suit against the Oregon district director of the INS. Jorge Luis Rodriguez charged that when he was living in Astoria, Oregon, with five other men, and five days after he found a job as a tree planter in January, INS agents knocked on his apartment door, forced their way in without a warrant, and interrogated him. He was arrested, detained five days in an Astoria jail without being allowed to use a telephone, and then placed on a bus with fifteen Mexican nationals and dumped in Mexicali.

• In September 1978, a group of restaurant and bar operators in the California farming community of Dinuba filed suit in U.S. District Court charging that Dinuba police made illegal searches of their prem-ises for Mexican nationals. The restaurant owner and two bar owners asserted the raids were made without warrants and resulted in a loss of profits to their business establishments.

• In January 1979, Hispanic residents of El Monte, California, took their complaints of harassment by local police during raids of restau-rants and bars to the city council. Said spokesperson Ernie Guitierrez of the San Gabriel Valley Concerned Citizens Organization, "The El Monte police department on at least five different occasions has felt it had the authority to go into a place . . . and pull people out and give them sobriety tests." Mexican-Americans, he noted, felt it degrading to be checked in public for their citizenship "just because of the color of their skin."

• In February 1979, Umatilla County, Oregon, in an out-of-court settlement, paid $1,000 to Trinidad de La Cerda, a legal migrant worker, who was jailed after he went to the county jail to act as an interpreter for a friend. He said he spent three days in jail without being told why. His suit against the INS was still pending when the county decided to settle.

• In March 1979, a group of legal residents and citizens of Paterson, New Jersey, formed the United Mexican-American Organization of New Jersey to protect the rights of Mexicans legally living in the U.S. The group was formed after an INS stakeout of the Garfield, New Jersey, Presto-Lock plant resulted in the seizure of Amador Sanchez, a legal resident. A scuffle ensued in which Sanchez was beaten badly enough to miss three weeks of work at the plant, where he was a night-shift machinist. Sanchez was put on trial for allegedly assaulting the agents, but, as he explained, the agents failed to identify themselves when they grabbed him and beat him as he got out of his car. He said he lost consciousness when they knocked him against a fence. The agents, however, testified that they had identified themselves and that Sanchez ran from them. A municipal court judge told Sanchez he could either be found guilty or sign a release clearing the agents of any possible charges. Sanchez signed the release, knowing that a guilty finding would go against him when he applied for citizenship.

Headlines of Hysteria

Just as INS enforcement policies have done little to end the wetback syndrome, some newspaper editors seem to have done all they could to stir up hysteria against Mexican illegals. Topping an article on medical problems in East Los Angeles barrios, for example, was this 1973 Los Angeles *Times* headline in bold, 72-point type: "Epidemics a Barrio Specter" with the subhead "TB, Typhoid, Hepatitis Linked to Illegal Immigrants." Concluding the article with a dramatic specter of fear was this anecdote from the director of the county's Department of Health Services: "A woman brought a 4-month-old baby to the center last weekend. Preliminary test showed the baby 'possibly had meningitis' but the mother disappeared into the barrio. Doctors called the police for help and messages were broadcast over Spanish-speaking radio stations, but with no success, he said. 'She probably was an illegal alien who gave a false address. There's no chance of finding her now,' he added."

The New York *Times* added its more discreet contribution to hysteria in 1975 with a special report from Fort Worth headlined, "TB Rise

Sparked by Illegal Aliens." The story led with the statement, "Illegal aliens entering the United States from Mexico are increasing the danger of Americans contracting tuberculosis." The single source for the story was not an immigration specialist, but the head of the state's Tuberculosis Advisory Committee. The article continued, "Mr. Wiggins says the influx of between 10 million and 12 million illegal Mexican aliens has kindled an outburst of tuberculosis in this country with a type of the disease that is more difficult to detect and control than Americans have known in the past." Wiggins went on to note that "Texas alone may have as many as a million illegal Mexican aliens."

And in similarly hysterical style, smaller papers followed suit. Typical of the renewed spurt of interest in epidemics spread by wetbacks was a Los Baños (California) *Enterprise* report headed "Caused by Illegal Aliens: High rate of TB found in county." A county supervisor, commenting on reported increased TB rates, said, "I believe this identifies the seriousness of the illegal alien problem more than money." Data cited by the article to support its headline were "In 1977 there were 33 cases of tuberculosis in Merced County. Three of those were definitely 'imported' by illegal aliens from Mexico."

In 1978, after a private study indicated that U.S. population growth was increased by legal immigration as well as by an undetermined number of illegal immigrants, the old argument against foreigners was again dragged out of the closet and began appearing in headlines such as this one from the Pasadena (Texas) *Citizen,* Illegal immigration linked to overpopulation." The collection of hysterical headlines is vast, including such gems as "Third World Establishing Beachhead in U.S." and "Brown Tide Flooding California."

Newspapers were not alone in contributing to a rising level of hysteria about the "brown tide." Traditionally, nativist groups have been re-emerging since the early 1970s, generally lobbying for restrictive legislation at the state level. California, for example, enacted a law in 1972 making it unlawful to employ "illegal aliens." Texas decided to charge tuition for schoolchildren of undocumented immigrants, thereby excluding not only the children who had been brought into the country unlawfully by their parents, but also those who could not prove that they were here legally. The latter might include those whose birth records were lost or impossible to retrieve in the bureaucratic mess at some out-of-state county clerk's office, or those who had no certificate because they were born in American boxcars, or barrio homes, or farm labor camps without a doctor. (It is to people such as these latter, adults as well as children, to whom the unofficial phrase "undocumented" applies. This phrase also encompasses those eligible for "documents" establishing their legal right to live or work in the U.S. but who are engaged in a years-long struggle to pry the documents out of a nearly dysfunctional INS service system. It is a phrase used by volunteers trying to help immigrants formalize their status in the U.S. and distinguishes these from those who have no legal claim to either U.S. residency or citizenship under current immigration law and therefore cannot obtain "documents.")

Meanwhile, in California, where the 1972 law had never been successfully enforced, a group began collecting signatures for a 1979 ballot initiative that would require every worker to get an ID card from the state employment office. The proposal would ensure that such cards were given only to those entitled under law, including immigration law, to work in California, and would penalize any employer who hired a person who did not have such a card. During the seven intervening years, more than a dozen other states had enacted employer-sanction laws similar to California's 1972 law.

Perhaps best crystallizing nativist sentiment was the small-press book *Give Us Your Poor: (The Immigration Bomb)* by James Farrell. First published in 1975, the short book found a ready audience in right-wing circles and went into a second edition the year after. The book forcefully argues that the U.S. has dwindling physical resources. These, it says, are not enough for Americans, let alone for millions of illegal Mexican (and other) aliens. The book's unwritten but logical conclusion was that to protect the nation for our children, we should build and patrol an iron curtain around the country and stop letting any more people in.

The tenor of the Farrell book, which is recommended reading by some right-wing groups and far-right groups including a California Ku Klux Klan group, is summarized best in this brief quote: "Telephone numbers of people to contact in a nationwide network of individuals and organizations, with hideouts and even sources of bail, are a part of the illegal alien's kit. The whole procedure is startlingly reminiscent of the infiltration of enemy agents in a wartime operation."

Nativists Organize

U.S. Representative John Ashbrook is among the more articulate right-wing members of Congress and has become a spokesman for U.S. nativists. Coming out against even emergency medical care for indigent aliens in 1977, the Ohio representative told Congress, "In a time when the average workingman's family can be ruined by a major illness, we have no right to offer free medical care to anyone who has just reached our shores."

In one of his periodic entries into the *Congressional Record*'s Extension of Remarks, the implications of Ashbrook's nativism become apparent. In 1978 Ashbrook cited the fact that Sweden had its first race riot a year earlier between native Swedes and a tiny "minority of Assyrians [sic] in the town of Södertälje." Immigration, wrote Ashbrook, "has led to major racial confrontations in Britain and in most other countries, yet liberals act like it just does not happen or will not happen." He concluded his column-and-a-half essay with the warning, "Our country is full of people. If we bring in more, it will not so much improve the status of immigrants as it will lower the living standard for our own working people to the level of those in the world's poor countries. Marxists, of course, would be happy with such a situation. They would then have the land they want America to be, a land of the rich few and the starving masses, ripe for revolution."

The American Legion, one of the oldest nativist organizations, in 1978 also added its bit to the growing nativist movement, this time covering it in what, on the surface, seemed like nonracist rhetoric: "The principal concern of The American Legion with regard to illegal aliens is that they are increasingly competing with veterans in a tight job market. That competition especially affects the employment prospects of unemployed black veterans." That same year, another traditionally nativist group, the Veterans of Foreign Wars, endorsed an anti-alien resolution at its national convention.

Local nativist groups have also taken up the call. The Citizens for Immigration Reform in North Carolina distributes copies of newspaper articles headlined "Illegal Aliens 'Out of Control' " and other such zesty bits from newspapers like the right-wing Manchester (New Hampshire) *Union Leader*, and urges its members and friends to protest liberal immigration laws by writing their representatives in Congress. A California group calling itself the Non-Partisan Political Action Committee (N-PAC) launched a campaign to stop illegals by trying to collect twenty-five million signatures on a petition to the President and Congress. N-PAC chair Wes Marden explained, "In actuality they [undocumented aliens] are people with no interest in the United States. They represent political power to the terrorist and the Third World, including the Red Brigade whose political assassinations have become almost commonplace in Mexico."

Nativism found a hold in New York City as well, where a group called

Citizens Committee Against Illegal Immigration attempted to get half a million signatures calling for a law to end the employment of "illegal aliens."

Nor was the return to nativism without its more extreme backers. Among these was George S. Benson, president of the National Education Program in Searcy, Arkansas, who had made a lifelong career of his fight for "traditional American" values. In a 1978 column syndicated in several newspapers and mailed out by some right-wing organizations, Benson warns that the U.S. had better regain control of its Mexican border because Mexico may be the next Cuba. He cites examples of what he believes to be the growth of Soviet activities in the Mexican political scene.

Nativism finally reached the violence-prone fringes of the racist cults, becoming a theme song for several domestic Nazi and Ku Klux Klan organizations by 1977. Spurred on by articles in the white supremacist press, including the *Klansman*, the *Thunderbolt*, *Spotlight*, and the *National Vanguard* (formerly *Attack!* Its motto is "Toward a New Consciousness; a New Order; a New People"), California Nazi organizers circulated leaflets calling for the organization of vigilante groups to deport brown aliens from the state. And, in 1977, the Nazi-leaning California Klan (whose leader had recruited dozens of U.S. Marines into the Knights of the KKK) took action along the border.

The group made a media event out of its first "border patrol," and journalists arrived from around the country to find only fourteen Klansmen had showed up. The incident rated front-page coverage in many newspapers and made national television news. But the reporters, obviously embarrassed by giving so much free publicity to such a tiny band, abandoned the Klan story to the back pages of the local press. Meanwhile, the group continued to organize around the issue, bemoaning the fact that it could only afford black-and-white printing for its literature, so the brown-skinned wetback turned out black in print.

Despite warnings from the INS the patrol continued. On April 3, 1978, a resident alien was allegedly kidnapped by Klan members and turned in to the INS. In November, two men were indicted by a federal grand jury for the April 3 incident involving Mendez Ruiz, a legally documented, Mexican resident alien. The indictment charged that two men, reportedly Klan members, had picked up Ruiz as a hitchhiker and dumped him at the freeway INS checkpoint at San Clemente, reporting him as an illegal alien. The indictment alleged that one of the men threw Ruiz's documents out the window of their moving car as they drove to the checkpoint, where they unloaded him as a wet. Fortunately for Ruiz, the Border Patrol believed his story, retraced the route of the car, and retrieved his documents. The two men, Carl Leroy Shipton, Jr. of San Bernardino, and Robert L. Cole of Libby, Montana, were eventually located. In January 1979 Shipton pled guilty. Charges against Cole, allegedly a former Klan member, were dismissed for insufficient evidence.

In 1979 a national media turned off by its first contact with the Klan border patrol failed to report what a local journalist found: about seventy-five Klansmen arrived at the border with Mexico at 8 P.M., February 17, in twenty-five cars and vans for a peaceful demonstration against the "brown tide." Police monitored the demonstration. The only violence they observed was that of Mexican nationals on the south side of the border throwing rocks at the Klan. The demonstration ended at one-thirty in the morning. The tiny band of fourteen who had been laughed at by the national media little more than a year before had grown fivefold. Their uniforms had also changed. Instead of robes and hoods, they wore black jackboots and helmets.

Community Tensions

As a special cabinet-level committee created by President Ford reported in 1976, rising anti-alien sentiment has greater ramifications for the nation than nativism. "More important," the committee noted of anti-alien organizations, "they create severe polarization within impacted areas which results in generalized suspicion toward 'foreigners' regardless of their legal status, and a menacing form of scapegoating which ties the problems of housing, urban flight, overburdened services and the [deteriorating] quality of life to the presence of illegal aliens." Such sentiments, the committee wrote, "will be felt most keenly by the legal immigrant and ethnic populations."

The "generalized suspicion toward 'foreigners' " noted by the Ford committee has resulted in outbreaks of not only interracial and ethnic violence, but intra-ethnic violence as well. In 1969, for example, as the population fleeing the Dominican Republic for New York City began to grow, some schools began showing changes in their ethnic composition. George Washington High School, on Manhattan's Upper West Side, for example, had a predominantly native black population until a shift began in the ethnic composition of the student body. By 1971 Dominican students composed more than half the school's population. Concurrent with the change in ethnic ratios were frequent episodes of fighting between the Dominicans and black students. One such incident in 1971 resulted in a brawl that ended with four injuries and four arrests. Dozens of windows were broken in the school and tires were slashed on cars parked nearby. As one Dominican student explained, "It's not the skin color – a lot of us are as dark as they are. It's just a question of style. The blacks and Puerto Ricans get along fine. They go to the same parties, dress the same, enjoy the same music. We're not used to it yet. A lot of us don't even understand English."

An earlier chapter noted the increase in violence along the Mexican-American border against border jumpers. Similar incidents are also present in communities with large immigrant populations. The Justice Department in 1977 labeled this wave of crime and demonstrations as "mini-blow-outs" against not only undocumented Hispanic aliens, but, increasingly, Hispanic American citizens mistaken for illegals.

Gilbert Pompa, an American of Mexican descent and head of the Community Relations Service of the Justice Department in 1977 explained, "In the last three years our caseload of all types of Hispanic community tensions has increased from two percent to fifty-two percent."

Pompa noted that the friction factor also expressed itself within the Hispanic community. "We've seen confrontations between Chicanos and illegals in New Jersey. It's becoming quite common." New Jersey also has a sizable population of 'illegal' Poles. They have yet to be attacked by the Chicanos; apparently the wetback syndrome, the myth that an illegal is a person with brown skin, has affected Chicanos as well.

American citizens of Mexican descent can be described, at best, as ambivalent about illegal border crossers from Mexico. In Fort Worth, the first Mexican-American to be elected to the city council said, in 1978, that the tensions between the new and presumably illegal Mexicans and the legal Mexican immigrants and citizens were growing. "We are sitting on a powder keg that must be defused by mutual understanding and respect," said Councilman Louis Zapata. The problem identified by Zapata was community concern about increased vandalism and street littering attributed to "illegal aliens." An additional problem cited by Zapata was that accessibility to some post offices had been hindered because of the number of illegals sending money home. (It is possible that among those in line were documented resident aliens also sending money to families in Mexico.) Zapata charged that increased vandalism may have been due to the illegals' frustrations over not getting the employment they had come to Fort Worth in search of.

Further comments about Hispanic-American ambivalence toward presumed illegal immigrants were made by Dr. Gilbert Merkx, a University of New Mexico professor, who discussed a July 1978 incident that ended by community members calling in the INS. The illegals, according to Merkx, had been taking over northern New Mexico-area bars and "moving in on the local girls." Merkx also cited an additional incentive for the apparent ambivalence of New Mexico's long-established and powerful Mexican-American community. "Community leaders," he told a local reporter, "will also comment in private on the difficulty of building stable community institutions in the face of a consistent and rapid circulation of outsiders who are in the Chicano community but not of it. Their familial and community loyalties lie in a Mexican town to which they will return."

If feelings within the Mexican-American community about "wetbacks" are ambivalent, they are hostile, at best, among many black community leaders, who fall into the wetback syndrome and fail to recognize that many of the illegals are black Jamaicans and Haitians, and blame the brown-skinned illegal for high unemployment in their own communities. At a regional NAACP meeting, Marion Hill said, "I want stiff immigration quotas to be put back into effect. They're [wetbacks] ruining our labor. I'm concerned about unemployment in the black community." The Los Angeles delegate's statement appeared to reflect the views of many NAACP delegates.

Increased tensions between blacks and Hipanics roused by controversy over "illegal aliens" could be counterproductive for two populations sharing similar problems of poverty, unemployment, and discrimination. The two minorities together could represent a sizable voting block able to effect political change for their mutual benefit. If the issue of immigration drives them further apart, then both minorities (and all people sharing similar problems of seemingly endemic poverty) shall surely lose. Concerned over just such issues, several national organization leaders representing both minority communities met in 1979 to attempt to come to an agreement about their common goals and aspirations, and to talk about the differences that still obstruct the formation of a viable political alliance. Raul Yzaguirre, president of the National Council of La Raza, one of the initiators of the 1979 meeting, who believed that the issue of immigration was a formidable roadblock to an alliance between the two minorities, said, "There's been a lot of playing off of one minority against the other. We're going to put an end to that."

Any end to differences between two groups who have much to gain by standing together, but who are becoming increasingly polarized by the issue of immigration, will have to be based on an understanding of the facts surrounding the issue, faced with eyes unblinded by a wetback, or any other, syndrome.

15: THE UNDERGROUND WORKFORCE: WHO GAINS?

Who are the people and institutions who make a profit from undocumented immigration? It first appears that the prime beneficiaries of the underground slave trade are the poverty-stricken foreign nationals who come to the U.S. in search of work. Even one dollar an hour is more than most could earn for their work in their home countries. Wages of two or three dollars an hour sound like King Midas's gold to most of the people of the world.

King Midas's wealth quickly changes to fool's gold at the U.S. border. Most immigrants apprehended each year by the INS are caught before they find any work. Of the more than one million deportable aliens located by the INS in the year ending September 30, 1978, for example, fewer than one-quarter were employed. INS statistics, of course, reflect the agency's emphasis on catching wetbacks as soon as they set foot on Yankee territory, and perhaps are not representative of the real employment picture for those working illegally in the U.S. But these numbers do reflect tragic stories for many would-be workers.

One study commissioned by the Mexican Intersecretariat in 1974 found that of those who crossed into the U.S., 52.3 percent never found work, and of those who did, the average number of days worked was sixty-two. Another study, conducted by Dr. Jorge Bustamante of El Colegio de Mexico, the nation's most noted authority on immigration, was based in part on interviews with 493 people held in INS detention centers in California and Texas. It found that "more than 50 percent were apprehended without having gained employment in the United States," and concluded, "for hundreds of thousands of Mexicans originating in the most economically depressed sector of Mexico, to emigrate to the United States carries the consequence of adding to their poverty."

President Ford's committee on undocumented immigrants also noted that "some studies indicate that a number of illegal aliens have considerable difficulty in finding jobs. One study reported that finding a job presented far more difficulty for the illegal alien than eluding the INS. A second study indicated that only 47 percent of the voluntary departures interviewed were able to find a job. An earlier study indicated that most illegals are unsuccessful in locating a job."

Findings such as these are myth destroyers. Many may be apprehended, but few find work. Of those who do, their work tends to last only an average of three months. Of the people hunted by the INS, many become poorer than when they first decided to emigrate.

Those who do find work often help to support their families back home in a kind of underground foreign aid program. The underground program has the benefit of directly helping the poor without the inter-

ference of the middlemen who handle official foreign aid programs—middlemen who often see to it that the truly poor, the most in
need, benefit least from the aid.

This underground foreign aid program is not without critics, who
charge that the flow of Yankee dollars to foreign countries is a drain on
the U.S. balance of payments, and therefore, in the end, bad for the U.S.
economy. This argument falls in light of the fact that most countries
from which undocumented workers originate are not only deeply in
debt to the U.S., but also import most of their products from the U.S.
Seventy percent of Mexico's foreign trade, for example, is with the
United States, and 70 percent of its foreign debt is also to the U.S. So
the Yankee dollars are, in reality, used to buy U.S. goods and pay back
Yankee loans.

How much do the workers send? David S. North and Marion F.
Houston, as part of their study of "illegal aliens" for the U.S. Department of Labor, found that out of an average gross weekly wage of $120,
their entire group of 793 apprehended aliens being deported sent home
an average of $105 per month. This average included those who sent no
money. The Mexican deportees reported the lowest weekly wage, $106,
and sent the most home, $129 per month. Other Western Hemisphere
deportees were ranked second. They reported average weekly wages of
$127 and payments home of $76 per month. Eastern Hemisphere deportees, meanwhile, earned the most, $195 a week, and sent home the
least, $37 a month. The two researchers tentatively estimated that
Mexican dependents may be receiving a total of $1.5 billion annually.
Another study, conducted in Mexico by an American professor, Wayne
A. Cornelius, surveyed 505 one-time U.S. workers. Cornelius estimated
the amount sent by Mexican workers in the U.S. to be $2 billion. The
U.S. Secretary of State, meanwhile, estimated $3 billion was sent by
undocumented workers to dependents in Mexico. (By contrast, direct
U.S. foreign aid to Mexico for the thirty-year period 1946 to 1976 to-
taled only $77.6 million, slightly more than $2.5 million per year.)

North and Houston also calculated the number of dependents their
alien sample helped support back home. Mexicans, they reported,
helped an average of 5.4 dependents outside the U.S., other Western
Hemisphere natives helped an average of 3.6 dependents, and Eastern
Hemisphere natives assisted only an average of 1.8 dependents abroad.

It might be expected that this underground foreign aid program
would bring substantial improvement to the lives of the aliens' families
back home. Cornelius, who concentrated his studies on the small towns
and villages of Mexico's backlands from which most Mexican illegals

emigrate, reported that the money and skills community members gained during their stays in the U.S. have, on occasion, benefited those communities. But, he added, they have not significantly improved conditions. Emigration, according to Cornelius, has probably kept the Mexican towns and villages from becoming considerably worse off than they would be if they had not sent their sons and daughters to the U.S. to work. In other words, the underground foreign aid has been, at best, a holding action only, enough to sustain the poverty at the same level it has always been in these small towns and villages, so far from the mainstream of Mexican economic life.

The villagers of Inticaputa, El Salvador, who began a migration to the U.S. in the mid-1960s, reveal a similar story. The money sent home has made the village rich. It has built cement houses where once there were only wooden shanties; it has bought shoes and socks for the children's feet. But as one Inticaputan immigrant admitted to a reporter from the Washington *Post*, the money has done little else. Were the Inticaputan to return, he would find nothing changed except the exterior of the village. Nothing in the surrounding economy has changed; were he to go back, he would return to the same grinding, hopeless poverty he was born into. He has resigned himself to never returning to see his family or children again, hoping only that the money he can send them will at least be enough to feed them.

Mexico, El Salvador, and perhaps other countries like them, viewed as economic and political institutions, benefit from even this condition, according to one writer whose thesis is supported by many social scientists who have studied the situation. Portes Alejandro, in his article "Return of the Wetback," explains that the flow of migrants to the U.S. benefits Mexico institutionally in two ways. First, the migrant flow alleviates some of the social tensions resulting from the extreme maldistribution of income by providing the poor with an alternative to starvation or rebellion, and second, the money sent home to migrants' families helps keep the poor on their feet (and not arming themselves to join a new revolution). This is the "social valve" theory. If all the poor were forced to stay where they were, without hope for a better future, it would be an easy thing for a social agitator to organize a revolt.

These few facts, reasoned estimates, and informed opinions lead to a few intriguing answers to the question of who gains from the slave trade. Mexico and other nations, in exchange for the labor of the strongest, most fit, and most highly motivated of their poor (the prime cut of potential revolutionaries), get "foreign aid" to keep some of their poor from facing the alternatives—starvation or rebellion. The resultant situation is a kind of stability, alleviating the social tensions that would otherwise make Mexico and other countries like it unsafe for investment by multinational corporations constantly on the move for new markets to exploit, greater tax savings in their foreign operations, and cheaper labor in the so-called stable countries. In summary, there are two beneficiaries of the slave trade: Mexican political and economic institutions perpetuating the country's maldistribution of income between the very few rich and the multitudes of the very poor; and multinationals not only operating within Mexico, but trading with her and other nations as well.

Winners in the United States

The most obvious U.S. beneficiaries of the slave trade are those who purchase the undocumented alien's work. Evidence of the benefits that are to be derived from such a workforce is abundant, especially when illegals make up most or all of the workforce. The first benefit is the lower payroll the boss must meet, in contrast to the salary he would have to pay for workers who demanded "American" wages.

Bosses who engage in illegal practices (hiring an alien is not illegal in most states) can save substantially more by not paying payroll taxes for his or her workforce. This can make a double profit if the boss tells his workers he is paying the taxes and then deducts them from their wages and pockets the money. This appeared to be the practice when, as described in an earlier chapter, reporters found check stubs with phony social security numbers attached to tax deductions. Alternatively, the boss can pay cash wages. Margo Cowan of Tucson's Manzo Area Council said, "There's a double wage scale in some places—cash for undocumented workers at a lower wage in some places, and paychecks for the others." North and Houston, in their study, reported that more than one-fifth of their sample said they were usually paid in cash.

Additionally, the employer of an undocumented, and, therefore, statistically invisible workforce can save money by neglecting other laws—health and safety laws, minimum wage laws, child labor laws, and overtime laws. As studies of industries known to have large illegal workforces in California have shown, the employer of undocumented workers often violates labor laws. There is no reason to expect that employers in other states don't follow the California pattern.

A 1976 government commissioned study, for example, estimated that there were about 9,000 undocumented workers employed in San Diego County, and that 63 percent earned less than $2.50 an hour. The average wage found was $2.00 an hour, thirty cents less than the federal legal minimum for that year.

At the beginning of 1979, Frank Mercurio of the U.S. Department of Labor served notice that he was "declaring war against unscrupulous employers" in Manhattan. His federal strike force, he said, would concentrate on four hundred contractors who operate garment factories employing more than ten thousand predominantly Chinese workers within a thirty-five-square-block area. Mercurio estimated that up to two-thirds of the employees were working in violation of immigration laws, and that they earned $100 or $120 for a work week lasting between fifty and sixty hours. Deportable aliens, he noted, are "forced to accept whatever their unscrupulous employers elect to pay." Mercurio's project was launched after a six-month pilot study which, he said, uncovered many labor law abuses.

Another money saver for unscrupulous slave trade profiteers is calling in the INS for a raid of their own shops the day before payday. The INS obligingly rounds up the suspected illegals, who are not given time to collect the wages due them. In this manner, according to several sources, employers have saved paying for an entire week's work or more. A study made by the Mexican government in 1972 found that 67 percent of those interviewed on their return from the U.S. said they were not paid regularly and/or were still owed wages when apprehended.

It was not until August 1978 that Mexican officials made a serious move to correct this injustice by setting up a consular office near the California border. In a historic first, celebrated with appropriate fanfare on October 28, 1978, Jesus Rodriguez Navarro, the Mexican consul general posted in San Diego, distributed nearly $10,000 in checks for wages owed to 142 deported Mexican aliens. A similar amount, Navarro said in the Tijuana ceremony, would be distributed to another group of deported Mexican nationals the following week.

The final advantage of an underground workforce is its docility. Employers with no desire to violate any labor law simply prefer a worker who is uncomplaining, diligent, and in continual fear of losing a job; one who shows up for work on time every day and never complains if a coffee break is missed or if there are a few extra hours of work to be done. Economist Michael Piore, of the Massachusetts Institute of Technology, studied Boston's secondary labor market and its employment of undocumented workers in the mid-1970s. Piore observed that fundamental changes in this market began in the late 1960s. In the mid-sixties, Piore said, the secondary labor force was dominated by older immigrants and black workers who had migrated from the South to urban ghettos. By the end of the decade, said Piore, "these workers reportedly became a good deal more difficult to manage. Clashes between employees and supervisors and among employees themselves became more frequent." This he attributed in part to the generally prosperous economy of that time and a consequent rise in worker expectations. But rather than improve wages and working conditions, according to Piore's observations, bosses began to recruit a wave of new immigrant workers, both legal and illegal. These included citizens from Puerto Rico and immigrants from Haiti, the Dominican Republic, Mexico, Guatemala, and other Latin-American nations. By 1975, according to Piore, illegals constituted almost three-fourths of the minority labor force in Boston.

Other Beneficiaries

President Ford's committee to study the impact of "illegal aliens" in the U.S. represented a fairly comprehensive review of many factors surrounding the cause of illegal immigration to the U.S. and its effects. A section of the group's report dealing with "Domestic Impact of Illegal Aliens," although admitting there were few hard data to work from, analyzed the distribution of real income, and the effects of illegal immigration on the labor market and on the U.S. economy as a whole, on the basis of what it felt were generally accepted economic theories. The analysis was revealing in terms of answering questions about the beneficiaries of illegal immigration.

The report states unequivocally that "the total real output (GNP) produced by the economy increases in response to the greater employment supply due to immigration, whether legal or illegal. Even the *total* real income of those already residing in the United States increases." (Emphasis added.) This uplifting statement was followed by the caveat, "However, the gain in real income is not shared uniformly."

The committee reports that relative wages for undocumented workers decline as more illegals enter the job market. Therefore, owners of firms employing illegals, the committee says, "tend to gain through higher profits," which is little surprise. Also benefiting, according to the committee, are American consumers. The logic behind this conclusion is that since the illegal workers cost less, the products of their labor—services or tangible items—are priced lower. The report cites one fact in support of this hypothesis (which presumes that employers automatically pass on savings to consumers, a theorem of the free-market economic model): after the Bracero Program was ended in 1965, domestic farm laborers began to earn more money *and* the price of food rose, implying a direct connection between the two. Labor costs, however, account for a very small percentage of the consumer price of any hand harvested crop. One suspects that the rise in the price of food was related to the rise in costs other than labor.

Despite these observations, the Ford committee report is firm in its conviction that the prices American consumers pay for labor-intensive products are kept down by the presence of exploited, unskilled illegal workers (and the more of them, the lower the prices). As a result, some of us benefit in terms of lower prices and the consequent rise in real incomes. Perhaps on a macroeconomic scale these observations are valid, but it is doubtful that any individual consumer would notice a difference in price if the Manhattan garment worker were paid $120 for a forty-hour work week instead of a sixty-hour work week, or if the deportable alien washing dishes at the local restaurant were paid the minimum wage.

A Surprise Beneficiary

Among the more controversial topics in discussions of today's slave trade is whether the underground worker uses more in welfare and other transfer payment programs than he or she pays in taxes. Much of the heat on this issue is generated by local governments, which must pay for whatever public services ineligible aliens use, but are not reimbursed by the federal government in revenue-sharing or other funds because, officially, illegals—who don't appear as part of the census data supporting revenue-sharing claims—don't exist.

Several studies have explored the cost of public services used by "illegal aliens," including one prepared by the General Accounting Office in December 1977. The GAO report concludes that not enough is known about the impact of undocumented immigrants on public assistance programs and recommends further study. The report does, however, enumerate specific public assistance programs that might be affected and provides some data about their use.

There are four major public assistance programs that illegals are *not* eligible for: AFDC (Aid to Families with Dependent Children), SSI (Supplemental Security Income—payments made to the blind, aged, or disabled person with limited income), Medicaid and/or Medicare, and food stamps. Since the issuance of the report, illegal immigrants have become ineligible for unemployment insurance, another impact area the report covered. Other public assistance programs included in the report are: public education, public housing, and a variety of school-related food aid programs. Individual states and/or localities may exclude undocumented aliens from these programs if they wish. Several public school districts in different states, including New York, California, and Texas, either do not allow illegals to attend, attempt to charge them tuition, or levy special taxes to pay for their education.

Some illegals do make use of these programs, even when they are, by law, not entitled to. How many, or what percentage of them, use these programs either legally or illegally is an issue that concerns many tax-conscious Americans. The answers to such questions are fairly straightforward, despite claims by the GAO that information is insufficient. The GAO found, in its own survey of 120 deportable aliens, that none had used AFDC or SSI. One of the 120 had used food stamps. Other studies of much larger samples than its own cited by the GAO showed that the range of undocumented immigrants found to be using these programs was from less than 0.5 percent in most areas to a maximum of 2.6 percent of all users in Los Angeles County, which was under a court order to provide AFDC payments until it could prove that applicants were ineligible. Two studies of one-time alien workers in the U.S., one by Wayne A. Cornelius and the other by North and Houston, reported very low usage of these programs. Cornelius reported that 2.2 percent of Mexicans he studied had used welfare in the U.S., and North and Houston found that only 0.5 percent reported using welfare in the U.S. (These studies did not distinguish between AFDC and SSI.)

A report prepared by the House Select Committee on Population a year after the GAO report concluded that "every study of both apprehended and unapprehended illegal immigrants shows that reliance on welfare (AFDC or SSI) is between zero and three percent. Use of food stamps is similarly low (1 to 4 percent)."

Don I. Wortman, acting commissioner of social security, testified before a 1978 Senate hearing that it is the opinion of his department that an "insignificant fraction of 1 percent of all applicants are undocumented aliens who succeed in receiving assistance."

Almost all authorities agree that the major impact of undocumented workers is on medical care and public education programs. The GAO found 12.5 percent reporting that all or part of their medical care in the U.S. had been free. Cornelius found that 15.4 percent of his Mexican sample had received free medical care in the U.S. North and Houston, meanwhile, reported that only 4.6 percent of their sample said they had received free medical care.

Because states are not reimbursed for their treatment of un-documented immigrants (nor are most counties within states that have their own programs), the issue of health care for the deportable alien has become volatile. Los Angeles County, for example, claimed in 1979 that it spent between $50 million and $60 million each year on health care for illegals. New York officials, meanwhile, estimated that they spent anywhere from $3 million to $30 million each year. It is obvious that neither municipality knows what it is talking about. New York, most observers agree, has an illegal population either equal to or greater than that of Los Angeles. As the population committee report concluded, figures supplied by county and state officials are suspect both "because of the difficulty of determining who is an illegal immigrant and because hospitals have a vested interest in supporting the highest possible estimates." Los Angeles County's vested interest was its attempt to get the federal government to reimburse its expenses.

The law requires that public hospitals provide emergency treatment to whomever needs it, citizen or noncitizen. Some regions, like New York City, voluntarily provide nonemergency care. Others are not so generous, like Orange County, California. In any event, the population committee deemed that use of free medical services by illegals was "moderate."

Falling through the cracks of the health care controversy are children like Isidro Aguinaga, Jr., whose parents claimed they *could* pay for their child's care. Isidro was apparently suffering from a respiratory infection and dehydration when his parents brought him to Plains Memorial Hospital in Dimmitt, Texas. A hospital staff physician had examined Isidro at a public clinic and prescribed emergency treatment at the local hospital. The child's parents took Isidro to the hospital and were told, they said, that their son could not be admitted unless they paid a $400 deposit. Hospital officials denied telling the Aguinagas that, saying that since they did not speak English, the parents misunderstood. The Aguinagas eventually left Plains hospital and drove to a county hospital thirty miles away. Officials there denied Isidro admission because the family did not live in the county.

Isidro died on the return trip to Dimmitt.

Discussion of unemployment benefits is by now outdated, since a federal law now prevents people who are in violation of immigration statutes from collecting unemployment, even if they are otherwise eligible. While the program was still legally available, unless barred by state law, 2.4 percent of the Cornelius sample reported receiving unemployment benefits, 3.9 percent of the North and Houston sample did so, and 7.5 percent of the GAO sample reported receiving benefits. The pattern of these statistics is interesting because they tend to support the thesis that those who enter the U.S. without inspection (EWIs, in INS parlance) are the lowest users of tax-supported services. The Cornelius sample were virtually all EWIs. Sixty-nine percent of the North-Houston sample were EWIs, and, they noted, visa abusers were more likely to draw unemployment than EWIs. Sixty percent of the GAO sample were EWIs.

Although America's system of free public education is one of the things that undocumented workers comment most favorably about in the United States, it is, apparently, a system that many of their children will never see. As of the end of 1978, the highest estimates from research on undocumented populations found only 7 percent had foreign-born children in U.S. public schools.

A similar pattern of low EWI usage was noted by both the GAO and North and Houston in public education. North and Houston concluded, "It was the non-Mexican illegals, who were the least likely to be apprehended by the INS, who were the more likely to have taken advantage of tax-supported programs."

Aside from the cost of enforcing relevent sections of the Immigration and Nationality Act, the above data account for most of what illegals take out of the public system. What do they contribute to it? The same dues that each American must pay: taxes. The House population committee report said, "Precise data on tax payments are lacking, but it is clear that most illegal aliens work and that a substantial portion have Federal and State taxes withheld from their pay. The results of six studies of apprehended and unapprehended illegal immigrants in San Diego and Orange County, Calif., New York City, and other areas throughout the United States are remarkably consistent. In each study, between 69 and 81 percent of employed undocumented workers had Federal and/or State income taxes withheld from their pay, and 62 to 88 percent paid Social Security taxes."

Even if the workers do not file income tax returns, it is likely that something has been withheld from their checks. And even if employers take what should be withheld for themselves and do not turn it over to the government, there are still unavoidable taxes: gasoline taxes, excise taxes, sales taxes, and property taxes (even if paid indirectly through rent).

Two California counties attempted to estimate overall tax contributions made by undocumented workers within their boundaries. San Diego County estimated that its 9,000 undocumented workers contributed a total of $49 million in taxes to all levels of government – some 17 percent of their wages (a low percentage compared to the average American worker because the undocumented worker, earning less, falls into a much lower tax bracket for federal and state income tax purposes). Meanwhile, San Diego County estimated that illegal aliens may have cost it about $2 million for medical care services. Orange County estimated that tax payments by undocumented workers within its boundaries totaled at least $83 million and perhaps as much as $145 million. Medical care for the population cost the county $2.6 million (it pays only for emergency care). These figures are based only on estimates of the number of deportable aliens thought to be present and working, but even the cautious House population committee concedes, "the consistency of the findings from a number of different sources suggests that many illegal immigrants do pay taxes and that these payments must be taken into account when assessing their use of public services."

David S. North contends that illegal immigrants, especially EWIs, may contribute substantially more to the system than they withdraw from it. Using the same data base and assumptions he earlier used to conclude that illegal immigrants were sending $1.5 billion annually home to their families in Mexico (presuming one million illegal Mexicans are, at any given time, employed in the U.S.), he estimated that social security contributions by aliens and their employers total more than $500 million a year.

Those who work with immigrants have many compelling stories to tell about people who have worked in the U.S. for years and, because of their fear of deportation, or from lack of knowledge that they might be eligible for the permanent residency status that leads to citizenship, have never collected a dime of public money. Among the more compelling is one pulled from the files of Sister Adela Arroyo. "Here is a sixty-four-year-old woman who was brought to this state illegally by her parents when she was two years old. She has lived here ever since. She married in 1932. All her children were born in the United States. For twenty years she has been trying to document her existence to INS. But either the U.S. consulate in Monterrey [Mexico] can't find her records or INS has misplaced her file. Now we have eventually made progress. Through her children, she will be eligible for naturalization in five years.

"But she has lived here for sixty-two years. She paid the taxes on her little house and paid into income tax and social security. Her children,

also, pay their taxes. But because she is illegal, she can't draw the benefits from the years of her labor. There are many like her. The rule is: no
status, no rights."

A sociologist from the University of Texas at El Paso, E. R. Stoddard,
the author of several articles on Mexican migration, talking at a 1977
conference on "Immigration and the Mexican National," summarized
the situation: "As has been suggested this morning, a study in San
Diego shows that they put in about forty-two million dollars into certain kinds of income tax deductions . . . and took out about two million
dollars, which means that we ripped them off for about forty million
dollars that year in San Diego County alone."

16: THE UNDERGROUND WORKFORCE: WHO LOSES?

> Of course blacks feel the aliens take away jobs. Why do
> you think blacks can't even get jobs as dishwashers or in
> gas stations anymore? Drive into any gas station and
> they're all foreigners, don't even understand when you
> talk.
>
> —*Mother of two, Washington, D. C.*

A survey of the beneficiaries of the slave trade is a task almost as simple as marking sections in the Great Plains where there are no canyons
or mountains to tangle the surveyor's chain. Mapping the measure of
the loss to the U.S. is much more difficult. Rivers once charted no longer
lead where they once did, assumptions, once dogma, can no longer be
relied upon, and only one truth seems to remain: employers are still
hungry for cheap labor and will find it any way they can. Of the assumptions that demand questioning is the belief that "illegal aliens"
take employment away from job-hungry American citizens and resident aliens lawfully entitled to work.

Every map that was ever drawn has a base point, a geographic fixture that could be returned to by later generations of map makers who
could say, "that mountain was the place they began their survey." The
only base point in reference to the slave trade is the fact that there are
illegal aliens in the U.S. and that, in fact, some of them do work. Many
of the other assumptions are based on markers as shifting as the dunes
of the Sonora Desert. We are given a general profile of the Hispanic
illegal worker. Poorly educated and not speaking English, he or she is
most likely to find a job at the lowest end of the employment scale: as a
farm worker or maid, as a dishwasher or part-time janitor, as a
seamstress or cutter in a nonunion garment sweatshop, as a general
laborer paid three dollars an hour when the union man gets seven, as
an assembler at a small plant, putting together every sort of thing from
car stereos to mobile homes at wages far below the prevailing industry
wage. We can only make assumptions about the other undocumented
workers. Virtually nothing is known about the visa abuser from
Canada or Europe who, presumably, can compete successfully for better
jobs than his or her fellow illegals because of better education, vaster
work experience at home, and better command of English.

It is almost a certainty that many of the jobs held by Hispanic workers are jobs no American wants. These include harvesting citrus for less
than $2 an hour, working a fifty- or sixty-hour week in a garment
sweatshop for $120 a week less taxes, where cockroaches crawl over the
clothing and the plumbing leaks onto the floors and an injury means

firing, or washing dishes at a minimum wage but with no overtime, where a day of sickness means the end of a job, or working at a laundry facility at a job that costs $200 just to get. Some people say, however, that if the aliens were all gone, these jobs would change, that they would become jobs that Americans could live with, perhaps even survive on. Such an assertion runs contrary to a vast history of American employment practices that show that if cheap and docile workers cannot somehow be replaced with others like them, the sweatshops and restaurants will close, and the farmer will switch to a crop that can be harvested by machine, or sell out and move on to a job somewhere else.

Some organizations, like the American Enterprise Institute, say there are jobs held by undocumented workers that already pay enough for an American to want. The AEI cites Detroit to back up its case. There, they say, during the period between February and October 1976, 1,500 deportable aliens were apprehended. Of these, 900 had jobs and 31 percent earned more than $6.50 an hour, while 39 percent earned between $4.50 and $6.50. The AEI report, distributed to legislators considering illegal immigration, defeats its purpose: unemployment was 40 percent. And if Detroit was so typical of the underground job market, why wasn't data included from other cities?

But this is no answer to the charge of the District of Columbia mother, who sees jobs once held by people from her own community now taken by foreigners. She reports that her brother was lucky one day when he stopped by a pizza parlor a few hours after the INS swept it clean and got a job. He was lucky, for by the next day a new illegal crew would have filled all the jobs.

So, at least from one mother's testimony, we have another benchmark. Adding to her complaints are thousands of other Americans who call the INS to complain they have lost their jobs when the boss fired them and replaced them with foreign workers, or who complain that they cannot get a job because the only people who are ever hired are foreigners. So there are jobs held by illegals that American workers would like to have. What kinds of jobs are these? They are, as far as any of the social scientists have been able to tell, dead-end, minimum-wage jobs that Americans take when they can get them and hold onto only until they think they can find something better. They are jobs that require no skills but obedience; jobs that develop no skills.

Even these dead-end jobs going nowhere concern the black mother, who saw that the black teen-age unemployment rate was, according to official statistics, more than 39 percent in 1978, while unofficial rates that include those who work only a few hours but want to work full time, as well as those who have given up searching, were higher than 60 percent. Black unemployment in the twenty to twenty-four age group was not that much better, holding at an official rate of 20.7 percent. Black teen and youth unemployment stood, in 1978, at twice what it was a decade earlier when urban riots reached their peak. To the black mother in Washington, the jobs may have been dead-end, but the foreigners who held them threatened her. She saw a job, any kind of job, as a beginning, as a place where a young person learns not only a pride in work, but the reinforcement of a salary increase – an education for a life of employment instead of ghetto crime. To her, the employment market seemed like the credit market: you can't get credit until you have already established it somehow. Jobs were the same: you can't get one unless you have a reference from an earlier job. To her, even the dead-end job was an essential entry into the labor market for her children.

To Herbert Hill, former labor director for the NAACP, the unemployment statistics meant more: "It is evident that a permanent black underclass has developed, that virtually an entire second generation of ghetto youth will never enter the labor force."

To people such as Hill and the Washington mother, arguments that the underground labor force hold jobs that are degraded below even the most desperate American's needs, don't wash. The jobs, good or bad, are jobs that should be filled by the unemployed. And if employers do not pay a minimum wage, they should be forced to do so.

California, in 1975, tried an experiment to see if illegals who were removed from their jobs would be replaced by Americans and legal residents. In June the INS rounded up 2,154 suspected illegal immigrants working in Los Angeles and gave information about their jobs and places of work to the state so it could fill these vacancies. After a month, both the state and the INS declared the experiment a failure. Nearly 99 percent of the employers contacted by the state refused to accept help in hiring workers to replace those they had lost to the INS. Although no one admitted as much, the only conclusion that could be drawn from this experiment was that these jobs were reserved for illegal workers. The employers were interested only in an exploitable labor force, and did not want to face paying the minimum wage or to meet other state requirements.

Many jobs in the underground labor market apparently fall into this category. They are controlled by bosses who do not want to hire American workers and the rights they bring with them to the workplace.

Interestingly, the Ford committee on "illegal aliens" reported that the illegals were, if they competed in the marketplace, most likely to compete against and perhaps displace teen-agers, legal immigrants, and disabled people in the nonskilled or secondary labor market sector. (Disabilities in the American labor market today include both race and gender.) The Ford committee's model of possible job displacement would tend to support the black mother's feeling that her children would be unable to find jobs because of the presence of undocumented workers. However, the single group apparently most vulnerable to such a "displacement effect" would be, in the Ford committee's model, unskilled Hispanic-American youth. At this juncture the committee's model fails. While unemployment among Hispanic-American youth is high, nearly 20 percent in 1978, this unemployment rate had steadily decreased during the previous three years, when the flow of undocumented Hispanic peoples into the U.S. was thought to be increasing. In 1975 Hispanic-American youth unemployment was 27.7 percent.

Obviously, there are other processes at work in the relationship between illegal immigration and employment of which we are not aware, or, alternatively, there may be no relationship between the two at all. In another model, Hispanic illegals may actually increase employment, primarily in the Hispanic-American regions and neighborhoods of the U.S. Some economists, like Sheldon Maram of California State University at Fullerton, support this model, believing that the foreign workers are not only good for the economy, but that they create jobs for natives as a by-product of their consumer purchases here.

An excellent example that would appear to substantiate Maram's thesis comes from Houston, in a phenomenon that might well exist in Los Angeles, Miami, and other regions of the country where both documented and undocumented workers are mixed in city neighborhoods. Houston's late-1970s economic boom led to the migration there of not only Americans of Mexican descent, but Mexican nationals as well. Both populations are heavily concentrated in certain areas of East Houston. Some observers there (doubtlessly exaggerating) estimated that the undocumented population of the city may be as high as 200,000. With a large (whatever guess one chooses to make) population of deportable Mexican nationals, it is little wonder that community spokespeople, like the president of the Mexican-American Chamber of Commerce, estimate that in the hypothetical situation of a mass deportation of all unlawfully present aliens, business in East Houston would drop by 30 to 40 percent. J. Homer Garza, chairman of the board of the American National Bank, conservatively estimates the drop in business at 15 to 20 percent. Such a deportation, according to Garza, would have a "tremendous impact on employment" in local shops and businesses, which would be forced to lay off what he estimates would be from 20 to 25 percent of their employees.

The impact of the illegal immigrant on business is so real, says Garza, that when some Houston owners decide whether to expand or to start businesses in the Mexican-American neighborhoods, the presence of the Mexican national population is one of the things factored into their decision making process.

Maram is not alone is his positive appraisal of the effects of illegal immigration. A better-known voice than his, Massachusetts Institute of Technology economist Michael J. Piore, asserts that the presence of an illegal labor force may, in some ways, benefit low-skilled U.S. workers: "Instances where native workers share jobs with aliens and appear to suffer a dampening effect upon working conditions are not uncommon, but in many of these cases higher wages would either drive the industry out of existence or force major changes in technology, either of which would leave the native jobless. In this sense, the presence of aliens serves to preserve native jobs, and the proper way to deal with the problems of native workers trapped in such jobs would thus seem to be through equal employment opportunity, training and other programs which foster their upward mobility."

In any event, although a substantial number of community leaders believe that the aliens take away jobs that should go to Americans, the evidence is by no means completely in.

The only solid evidence of displacement of native worker by foreign worker is in farm employment, where employers conscientiously seek out foreign labor for the explicit purpose of keeping the cost of farm labor down. This situation will only become more aggravated in the coming few years. The U.S. Department of Labor estimated that between 1976 and 1985, the total number of available farm labor jobs will have decreased by about 34 percent. The number of other low-skilled jobs is also likely to decrease, the department predicts. Meanwhile, the projected growth in the labor market continues to accelerate in jobs requiring not only specific skills, but a combination of special advanced education and prior work experience in similar fields. In short, the future of the unskilled labor market in the U.S. looks bleak, not only for American citizens and permanent residents, but for undocumented workers as well.

The conditions begetting not only a permanent black underclass, but a shortage of low-skilled jobs at a survival wage, strangely parallels that of the so-called underdeveloped, or developing nations from which the foreigner tries to escape. Other conditions in the U.S. also parallel those of developing nations. Our national wealth of minerals, water, trees, and other assets are gradually becoming depleted. Contemporary America is a nation in decline as compared with other nations. Real per capita income for hourly workers is no longer the highest in the world; even managerial salaries are no longer the highest in the world; infant mortality rates are no longer the lowest in the world; and nutritional standards are not keeping pace with other nations. These are all symptoms of an "underdeveloping" nation.

The picture is similar in the farming industry. Robert McNamara, president of the World Bank, candidly remarked that "the whole thrust of the Green Revolution has been to modernize the methods of the already better-off farmers to the detriment of the poorer, who unable to afford the costly inputs it requires, are being progressively pushed off their land." McNamara, of course, was referring to other nations of the world. But his statement applies equally well to the U.S. farming industry, where concentration of capital continues to build in the hands of the already rich, as other farmers are being pushed off their land.

Vernon Jordan's "permanent underclass" parallels the permanent underclasses of other nations in which the U.S. has intervened and fostered a process of underdevelopment.

Employers controlling the greatest number of jobs in the U.S. are multinational corporations such as International Telephone and Telegraph. American-based corporations like ITT are no longer what they once appeared to be. They have become citizens of the world, and their loyalties have shifted, no longer promoting what is best for America and her people, but what is best for the "company" and its profit margins. Concentration of capital accumulated by these giants continues, making them less and less dependent on, or affected by, American consumers, American workers, or even the American government. Such remnants of free enterprise as remain within the U.S. are fighting an increasingly tougher battle for survival against the giants that are making it nearly impossible for the small business owner to compete, buying out the farmer, and either buying out, or underpricing, the small manufacturer.

Peter F. Drucker, a guru of multinational expansion as the key to world salvation, once made this revealing comment in reference to India: within "the vast poverty that is India," there is "a sizable modern economy, comprising ten percent or more of the Indian population, or fifty million people." They, he pointed out, are a consumer market ready for the products of multinational corporations. Following in the footsteps of Drucker's analysis, American and other worldwide corporations have targeted their marketing, their advertising, and their production to the developed and developing upper and middle classes of those nations who can afford to buy their products in a sort of "to hell with the starving masses" attitude.

If the Drucker thesis works in India and other nations, why should profit-hungry conglomerates not also apply it to the United States? The U.S. reportedly no longer offers the substantial military and CIA aid that once promoted the "stability" of foreign countries so that companies such as ITT could continue to profit without fear of expropriation. The U.S. no longer offers cheap labor, and taxes on profits are high. What reason is there to expect that ITT or any of the other major multinational corporations gives a damn about the minor problems of American unemployment or a developing underclass? There is, after all, nothing binding their loyalty to (nor, apparently, much else that is useful in) the United States. And, since the doors to the most populous nation and potential market in the world—Red China—have been opened, of what benefit is the U.S. from the corporate point of view?

This is, perhaps, a circuitous route to have followed in trying to plot the map of the losers of the underground workforce. But the analysis leaves serious questions about whether anyone loses anything from the presence of an illegal workforce. In fact, we are all, legal and illegal alike, in some part losers to institutions much greater than those we control.

17: QUENCHING THE NATIVIST THIRST

In 1975, when INS head General Leonard F. Chapman, Jr. told a nation suffering its highest unemployment rate since the Great Depression that there were twelve million illegal aliens in the U.S. stealing American jobs and robbing America's welfare coffers, he paved the way for a return to nativism. Quietly adding to the nativist fervor was a slowly changing ethnic composition brought to the country by her new immigrants. During the 1960s, for the first time in U.S. history, the majority of her immigrants (excluding pre-1865 black slaves) were not white. Fifty-one percent were either Asian or Latin-American. The trend continued into the 1970s, when about 70 percent of new immigrants were Asians and Latin-Americans. Chapman was addressing a nation that was not only confronting serious economic crisis, but was quietly undergoing changes in immigration trends similar to those that had brought on the harsh, racist immigration quota laws of the 1920s, which were enacted to "save America" from the invasion of "inferior" racial stocks from southern and eastern Europe.

The new immigration, while only accounting for a small fraction of the total U.S. population, nevertheless was sufficient to make a noticeable presence in a few states, especially New York (confronting economic troubles of its own), California, New Jersey, Florida, Illinois, and the District of Columbia. Were such immigration trends to continue, some population authorities speculated, California would, by the year 2000, join Hawaii and become the second state to have a white minority population. Meanwhile, experts predicted, black people, the largest American racial minority in 1970, might be outnumbered by Hispanics in the 1980s. Massachusetts, according to the U.S. Census Bureau, had made the change by 1976; Hispanics there already outnumbering the state's vocal, but tiny, black minority. Social conditions were ready for the nativist outburst: a projected minority population in excess of a quarter of the total population by the end of the 1980s, and a worsening economic outlook. Chapman merely gave a misleading name to the scapegoat that nativism needed: "illegal aliens."

Given this target, the issues of legal immigration were obscured. For example, when a 1976 UPI story on legally immigrated aliens reported that they were drawing in excess of $73 million per year in welfare benefits, those protesting illegal immigration saw only the headline "aliens," and mailed the article out along with their other anti-alien literature.

American opinion was also shifting toward the nativist position, as cities became more crowded and conditions in them appeared to worsen. A 1977 Gallup poll, for example, reported that 60 percent of Americans favored laws that would prohibit employers from hiring "illegal aliens," while 40 percent also responded that they supported a decrease in legal immigration. In order to effect such changes, 45 percent said they were ready to accept a tough national identification card program for all legal residents that would require them to carry, at all times, a card bearing their photos and fingerprints, along with other information about them.

The complex problems of legal immigration and its effects on the American economy and social fabric, however, were ignored as people focused on the target General Chapman had given them: "illegal aliens." It was a perfect target. No one could count them, and no one really had the answers to the question of whether they affected the American economy, and if they did, whether the effect was good or bad. But it sounded bad. And since the illegals were presumed to be brown people, it also became a quiet (and, at times, not so quiet) outlet for racial hostilities. It was a tailor-made political issue, and many politicians ran for election on the issue, especially in those states most affected by large numbers of legal Hispanic immigrants. It was tailor-made in another sense as well: there was a very simple solution to the entire problem. It was already illegal to transport aliens or to harbor them. The only thing that wasn't illegal was to hire them. Close this loophole, nativist thinking went, and the problem would be solved.

Nativists at first took their demands to their state legislatures, as they had in earlier eras. The logic of the hiring ban was best explained in 1978 by the Illinois Legislative Investigating Commission, which reported: "The only way that the state of Illinois can hope to deal with the illegal alien problem is through passage of legislation which would penalize those who employ the illegal aliens." Ironically, legislators in Illinois, whose industries were prime employers of undocumented workers, proposed such legislation several times, but, as of early 1979, had not passed a hiring ban. Similarly, the District of Columbia tried to enact a hiring ban, but it also had not passed.

But it was an appealing political issue. In 1977, Virginia Delegate William P. Robinson sponsored an employer sanction bill, saying that it would open up at least thirty thousand jobs in his district alone. His law passed and went into effect on January 1, 1978.

By mid-1978 fourteen states and Puerto Rico had enacted legislation imposing penalties on employers who knowingly hired workers who were in violation of the Immigration and Nationality Act. The states were: California, Connecticut, Delaware, Florida, Maine, Massachusetts, Montana, Nevada, New Hampshire, New Jersey, New York, Vermont, Virginia, and Washington.

The constitutionality of such laws is seriously questioned by the American Civil Liberties Union and Hispanic and Asian minority groups who believe their effect would be discrimination in hiring of anyone who looks "foreign." In the era of the wetback syndrome, such discrimination would affect Hispanic-Americans the hardest. In any event, as of early 1979, none of the laws had much effect. Not only did most attorneys feel they were unenforceable, but, at least during 1978, there was not a single reported case that any of these state laws had been enforced nor that employers had been prosecuted or fined because of them. As INS raids continued, in 1978 and 1979, to round up deportable aliens in California, New Jersey, New York, Nevada, Virginia, and Washington, there was no real evidence of voluntary compliance with the law. Virginia's first case testing the law was thrown out of court in 1979.

It is somewhat naive of the nativists to believe that employer sanctions, in view of the historical record, will open up any significant number of jobs for resident aliens and citizens. When the Bracero Program ended, for example, domestic farm workers got raises and their unemployment rate dropped during the first year after the program. In following years, however, bosses simply returned to their old source of cheap labor, the slave market. Employers, after a time, had come to like the Bracero Program and preferred it, in many cases, to the underground labor market. As one Texas rancher commented about the program, "We used to buy our slaves; now we just rent them from the government," apparently a much more satisfying way of doing business.

California's experience with employer sanctions (it was the first to enact them, in 1972), sheds some light on how employers manipulated the system to retain their cheap labor. As the law went into effect, a Los Angeles INS officer reported that his office was seeing about ninety aliens a day, a huge jump over previous numbers. All were seeking legal permission to document their presence and right to work. Most succeeded. The INS finally explained this curious phenomenon to their satisfaction. Employers, it seemed, were sending in those aliens who could qualify for legal status, and not sending those who could not qualify. As soon as the California law met its first court test, the INS reported, this sudden surge of employer-sent aliens ceased.

Despite evidence that state laws have done nothing to change the underground employment market, members of Congress continue to press for federal sanctions similar to the state laws. Even President Jimmy Carter jumped on the employer sanction bandwagon when he introduced his immigration proposals to Congress in 1977. There was, in his package, no money allocated for enforcement of such laws. Carter just smiled and said he relied on the law-abiding nature of the American public to comply voluntarily—as if America's age-old hunger for cheap labor would give way to a good-natured toothsome smile.

Although the politics of the 1970s produced some fairly strange alliances, perhaps none was so strange as that which formed on either side of the Carter immigration proposals. Vernon Briggs, an economist at the University of Texas at Austin, and a specialist in labor economics and the Chicano worker in the Southwest, commented, "It is the strangest issue I have seen in one sense. . . . It has united the Chicano community with its historic oppressors. The people in the past who have done everything to keep the Chicano community down are now in there holding their hands. . . . I am talking about the farmer, the ranchers, the conservative politicians, the people who want a dependent peon work force to do the work for them and a non-unionized work force. I would beg the Chicano community to at least ponder why it is that one of their friends, like the labor movement, they are now breaking away from. The black community. Blacks throughout this state tell me that this issue is going to break the civil rights alliance between the Chicano community and the blacks. . . . And the number of Anglos are beginning to raise questions too, a lot of them who are poor. The Catholic Church is split on this issue. Again, they have been a historic friend."

The alliances were indeed strange. Opposing employer sanctions were: most Hispanic organizations, the National Chinese Welfare Council, the National Association of Farmworker Organizations (which doubts that many citizen farm laborers could prove their right to work), the National Restaurant Association, The Conservative Caucus Citizens Cabinet, and the American Hotel and Motel Association.

Favoring employer sanctions were: Zero Population Growth, the American Legion, the Veterans of Foreign Wars, the national AFL-CIO, the National Urban League, the National Association for the Advancement of Colored People, and the National Council of Agricultural Employers.

Two employer organizations on opposite sides of the issue add caveats to their positions that are probably more revealing than anyone's talk of civil rights. The American Hotel and Motel Association, while opposing employer sanctions, notes that it would demand an expanded source of legal foreign labor, perhaps through liberalization of H-2 provisions of the current immigration law. (H-2 is the U.S. equivalent of a guest worker program for unskilled laborers, primarily used in agricultural areas.) The National Council of Agricultural Employers declares it also favors a return to the Bracero Program. The initial Carter proposals, most observers agreed, were put out as a trial balloon to see which way the winds were blowing. The winds were hard to read except from a careful analysis of the 1978 testimony taken for the U.S. Senate in Arizona. Here questions began to feel out the acceptability of U.S. adoption of a European-style guest worker program, which was heartily endorsed by employers who obviously would not accept employer sanctions unless, as in the past, they were accompanied by a loophole that still allowed for the employment of cheap labor. U.S. Representative Hamilton Fish, Jr. of New York presented written testimony after a tour of border regions:

> I wish to state my strong support for sanctions on employers who knowingly hire illegal or undocumented aliens. . . . However, I believe that employer sanctions are only one step of several that should be taken together to deal with the problem. If it becomes illegal to employ undocumented aliens, I suggest that there will develop legitimate needs for alien workers to come to this country [to fill jobs left vacant by undocumented workers but not filled by native workers]. . . . At the present time, with millions of undocumented aliens here who can now be legally employed, there is still a need for temporary alien workers, particularly in agriculture during labor-intense periods [who were requested through the H-2 program by farmers]. Employer sanction legislation will hopefully reduce the influx of available workers. When this occurs, I suggest that the need for alien workers, particularly temporary workers, will increase. Therefore, an improved temporary worker program [e.g., guest worker program] should be included in any legislation enacted.

The guest worker "option" is popular among many members of Congress. In the kind of crooked ways that politics work, it makes sense. The nativists are placated by an unenforceable law barring the hiring of ineligible workers, and the employers hungry for cheap labor get an expanded program to help them recruit it from abroad. In the end nothing is really changed except that the black voting bloc will probably be pitted against the Hispanic bloc, therefore preventing an effective alliance between the two groups with many common needs who, together, will soon (if they do not now already) make up nearly a quarter of the population. Even better, the program doesn't cost much. Employers comply voluntarily, so enforcement expenses are kept down; those who hire guest workers will pay for the maintenance of the program. Meanwhile, if necessary, the Hispanics can at least be divided, if not placated, with a law allowing those present in the U.S. continuously for the last seven years or so to become permanent residents. Organized labor, while unlikely to be very pleased by a guest worker program, can simply be given a few positions on whatever agency will monitor it. Employers who are turned down by the board in their request for workers will resort to the same underground slave trade they have always resorted to, except, with legal sanctions against them, the trade may become more brutal for the workers.

It is an almost perfect political strategy, a compromise satisfying almost everyone and costing almost nothing. However, it solves none of the pressing problems of the low-skilled domestic labor force of whatever race, nor does it offer anything to politically impotent farm workers who will soon join the swelling ranks of the permanent underclass as they are mechanized out of jobs.

It is the history of immigration politics and law repeating itself.

A European-style guest worker program, aside from being based on the unproven assumption that Americans are not available for, or perhaps not anxious for jobs that pay even a minimum wage, contains within it the seeds of future problems. It is possible that, like the old Bracero Program, its initial intent might be speedily abandoned. According to this 1949 recounting of the bracero experience as described by Ernesto Galaraza, then director of research and education for the AFL's National Farm Labor Union: "Stripped of its technicalities, the recruitment of [Mexican] nationals is a new phase of the old sources of low-cost, unorganized mass labor power. The original intention of the agreements as understood by some of their early advocates – the protection of wage and living standards as well as civil rights of imported workers and domestic labor in a time of great national stress – has been sidetracked."

After the Bracero Program ended, employers attempted to substitute for it the increased use of the H-2 program, an abbreviation for provisions of the Immigration and Nationality Act under section $101(a)(15)(H)(ii)$. H-2 has frequently been criticized as being inadequately responsive to employer's needs, doubtlessly because it is more difficult to get approval through H-2 than it had been earlier for bracero workers. H-2 is administered by the attorney general in consultation with the Department of Labor. Its regulations provide for the protection of domestic labor, but such protection is largely an administrative judgment that has varied from one administration to another. During the six years between 1966 and 1972, the number of foreign workers certified by the attorney general under H-2 ranged from 12,000 to 23,000 annually. The numbers stayed in this range until 1977, when the total number of foreign workers admitted under the program was a moderate 15,281. The Carter administration reportedly had begun an effort to cut down on the number of workers imported under the program, an act that pleased many of the Hispanic constituents who had helped swing the election for him. Carter, however, appeared to go back on his word in 1977 when some 800 Mexican nationals were certified to harvest onions in Presidio, Texas. He got in trouble again, this time with employers, in 1977 and 1978, as he attempted to substitute Puerto Ricans, Floridians, and other native migrant farm workers for the Jamaican H-2 workers the apple harvesters of the Northeast had been accustomed to importing.

The Jamaican controversy was still in court in 1979. Labor Department officials and lawyers for the Puerto Ricans who had been brought, at government expense, to the apple orchards but not given jobs, claimed the orchard growers conspired to violate provisions of H-2 that guarantee that domestic workers get first crack at available jobs. Apple orchard owners had sent a recruiter to Jamaica annually to line up the workers who would come, under contract, to work for them. Growers make no show of hiding their preference for Jamaican workers, claiming that apple picking is a highly refined skill (which can actually be learned in a few hours), that Jamaicans work harder, are more efficient, and demand less than do American workers. This latter statement is doubtlessly correct, for Jamaicans are in no position to demand anything unless they wish to be immediately deported. As then U.S. Representative William D. Ford of Michigan summarized:

While recent concern has centered on the illegal alien phenomenon . . . we have not focused on the wholesale employer violations of the Immigration Acts, which have resulted in the loss of thousands of jobs for American agricultural workers. . . . While some 2,500 agricultural workers from Florida and another 3,000 U.S. citizens from Puerto Rico were willing to come up to harvest the apple crops in the Northeast last fall, apple growers unashamedly claimed that there was no domestic labor supply, and then actively recruited Jamaican workers. . . . By waiting until the last minute to recruit domestic workers and by refusing—for the first time—to pay domestic migrants' transportation costs to the orchards—while offering to pay such costs for Jamaican workers, the employers blatantly manufactured the very situation, that is, an unavailable domestic labor force, which then permitted them to recruit this Jamaican labor. And this was at a time when over 100,000 American farmworkers were unemployed.

Rather than comply with the law, provide decent working conditions, and hire American workers at a fair wage, these employers continue to flout the Immigration Act, so they can obtain a foreign work force that is more susceptible to their strong-arm tactics. . . . With this situation threatening to occur again this year, there is the increased danger that the apple growers' successful evasion of the law will have a ripple effect, spreading to other seasonal work, such as construction, retail services, and light industry.

The story repeated itself in 1978. And, while the practice has not yet spread to other industries, the idea caught on with other farmers. In August 1978, a Medford, Oregon, pear growing firm became the first West Coast agricultural enterprise to be approved to import foreign harvesters since the termination of the Bracero Program fourteen years earlier.

Also in 1978, Virginia and North Carolina tobacco growers, after having lost about seventy-five Mexican workers to INS raids, formed an organization to try to get approval to import legal, H-2 Mexican workers for its 1979 tobacco crop. The growers association retained the same law firm that had been successful in getting H-2 approval for the Jamaican apple harvesters. The attorneys advised them that legal fees might be as high as $30,000 but apparently the money was worth it to the growers, who agreed to pay the firm a retainer.

The tobacco growers' alliance is a portrait of a future including federal sanctions against the hiring of ineligible workers. Such sanctions would be nearly impossible to enforce, so many employers would continue to recruit from the ranks of the underground slave trade (as did the Virginia tobacco growers in 1978, despite state law). Were such sanctions accompanied by the now-available H-2 program or a new guest worker program, employers would doubtlessly resort to it in preference to hiring domestic workers, who bring their civil rights with them into the fields. A new guest worker program might also tend to open up new illegal routes of entry to the U.S. Arthur Martori of the Arrowhead Ranch, for example, (apparently having learned that even deportable Mexicans can and do organize to improve their working conditions) testified during 1978 that he was trying to get approval for some six hundred H-2 workers from Costa Rica. Those ineligible for such workers would perhaps be forced to go even further underground in their search for cheap and uncomplaining labor. Additionally, greater importation of either H-2 workers or guest workers would leave behind residual communities of foreigners ineligible for legal immigration, as happened during the Bracero Program and during the massive importation of H-2 workers to the Virgin Islands and Europe as well—communities that remained long after the termination of the programs that brought them there.

The circle would begin again: greater exploitation of those not legally entitled to work; greater importation of foreign workers, leaving behind residual foreign communities in addition, perhaps, to opening new routes of illegal immigration; and perhaps massive roundups like that of 1954—a time bomb ticking slowly until the next economic downturn, when someone rediscovers the fact that American jobs are being held by foreigners, and nativists are roused once again.

18: TOWARD A SANE APPROACH

From the date thirteen colonies declared their independence from England and formed a nation, America accepted an immigration policy based on both racial bias and business profit. The law that was written into the Constitution of their nation was a compromise measure: the slave trade would be outlawed in 1807. After 1807 the nation continued the outlawed trade, and it became a de facto immigration policy. A Civil War broke the back of this policy, but de facto slavery found other forms, always maintaining its ties to racial bias and business profit. As the United States passed its bicentennial celebrations, it entered a third century with a body of immigration law second in complexity only to its tax laws. And, huddling next to it, creeping through the cracks between the law and its enforcement, and the gaps of the boundaries of the nation, was a de facto immigration policy based, as it always was, on race and profit. The meeting of business in search of cheap, docile labor and those who would supply this market make up a contemporary slave trade extending to virtually every state in the Union, pausing at no Mason-Dixon line.

There is a crime in this that goes beyond denunciation, as, each day, American coroners swear out death certificates naming the causes of death—"death by asphyxiation," "death by drowning," "death by dehydration," "death by stabbing," "death by shooting"—and do not inscribe the real sickness that led to the cause of death: bondage and persecution and perpetuation of slavery.

There is a crime in all the debate over immigration and "illegal aliens." While others debate, people are hunted and hounded and studied like statistics, numbers that must compute into government economic models and foreign policy decisions, must fit into some future-studies scenario that does not have the space to encompass the humanity of it. Numbers are gathered. And numbers cannot be translated into people, human beings no different in their longings, hopes, and aspirations from those who discuss them, compute them, and those who hunt and hound and try to count them. Immigration policy never has had, and still does not have, any room for the human suffering caused by it, and there is a crime in this.

On the night the United States of America announced her entry into a third century with drum corps and drill teams and fireworks, two, or three, or four, or who knows how few or many thousands of Mexicans, El Salvadorians, Guatemalans, Colombians, Ecuadorians, and others from other nations, were trying to cross deserts and waterways, to pass a line drawn on paper that separates industrial prosperity in the north from starvation and poverty in all that is south. An unknown number died trying to cross. An unknown number were raped and beaten and robbed. An unknown number were killed. Those who survived the crossing of a line drawn on paper were distributed to employers hungry for them, hungry to eat the toil and sap the strength of them, in Los Angeles garment sweatshops, Chicago small industries crowded along Interstate 80, Massachusetts textile mills, District of Columbia restaurants, and points everywhere in between. If they were lucky, they would, always shackled by fear, find a job that paid enough to send money orders back home to families in other countries who depended on them. If there were no money orders, fathers, aunts, uncles, brothers, sisters, grandparents, mothers, children, would continue a slow dying, the kind of day-by-day eating away of life that malnutrition and not enough money for doctors and medicines bring.

On the East Coast they joined their fellow vassals of the economic machinery of the underground labor market, slaves imported from Poland or Italy, or who jumped ship from Greece, or stowed away under a load of bananas from El Salvador, or got through somehow on a faked or stolen birth certificate or on a tourist visa bribed from someone, from Haiti, Jamaica, the Dominican Republic. On the West Coast they joined Koreans, Filipinos, and Chinese, doing any job they could get for salaries too low for Americans to live on, in conditions that, were they free instead of in bondage, they could protest. In Florida they joined those trying to come by boat, maybe twenty-four in a boat made for six, Haitians fleeing death in Haiti, or kicked out of their one-time sanctuaries in the Bahamas and Cuba.

Across America they traveled whatever way they could, in the trunks of cars—maybe five to a trunk—underneath freight trains two inches from the wheels, or by foot. They traveled to do the jobs that needed doing: milking cows and shoveling manure; bending over sewing machines to make bikini swimsuits; stitching shoes together; rolling irrigation pipes across Idaho fields; shaping metal and fiberglass into mobile homes and recreational vehicles; picking mushrooms in dark cement compounds, hands guided by miners' lights; putting together parts for cheap stereos; planting trees in Oregon and Washington; mending fences in Montana; holding out in open-air hobo jungles to harvest every crop from avocados to tobacco; swinging shovels and pounding hammers at construction sites; serving food and cleaning tables and washing dishes; picking up after travelers in motels and hotels; minding the children and cleaning the house and feeding the family as thirty-three-cents-per-hour maids; turning cotton and wool into textiles; painting; gardening; laying down carpets—whatever jobs they were brought to do or could find at whatever the boss was willing to pay, minus deductions. Fake deductions pocketed by some bosses, and real ones for taxes. Deductions for the cost of the job. Deductions for sleeping on a mattress in a pizza parlor basement. Deductions for transportation; hunched in a U-Haul truck, hungry as a pack of beaten down hounds, or a four-day forced march through low sand-blown deserts, high cactus-strewn deserts, and barren mountains, littered by the bones of those who tried to go before them.

When they were sick and sometimes dying they hid out through their sickness, afraid of hospitals that might turn them in and send them back to wherever they came from—no matter that the taxes that were deducted from their wages helped pay for the programs that treated other people.

When they were robbed and beaten and sometimes raped they told no one, afraid of men in uniforms who might report them and send them back—no matter that all they had done was a misdemeanor and the rapists were felons.

When their jobs were done and they were kicked out by whoever first wanted them, or maybe fired for asking to be paid, they scrambled for other jobs at those kinds of places that hired the ones who had to hide. Jobs to pay rents that cost too much because there is great profit to be made in renting to people who have nowhere else to go; to pay double or triple the price for food because there is no choice but to buy it if you are hungry; to pay for the money orders for mothers and fathers and brothers and sisters, children, uncles and aunts, nephews and nieces, and grandparents back home.

They lived and continue to live among us, doing the jobs that need doing, hoping to put together enough money to make a difference between a life and a slow dying. And most of the people in the United States never saw them, for they were hiding in fear, because it is they—not the Canadian or the Britisher, who are hunted, stopped in streets, chased from job sites, trapped in apartments that are broken into in the early morning and searched for an ID that proves their right to work and live, and questioned, and kicked out of the United States of America, the nation built on labor just like theirs.

They are described in numbers and equations by social scientists trying to figure out how many, and how, and why, they are "exploited" and what their exploitation does to the rest of us (as if a moral cost could be tabulated). They are headlined in newspaper articles and editorials as part of some "illegal alien problem," as some "tide of aliens flooding the country." They have no voice in this country and few speak for them.

We are never confronted with their death and dying and misery and humanity.

Fear alone holds them in bondage. Fear of fugitive-slave catchers: the police, the sheriffs, the Border Patrol with its green wagons and helicopters and light aircraft and detention camps.

Somewhere along the line human beings were turned into numbers and became a part of economic policies, foreign relations programs, politics, and employer profits. And American citizens – scared and intimidated and made frightened by the headlines and the editorials, afraid of numbers that do not distinguish one brown or black or yellow person from another who might have a right, under law, to live here – are not likely to emancipate the people from their fear and slavery. Some want to round them all up, these people who look like "foreigners," and "send them back where they came from." Others made angry by the reports of foreigners taking their hard-earned money, or taking their jobs, and fearing for their own families and futures, demand Berlin walls on the line drawn on paper that separates the starving from the jobs that need doing, and demand more fugitive-slave hunters and trappers and catchers, and more military equipment along the line. And only a few, who know the fear, the hunger, the anguish, call for pardon, or parole, or documentation for the people in bondage so they can get treatment for their illnesses, so they are free to call the police when they are shot or raped, so they can protest the conditions of their bondage without fear of losing what little they have and being kicked out, on thirty minutes' notice, back across the line on paper that separates the hungry from the fed and housed and clothed. Meanwhile, the others, the ones who are citizens, blindly demand new laws, something to solve the "problem."

Toward a Solution

Perhaps there is no humane solution, no moral solution, that can be put into law and passed by Congress. And maybe we don't need new laws just yet. And certainly no law at all is better than one built on hysteria and fear and polarized political influence groups growing increasingly apart from one another.

It does not necessarily take new laws to alleviate some of the terror and suffering. We have plenty of laws, laws that have fallen apart because no one really wanted to spend the money to make sure they were enforced.

We already have laws that are supposed to ensure something approaching decency in the way people live and work. These laws ensure a minimum wage. They ensure certain safety and health conditions in the places where people work. They ensure certain standards of housing. These laws ensure that bosses make fair deductions and not fake ones. They ensure that some of the foreign-born brown people and black people and yellow people working here can become citizens—if only they knew the law and were not afraid to ask that it be enforced.

If we wanted to, we could spend time and money to enforce these laws. And where there is no money, Americans could take time, as they take it to see that environmental laws are enforced, to help enforce them. And to those who declare that workers from other countries have broken a law by crossing some border drawn on paper, we should say that the employer who pays a wage less than minimum, who refuses to pay for overtime, who keeps a shop that is unsafe to work in, is the greater criminal.

Enforcement of the laws would not only help the indentured worker, it would help build jobs to the standards they are supposed to be, and would give the employer less cause to look for slave labor when he might find people standing in line for the jobs he says are too "dirty" for Americans to do.

We have laws that say some of the brown people, the yellow people, the black people probably have a right to be here and to work. But they cannot prove it and free themselves from bondage until they know the law, and until the Immigration and Naturalization Service and the State Department process them. So they wait without documents, in fear of deportation, until the INS and the consular officials catch up on a backlog of paperwork. Sometimes they must wait two, three, sometimes four years. One has waited more than twenty. And sometimes it is just easier to live without papers and documents than to endure the endless bureaucratic delays. If we could speed up the workings of these laws, could catch up on all the paperwork piled on desks and shoved in files and sometimes lost in the mess—if we could do this in a year—then maybe some of the people now counted as "illegal aliens" would be removed from those rolls, and the numbers could be reduced so that there would be less fear, both among the citizens and the people who are waiting for their papers. Let us process all the papers for all who are here before we begin to count the number who are here without legal right. We may be surprised at the results.

We also have laws already on the books to punish the slave traders, the ones who transport and harbor their human cargo. But what effect do they have when most of the guilty are let off on probation (sometimes to be caught again)? And what is the purpose of the laws when a woman helping to bring twenty-three El Salvadorians into servitude in the U.S.—two of whom died in the middle of the California desert—is sentenced only to five years in prison, when the sentence could have been five times twenty-three? And what is five years to another woman who has made a quarter of a million dollars or more buying, selling, and transporting human cargo into bondage, when the money will be waiting in the bank when she is released? And usually the sentences are much shorter, if there are any sentences at all. Most often there is probation. Meanwhile, the underground immigrant who was traded and sold and transported has spent more time in jail waiting to testify than the felon who has violated the law but has thousands of dollars ready for instant bail. Where is the justice in punishing the slave, who has committed only a misdemeanor, and letting the felon go free?

Tiny adjustments in some laws could relieve much of the pain of those who live in fear within our boundaries. If the worker who has paid taxes that help to support a health care system for the needy becomes too poor to pay for medical treatment because the boss kicked him or her out, why can't she or he be treated in a hospital like other victims of poverty? Why can't the hospitals get back from the federal government what is their due for treating the worker, regardless of his or her legal immigration status? If the hospitals could be reimbursed as they are for their other indigent patients, much of the hysteria surrounding the issue of "illegal aliens" would be silenced, and a nation might be able to come to grips with the situation. And why must the hospital be forced to report the immigration status of the indigent seeking its help? It is this practice that has led some to die without treatment, fearing the hospital report and the deportation. All of the data suggest that the alien who has come here unlawfully in search of work, or who has been brought here recruited for work, pays enough in taxes to subsidize the cost of his or her medical care. Why is it that hospitals can only recover their expenses for treatment of the citizen poor, but not the unlawful immigrant or the out-of-status immigrant? No evidence has ever been found that suggests any of these aliens are driven to the U.S. merely because they want free medical care. They want only to work, and from their work their taxes sustain a host of economic programs. Surely, they should also subsidize treatment costs for the man who has lost a leg under a train, or the woman who has been raped, when they cannot pay for their own treatment.

Another tiny adjustment of the law might also help. Bosses who buy their workers from slave traders do so because they want people who cannot complain about poor wages or too much unpaid overtime. Slaves are voiceless against oppression. And so the jobs once held by slaves, if they are taken away by the INS, are never opened to the public, they are held open only for other slaves. What if all employers were required, not to police who is legal and who is not legal as legislation has suggested, but to file all their job openings with state employment departments? The boss in search of slaves does not want to file because he must meet the conditions of the laws of wages, and overtime, and health, and safety. So he does not use the agency. He merely waits for a new delivery of workers if some are taken away by the INS.

Such an adjustment might be costly, because the employment agencies we have now do not work. They would have to be made to work – so that when an unemployed person goes to look for a job, a job will be open. Farmers, claiming they cannot get farm workers – while one hundred thousand farm workers in the U.S. are unemployed – might, through an effective agency, be able to get the workers they need. Workers might get the jobs they need if only we could make the system, along with the interstate job placement agencies, work efficiently. And if it cannot be made to work, we should replace it with another. Because it is not only a system that helps to perpetuate the slave trade, it is a system that helps to perpetuate race, gender, and class discrimination. Most workers find out about job openings from other workers, not from want ads or government employment agencies. Such a system ensures that only the people now working have access to new jobs. America claims to have an employment system for the unemployed. Either it should be made to work, or it should be scrapped. And employers, faced with the prospect of policing immigration laws, might prefer instead to cooperate with the system, fulfilling a legal requirement that they place all their job orders with the agencies.

And too, America needs some major changes in her priorities. Part of the reason people are willing to give up freedom in favor of a national identification system, and to build Berlin walls and to have massive deportations, is because the American system has not worked for them. They cannot get jobs and their children cannot get jobs. And they live poorly when there are no jobs, degraded either by welfare or by crime, and they do not seek this degradation. They seek jobs, for jobs bring a tiny ray of hope for a better future, and may bring in the few extra dollars that mean the difference between mere subsistence and a life.

This is what needs fixing. And the government cannot do it alone. Private corporations must be part of the program. They must provide opportunities for training and upward mobility so that once again the janitor can aspire someday to become a manager. And unions must be part of the solution. As unions are structured today, the worker who begins as a dishwasher will always be a dishwasher. An effective union could, on the basis of seniority and merit, arrange to move the dishwasher from one restaurant to another where he might become a supervisor. Not only must corporations open their doors to the person who has never worked but is willing to take an entry-level position, but unions should do so as well—without racial bias or gender or age discrimination.

America can build all the iron curtains it wants to surround her boundaries. She can station them with millions of troops. She can mine the rivers. And none of this will improve her internal problems. Tossing out all the foreign looking people will not make medical care affordable for the middle- or lower-middle-class worker not covered by private health plans and ineligible for welfare. It will not bring down the cost of food, nor reduce the cost of housing. It will not end discrimination. It will not end the rottenness and sickness of urban centers abandoned by factories that have moved south or to foreign countries. Kicking out the aliens won't stop the rats from biting ghetto children, nor will it prevent rural children from getting diseases that they would not get if they had clean water, decent housing, adequate food, and shoes. How can any immigration law fix it so that all children get a decent education? Such basic needs as these have raised the howl for harsher immigration policies, but the needs will remain the same, immigration law or not.

Even the hysteria mongers have facts that demand attention. Their facts are inescapable and demand solutions, and the solutions they demand must be made outside the lines on maps dividing the USA from the rest of the world. There have been enough studies and projections and numbers, enough research, enough meetings and discussions, to make one thing very clear: Mexico, who currently sends the largest number of immigrants, legal and otherwise, is crumbling from the wealth of the few and the poverty of the many. The poverty of the many makes a people seek security for themselves in a new generation. There is no social security program in Mexico (nor Haiti, nor most of Latin America), and their security is children. So the population swells from the poverty and finds no work, and swells again from even worse poverty. And no leaflet promoting birth control will ever convince the rural poor that their chances for survival when they are too old to work do not lie in their children, and the chances are not greater with four children rather than two.

If Mexico sends her poor to work in bondage in El Norte today, how many will she send in twenty years, when her population is doubled? Or in forty years, when it has doubled again until there is no longer land, or air, or water, or space, or anything else to support her people? Even today the pressures for a revolution against poverty and unemployment are great and growing in Mexico, revolutions such as those in the People's Republic of China and Cuba. Poverty and hunger imposed by the wealthy few who hide in fear behind gates and guards, and who have bought homes in the U.S. in case they must leave, will bring the people of Mexico either to leave or to revolt. Faced with these choices, what will America, given her past history, then do? Build a better Berlin wall? Mine the Rio Grande? Send tanks and napalm and personnel bombs to someone trying to keep the peace by killing the people? A true revolution may be best for Mexico, but it is hardly conceivable that the U.S. would allow such a thing.

The United States of America and her dependencies straddle nearly half the globe; reaching into the tiny atolls of the South Pacific; dipping into the Caribbean to Puerto Rico and the Virgin Islands. A huge chunk of her stretches into the Arctic Circle, with Canada and the Soviet Union her nearest neighbors. And the rest of her, the "lower forty-eight," sits squarely on top of Mexico and Central America. And under them stretches a continent more vast than Europe.

Since the end of World War II, the nation's attention has been riveted to its wars in Asia, its interests in the Middle East and Europe, and its concern for an ambiguous "balance of power" in Africa. All of this attention spread around the world was interrupted for our nearest neighbors by only a few minutes of "good neighbor" talk and by invasions of the Dominican Republic and Guatemala, and by CIA maneuverings in Chile, Ecuador, Argentina, Brazil, and who knows where else. All of this attention to continents thousands of miles away, but nothing (save a CIA station) for the nation sharing a 1,945-mile border with us on the south; nor Central America, closer to Texas than Guam; nor Haiti, thirty minutes from Puerto Rico and closer to Florida than is Hawaii to California. And while we were busy looking somewhere else, many of these nearest neighbors have become virtual basket cases in the economic scheme and human scale of things. Mexico's unemployment and underemployment hover around 50 percent. Most of Central America is either in a state of revolution or under military rule as her poorest citizens starve to death. And Haiti has practically been written off by the world. Her per capita annual income has finally reached about $200 — mostly going to the very rich, with little going to the very poor, and none going to the many who have no income at all — while 90 percent of her people are illiterate and 200 of every 1,000 infants born die before they have taken their first breath, a mortality rate even worse than that of Bangladesh.

None of these nations started out underdeveloped. It takes someone or something to develop or "underdevelop" a nation. It takes the rich few, and it takes (as in this century) economic policies of foreign corporations to "underdevelop" a land — to take more out of it than they leave or put back in. It is time, in our own self-interest, to find a way of helping to reverse underdevelopment and make development a reality for our nearest neighbors — in a way that works to benefit the people who are hungry and sick, with a bit less for the already wealthy. For only hungry people will make a revolution, and only hungry people will try to move on to somewhere else, where they think there are jobs that need to be done, work that can provide money to feed their families.

It is a major change in attitude that we must undertake, one that will enable us to work in cooperation with nations trying to develop themselves, with a respect for the independence and dignity of our neighbors. No longer can we afford to treat neighbors as banana republics — producing profit for corporations and little for the people — at the whim or will of our government or the corporations' boards of directors.

We must begin more talks with our neighbor countries to determine how we can cooperate with one another. If we must have a year of Camp David discussions, then we must do it. Each day of delay makes the problem worse, not better. And someday too much delaying will cause a breakdown that cannot be repaired. We must get about this business before then, while we can still do things besides build walls, mine rivers, and ship napalm and tanks and missiles. And we must be prepared to fail, because every compromise is made by two sides. If a neighbor nation is unwilling to compromise, then no compromise can be made. If we are unwilling to compromise, there will be no compromise.

Yet you cannot throw out a used-up country like an old-model car or a rusty nail. The country stays there and its people still live and die and reproduce themselves and fight and make revolutions and wars.

There is the recent impression that since Mexico has oil we no longer have to remember her. Iran also has oil, but the people's lives were not changed. Venezuela has oil, but her people are still hungry. Oil or no oil, we must work with the people who are our neighbors in a spirit of cooperation.

A New Look at Immigration

It is also time to overhaul the Immigration and Nationality Act. The INA is' fundamentally the same law that was passed by Congress during the peak of the cold war, and even that law was little changed from the laws preceding it by three decades. These old laws don't fit a world that has looked at itself from the moon, nor do they fit a nation that has shipped Coca-Cola to Red China. All the changes in the INA over the past few years are just small patches covering up the holes of a tire that needs complete retreading.

Some of the patchwork has even been done within the frame of a 1921 mentality. Rather than befriending Mexico, we cut her quota of immigrants, a patchwork job reminiscent of the racial bias still remaining in the INA. One piece of INA practice, for example, requires that Western Hemisphere people who want to readjust their immigration status while in the U.S. must return to their home countries for final processing. Europeans, meanwhile, are commonly allowed to change their status while in the U.S. A chunk of the INA regulating border entrance allows the Canadian temporary visitor a six-month visa. The Mexican gets only seventy-two hours. Another piece of patchwork primarily aimed at Mexican nationals is an INA amendment providing that, while a child born in the U.S. is considered a citizen, no special preference is given to the noncitizen parent until the child is twenty-one. As undocumented Mexican mothers—some of whom have been here several years—have found, if the Border Patrol finds them they have two choices: leave their U.S. citizen children behind where they can get free public education and all the other things that go along with U.S. citizenship; or take the children back to Mexico, where, as foreign nationals, the children have no rights.

These are faulty patches bound to blow out.

An INA overhaul would also look at some of its refugee policies—predating Coca-Cola in Red China and Pepsi in the Soviet Union—laws that say that no political refugee is really a refugee unless fleeing political oppression from a communist regime. Were not the Haitians fleeing from the killer rule of "anticommunist" Papa Doc Duvalier as politically persecuted as those who fled Castro's Cuba? And the Chileans who ran for their lives when the Allende government was toppled—were they not also political refugees?

And, as we look at the kind of immigration policies that are needed for the last two decades of this century, we must seriously confront the issue of our own population growth. It is among the oldest of the nativist and restrictionist arguments that we have too many people and too few resources. Until a decade or so ago these arguments could be laughed off. But now we have seen droughts, and energy shortages with their brown-outs, black-outs and gasoline lines, and our environment polluted by our own refuse. Today every urban American can breathe in the air and wonder, "Have we crowded ourselves in too tightly?" Current immigration law excludes immediate relatives from such quotas as we have. The law itself is creating its own geometrically increasing population boom as new family members become citizens and immigration brings yet more family members. Perhaps an examination, a head-on confrontation of such realities as droughts and resource depletions may force us into shaping unfortunate and terrifying moral and ethical choices in drafting a new INA. Perhaps we shall have to delegate to ourselves the role of an administrator of triage, determining who shall die and who shall live. But there is a chance that such a head-on confrontation, faced squarely and without equivocation, may yield new and different concepts about national boundaries and our role as a nation. Perhaps such an examination will conclude that we face not a population explosion, but a flaw in our economic and social structures. Perhaps such an examination will lead to such ideas as the formation of a common market in the Western Hemisphere. Perhaps other ideas will result. But no answers or ideas will be produced unless the questions are asked and faced.

As we examine the INA we should take a closer look at the foreigners already present in the U.S., not as numbers but as people, and see the reasons why they come. On the road to forming questions and policies we will find many kinds of people seeking refuge in the U.S. We will see political refugees fleeing death for their beliefs in all types of regimes, perhaps no longer definable as communist or anticommunist. Some South Koreans, North Koreans, Filipinos, Haitians, and others fit this model. Others come seeking religious freedom and the freedoms of assembly, speech, and the press denied to them at home. (We might also ask why we continue to pump money into the harsh dictatorial regimes of South Korea and the Philippines, and look beyond the military rationalizations into the humanity of it.) We will see economic refugees, too poor to have been bothered with politics. We will see yet others who are both political and economic refugees. We will see some who come only to work for a few months and then leave, as their fathers and grandfathers did before them. We will see others whose only wish is to join their families. We will see others who are none of these, who come merely to enjoy the cream of the material prosperity America has created. And we will see others who are slaves, recruited in foreign lands to do the jobs that need doing at wages and under conditions that are not only indecent, but also illegal.

When we make an estimate of the overhaul job the INA requires, we should look at the way it helps to perpetuate the underdevelopment of foreign nations. The law was changed in the nineteenth century to protect us from paupers, to keep out the tired, poor, hungry masses and wretched refuse of foreign nations. As the INA stands today, A. P. Giannini, founder of the Bank of America, would be denied entry, as would many others who arrived poor and contributed much to build our nation. As the law is structured now, we take from impoverished nations the richest portion, the best educated portion of their populations – those people presumably best equipped to look after the development of their own countries. And once they are here, we take their families. There is a certain irony in this. Data have shown that about 3 percent of our legal immigrants *do* become "public charges" before they become naturalized citizens, while a tiny fraction of 1 percent of undocumented immigrants make use of welfare programs.

Maybe, after nearly one hundred years, it is time to see our national interests in a new way, and look again at the words inscribed on the Statue of Liberty, words without meaning under the INA today:

"Give me your tired, your poor,
Your huddled masses yearning to breathe free,
The wretched refuse of your teeming shore,
Send these, the homeless, tempest-tost to me,
I lift my lamp beside the golden door!"

People such as these built the U.S., and then laws were written to exclude them. Perhaps it is time, once again, to open our doors to those who want to build, but who cannot build anything out of the mud and hunger of their poverty; to those who want to work, but who cannot work because there is no work; to those who thirst for freedom and democracy, but cannot find it because there is no freedom where there is hunger.

APPENDIX
SOURCES AND RESOURCES
INDEX

Appendix:
The Immigration and Nationality Act

Any discussion of immigration policy should be based on an under-standing of some of its definitions and key provisions. The 1921 through 1929 immigration laws were based on the concept of maintaining the balance of the "national origins" of the American population and in-cluded various quotas on the total number of immigrants who could come from any country. After World War II, various humanitarian measures were adopted for war brides, refugees, and others. In 1952 the entire law was rewritten, and a three-category preference system was included along with the national origins quotas. In 1965 the law was rewritten again and, finally, national origins quotas were stricken from the law. As a compromise measure, the Western Hemisphere was, in 1968, also to be included in the new quota system. The 1965 law al-lowed a maximum of 20,000 immigrants from any one country that ful-filled any of seven preferences, which were designed primarily to facili-tate family reunification and to protect the American labor market. Beyond the preferences, people who are spouses of American citizens, or parents of an American citizen over twenty-one, or a person under twenty-one whose parents are citizens may be admitted without regard to quotas. Earlier quotas had established a 170,000 limit on Eastern Hemisphere immigrants and a 120,000 limit from the Western Hemi-sphere. An amendment passed in 1978 changed this to a single world quota of 290,000, while maintaining the 20,000-per-country limit.

Below are some summaries of relevant definitions and provisions of the INA. Anyone who is not a citizen or national of the United States is an alien. Aliens can be divided into three classes: immigrants, nonim-migrants, and "illegal," or "undocumented" aliens—that is, those who have violated one or another American law to gain entrance into the U.S. Also falling into the latter category are "out of status" immigrants and nonimmigrants, those who have violated the conditions of their entry.

1. Immigrants: aliens who are admitted for permanent resident status are immigrants. Upon becoming an immigrant, the alien is given an alien registration receipt card by the Immigration and Naturalization Service. This card identifies its holder as a permanent resident alien and is often referred to as the "green card," although in past years it has been blue, or white. Permanent resident aliens gener-ally have the same rights and obligations as U.S. citizens except that they may not vote or run for public office. They are also deportable if they have committed serious crimes. After five years, permanent resi-dent aliens are entitled to apply for U.S. citizenship. Most permanent

resident aliens do apply for citizenship. However, many Mexican and Canadian permanent resident aliens move back to their countries but continue to work in the U.S. These are known as "green card commuters."

2. Nonimmigrants: Aliens granted temporary admission to the United States are nonimmigrants. The overwhelming majority of these are tourists. Others include foreign government officials, students, reporters, and people in transit to another country. Most arrive in the U.S. holding nonimmigrant visas.

Citizens of Mexico can also enter the U.S. as nonimmigrants with a document called a "border crossing identification card." This card allows the Mexican alien to visit the U.S. within twenty-five miles of the border for seventy-two hours or less or to remain in the four Southwestern border states of the U.S. for up to 15 days. Canadian citizens may generally visit the U.S. without any special document.

A few categories of nonimmigrants are permitted to do temporary work in the U.S. "H-1" workers, as they are called, do skilled labor or are athletes or performers. "H-2" workers are permitted to do unskilled labor if American citizens or permanent residents cannot be found to do the job. "H-3" workers are trainees. "L-1" workers are intracompany transferees—executives or managers of multinational corporations who are aliens.

3. Visas: Before aliens (except as noted above) can enter the United States, they must first obtain an immigrant or nonimmigrant visa at the U.S. Consulate in their native country. Border crossing identification cards are available at INS offices as well as at some American consulates in Mexico.

The consulate has the initial responsibility of evaluating the legitimacy of a visa or border crossing card application. Once the visa or border crossing identification card is issued, aliens may present themselves for admission to the U.S. A second inspection occurs at this presentation, and INS inspectors have the authority to exlude any alien they believe has presented an illicit visa or border crossing card or acted in bad faith when obtaining these documents.

Qualitative Restrictions on Entry into the U.S.

An alien may be denied an immigrant or nonimmigrant visa for a number of health, moral, criminal, or economic reasons. The burden of proof that the alien does not violate any of these restrictions falls on the applicant. Immigrant applicants generally supply character references, bank references, employment history references, and references from the local police to prove they will not become public charges, have no criminal record, and are "moral" people. Additionally they must be inspected for health by a physician chosen by the local consulate.

Quantitative Restrictions on Entry into the U.S.

1. Ceilings: Any nonimmigrant who is eligible can enter the United States. No quantitative limits have been placed on the number of people who can temporarily visit the U.S. Ceilings have been placed on the number of immigrants who may enter the United States each year. This is 290,000, and no more than 20,000 immigrants from any one country may be admitted.

2. Exceptions: Two classes of people may obtain visas without reference to either the per country or world ceilings. In other words, no quantitative restrictions are placed on their entry, nor are they counted as admissions within the ceilings. They are "special immigrants" and "immediate relatives" of U.S. citizens.

Special immigrants include former citizens who want to reenter the U.S., ministers of a religious denomination, and aliens who were employees of the U.S. government.

Immediate relatives are the minor (under twenty-one) children of U.S. citizens, the spouses of U.S. citizens, or the parents of a U.S. citizen if the citizen is over twenty-one years old.

3. The Preference System: Anyone else seeking admission into the U.S. as an immigrant must do so within the quantitative limits set by the ceilings. Immigrant visas are distributed on the basis of a seven-category preference system.

1. Unmarried sons and daughters (twenty-one or older) of U.S. citizens. (Maximum number: twenty percent of the worldwide ceiling in any fiscal year.)

2. Spouses and unmarried sons and daughters (regardless of age) of aliens lawfully admitted for permanent residence. (Maximum number: twenty percent of the worldwide ceiling per year plus immigrant visas not issued under the first preference.)

3. Members of the professions or persons of exceptional ability in the sciences and arts whose services are sought by U.S. employers. (Maximum number: ten percent of the ceiling.)

4. Married sons and daughters of U.S. citizens. (Maximum number: twenty-four percent of the ceiling, plus any visas not issued for the first three preference categories.)

5. Brothers and sisters of U.S. citizens if the citizen is twenty-one years old or older. (Maximum number: twenty-four percent of the ceiling, plus any visas not issued for the first four categories.)
6. Skilled and unskilled workers in short supply. (Maximum number: ten percent of the ceiling.)
7. Refugees – people who flee political, racial, or religious persecution from Communist-dominated governments or Middle Eastern countries. (Maximum number: six percent of the ceiling.)

An alien who is neither an "immediate relative" nor a "special immigrant" and is covered by none of the seven preference-categories may still be admitted as a non-preference immigrant, but only if the authorized numbers of immigrant visas have not been depleted.

Labor Certification: Before an immigrant visa can be issued for a third, sixth, or non-preference immigrant, the Department of Labor must certify that there are insufficient numbers of American workers who are "able, willing . . . and qualified" to do the skilled or unskilled work the immigrant intends to do. This requirement is designed to protect American labor. However, since all but a small percent of immigrants are admitted under the family-reunification provisions of the act, such certification is largely irrelevant as a means of "protecting" American labor.

Refugees and "Parole": Under the preference system, refugees are allocated six percent of the worldwide annual ceiling, for a worldwide total of only 17,400. However, in emergency situations, or when the refugee is ineligible under the seventh preference category, or when the number of refugees exceeds the total allowed by the seventh preference, the Attorney General may "parole" refugees into the United States. Hungarian, Cuban, and Indo-Chinese refugees have been paroled into this country by the Attorney General.

Special Bills: Members of Congress may enact special legislation allowing for the immigration of a person who has come to his attention as a humanitarian gesture.

Naturalization: Applicants for naturalization must be at least eighteen years old and have been a lawful resident of the U.S. continuously for five years. (Other provisions on residency are provided for "derivative" citizenship, that is, for people who have become permanent residents because their spouse, etc. is a citizen.)

The applicant must also have been physically present in the U.S. for at least half of the five years' residence.

The applicant must read and write words in common usage in the English language.

The applicant must demonstrate an understanding of the fundamentals of U.S. history and the principles and forms of government of the U.S.

The applicant must have been of good moral character, attached to the principles of the U.S. Constitution, and well disposed to the good order and happiness of the United States for the five years prior to filing a petition for naturalization, and continue to be so until citizenship is granted.

A person inadmissible because of moral character includes: a habitual drunkard, an adulterer, a prostitute, a polygamist, a violator of criminal law, a gambler, one who gave false testimony to obtain benefit under the immigration law, one in prison for 180 days or more, one convicted of murder.

Naturalization is denied to any person who, within ten years, has been a subversive, including communists and others favoring totalitarian government, or who were members of proscribed organizations, unless the petitioner was under sixteen or joined under duress.

Recent amendments: Among the important changes in the INA was one which permits persons who have been legal permanent residents of the U.S. for twenty years and are at least fifty years old to become citizens without being required to speak English.

Earlier acts: Three times in this century special laws allowed those who entered the U.S. unlawfully to apply for citizenship. The last such law applied to all living in the U.S. prior to 1948.

Sources and Resources

The references detailed in the following pages are the so-called secondary sources that went into this book. That is, they are the sources for actions and facts described that I myself did not observe. The selection of these resources was carefully weighed against the information provided by those people I spoke with and interviewed, who are acknowledged at the beginning of this book. So, the following list of materials is neither a comprehensive bibliography, nor does it represent everything that I weeded through to write this story about America's slave trade. Each work listed here, the product of someone else's mind and energy and talent, made some contribution, either large or small, to this book.

Books

The books selected below are excellent resources on the factors that create the need for poor people to leave their home countries in order to live: American domestic policies that create immigration patterns, American foreign policies that contribute to increased poverty and instability abroad, and policies of private corporations that do the same. Additionally, this selection reveals not only how U.S. immigration policies are shaped by nativist pressures, but how they are shaped by electoral politics in the U.S. A few of the books also reveal how immigration policies have been used not only to shape domestic activities, but to shape foreign policy as well. Some offer a superb portrait of American nativism, both as it has existed in the past and how it exists today.

Agee, Phillip, *Inside the Company* (New York: Stonehill, 1975). America's "underground" activities that have helped to shape Latin America today.

Barnet, Richard J., and Ronald E. Muller, *Global Reach: The Power of the Multinational Corporations* (New York: Simon & Schuster, 1974). The private sector's contribution to pressures for emigration.

Caute, David, *The Great Fear: The Anti-Communist Purge Under Truman and Eisenhower* (New York: Simon & Schuster, 1978). Various sections describe the involvement of the INS in the post-World War II witch-hunt, as well as some of the factors behind the 1952 Immigration Act.

Cockcroft, James D., André Gunder Frank, and Dale L. Johnson, eds., *Dependence and Underdevelopment: Latin America's Political Economy* (New York: Doubleday, 1972). Perspective on American policies by Latin-American scholars.

Cornelius, Wayne A., *Mexican Migration to the United States: Causes, Consequences, and U.S. Responses* (Cambridge, Mass: MIT Press, 1978). One of the first examinations from the perspective of sending communities.

Craig, Richard B., *The Bracero Program: Interest Groups and Foreign Policy* (Austin: University of Texas Press, 1951). A study of the impact of special interest groups in the U.S. on policies of developing a cheap and docile labor force.

Divine, Robert A., *American Immigration Policy, 1924-1952* (New York: Da Capo Press, 1972). Some of the more intriguing sections discuss the effects of the U.S. political process, specifically presidential politics, in creating immigration policy.

Farrell, James, *Give Us Your Poor (The Immigration Bomb)* San Francisco: Fulton-Hall, 1976). Definitely the best example of contemporary nativist arguments against immigration. Underscores the distinct distaste for racial minorities underlying domestic nativism.

Frank, Charles R., Jr., and Richard C. Webb, eds., *Income Distribution and Growth in the Less-Developed Countries* (Washington, D. C.: The Brookings Institution, 1977). A move toward reassessment of U.S. policies affecting underdeveloped nations.

Gamio, Manuel, *Mexican Immigration to the United States* (New York: Dover, 1971). A reprint of Gamio's 1926 study, one of the earliest and best books on the patterns of Mexican immigration to the U.S., both documented and undocumented. Few of the patterns explored by Gamio appear to have changed today.

George, Susan, *How the Other Half Dies: The Real Reasons for World Hunger* (Montclair, N. J.: Allanheld, Osmun, 1977). Particularly instructive in its discussion of how multinational agribusiness has contributed to underdevelopment and the poverty that leads those who can to try to makes lives elsewhere. In combination with the Agee, Barnet, and Cockcroft books, George paints a picture of America's responsibility for her so-called illegal alien problem.

Heizer, Robert F., and Alan F. Almquist, *The Other Californians: Prejudice and Discrimination Under Spain, Mexico, and the United States to 1920* (Berkeley: University of California Press, 1971). Notable for its section on how local politics at first tried to drive out foreigners from the gold fields of the Gold Rush era, and then, realizing a need for their labor, tried to lure them back.

McWilliams, Carey, *Factories in the Fields* (Boston: Little, Brown, 1943). One of the classics on American farmers' continual search for cheap labor.

_____ , *North From Mexico* (New York: Greenwood Press, 1948). Another classic discussing importation of Mexican labor.

Moquin, Wayne, and Charles Van Doren, eds., *A Documentary History of the Mexican Americans* (New York: Praeger, 1972). Collection of essays and articles from primary sources. Excellent primer on U.S.-Mexican relations.

Morse, Arthur D., *While Six Million Died: A Chronicle of American Apathy* (New York: Hart, 1967). Includes excellent descriptions of how presidential and foreign policy needs distorted immigration laws to exclude thousands of Jews fleeing Nazi persecution.

Myeres, Gustavus, *History of Bigotry in the United States* (New York: Capricorn Books, 1960). One of the best studies of nativist movements in U.S. history.

Novotny, Ann, *Strangers at the Door* (Riverside, Conn.: Chatham Press, 1972). Excellent history of U.S. immigration to the East Coast.

Poitras, Guy, ed., *Immigration and the Mexican National: Proceedings* (San Antonio: Border Research Institute, Trinity University, 1978). Brings together a diversity of views on immigration reforms proposed in 1977 by President Carter. Short essay on effects of guest workers on Germany.

Ríos-Bustamante, A. J., ed., *Immigration and Public Policy: Human Rights for Undocumented Workers and Their Families* (Los Angeles: Chicano Studies Center, University of California, 1977). Collection of essays covering the entire scope of Mexican immigration to the U.S. today.

Russell, Phillip, *Mexico in Transition* (Austin: Colorado River Press, 1977; also supplements, Spring 1978, Fall 1978, Spring 1979). An unusually clear picture of Mexico as she is, and not how either the U.S. or her own government would like her to be seen.

Samora, Julian, *Los Mojados: The Wetback Story* (Notre Dame, Ind.: University of Notre Dame Press, 1966). The definitive history of U.S. policies toward Mexican immigration, clearly showing the desire for cheap and docile labor, but not for the Mexican as citizen.

Tate, Merze, *The United States and the Hawaiian Kingdom: A Political History* (New Haven: Yale University Press, 1965). Demonstrates methods used by white business owners to keep contract labor going back to the early nineteenth century.

Periodicals and Essays

Bustamante, Jorje A., "The Historical Context of Undocumented Mexican Immigration to the United States," *Atzlan*, v. 3, fall 1973, pp. 257-281.

———, "Structural and Ideological Conditions of the Mexican Undocumented Immigration to the United States," *American Behavioral Scientist*, v. 19, Jan.-Feb. 1976, pp. 364-376.

Cardenas, Gilberto, "United States Immigration Policy Toward Mexico: an Historical Perspective," *Chicano Law Review*, v. 2, summer 1975, pp. 66-91.

Gutiérrez, Félix, "Making News–Media Coverage of Chicanos," *Agenda*, v. 8, Nov.-Dec. 1978, pp. 20-24.

Investigative Reporters and Editors, Inc., "Barry and The Boys, Highlights of the Crime Report on the Sunbelt," *New West*, v. 2, April 11, 1977, pp. 21-30.

Jacoby, Susan, "The Struggle to be Legal Immigrants from Mexico," *New Leader*, v. 58, April 28, 1975, pp. 14-16.

Kirsch, Jonathan, "California's Illegal Aliens: They Give More Than They Take," *New West*, v. 2, May 23, 1977, pp. 26-35.

Lando, Barry, "The Mafia and the Mexicans: Crooked Justice from the INS," *Washington Monthly*, v. 5, April 1973, pp. 16-21.

Martinez, Douglas R., "Hispanic Youth Employment: Programs and Problems," *Agenda* v. 9, Jan.-Feb. 1979, pp. 14-16.

Martinez, Vilma S., "Illegal Immigration and the Labor Force: an Historical and Legal View," *American Behavioral Scientist*, v. 19, Jan.-Feb. 1976, pp. 335-350.

North, David S., and Marion F. Houston, "A Summary of Recent Data on Some of the Public Policy Implications of Illegal Immigration," *National Council on Employment Policy*, Oct. 1976, pp. 36-51.

Piore, Michael J., "Illegal Immigration in the United States: Some Observations and Policy Suggestions," *National Council on Employment Policy*, Oct. 1976, pp. 25-35.

_____ , "The Illegals: Restrictions Aren't the Answer," *New Republic*, v. 172, Feb. 22, 1975, pp. 7-8.

_____ , "Impact of Immigration on the Labor Force," *Monthly Labor Review*, v. 98, May 1975, pp. 41-44.

Portes, Alejandro, "Return of the Wetback," *Society*, v. 11, March-April 1974, pp. 40-46.

Stoddard, Ellwyn R., "A Conceptual Analysis of the 'Alien Invasion': Institutionalized Support of the Illegal Mexican Aliens in the U.S.," *International Migration Review*, v. 10, summer 1976, pp. 157-189.

Government Documents

Federal:

U.S. Domestic Council Committee on Illegal Aliens. *Preliminary Report*. 1976.

Report of the Commissioner of Immigration and Naturalization. U.S. Govt. Print. Off., 1977. (INS Annual Report for 1976.)

Immigration and Naturalization Service, Statistics Branch. Deportable Aliens Located by Border Patrol, Fiscal Year 1978. Mimeographed.
_____ . Deportable Aliens Found in U.S. by Nationality, Status at Entry, Place of Entry, Status When Found, All Regions Consolidated, Investigations, Fiscal Year 1978. Mimeographed.
_____ . Deportable Aliens Found in U.S. by Nationality, Status at Entry,

Place of Entry, Status When Found, All Regions Consolidated, Border Patrol, Fiscal Year 1978. Mimeographed.

————. Deportable Aliens Found in U.S. by Nationality, Status at Entry, Place of Entry, Status When Found, All Regions Consolidated, Fiscal Year 1978. Mimeographed.

U.S. General Accounting Office:

Aliens are illegally entering the U.S. mainland through Puerto Rico and the U.S. Virgin Islands. Immigration and Naturalization Service, Dept. of Justice, 1975. "GGD-76-5, Sept. 8, 1975."

Better controls needed to prevent foreign students from violating the conditions of their entry and stay while in the United States. Dept. of Justice, Dept. of State, 1975. "B-125015, Feb. 4, 1975."

Smugglers, illicit documents, and schemes are undermining U.S. controls over immigration. Dept. of Justice, Dept. of State, 1976. "GCD-76-33, Aug. 30, 1976."

Impact of illegal aliens on public assistance programs: Too little is known. Report to the Senate Committee on the Budget, 1977. "GCD-78-20, Dec. 1, 1977."

U.S. Congress, Senate:

Committee on Labor and Public Welfare. Subcommittee on Migratory Labor. Migrant and Seasonal Farmworker Powerlessness. Hearings, 91st Cong., 1st and 2d sess., on border commuter labor problems. May 21, 22, 1969. Part 5-A and Part 5-B. 2v., U.S. Govt. Print. Off. 1970.

Committee on the Judiciary. S. 2252: Alien Adjustment and Employment Act of 1977. Hearings, 95th Cong., 2d sess., on S. 2252. Part 1. May 3, 4, 9, 10, 11, 16, 17, 18, 1978. U.S. Govt. Print. Off. 1978.

Committee on the Judiciary. S. 2252: Alien Adjustment and Employment Act of 1978. Hearings, 95th Cong., 2d sess., on S. 2252, to amend the immigration and nationality act and for other purposes. Part 2, Sept. 1, 2, 1978. U.S. Govt. Print. Off. 1979.

U.S. Congress, House of Representatives:

Illegal Aliens. A Review of Hearings Conducted During the 92d Congress (Serial No. 13, Parts 1-5) by Subcommittee No. 1 of the Committee on the Judiciary, 93d Cong., 1st sess. U.S. Govt. Print. Off. 1973.

Legal and Monetary Affairs Subcommittee, Immigration and Naturalization Service Regional Office Operations (Part 5). Hearings, 93d Cong., 2d Sess. Aug. 13; Sept. 12, 17, 18; Oct. 9, 1974. U.S. Govt. Print. Off. 1975.

Mr. Eilberg, from the Committee on the Judiciary. Report, together with Additional, Supplemental, and Dissenting Views. Amending the Immigration and Nationality Act, and for Other Purposes. 94th Cong., 1st sess. Sept. 24, 1975. U.S. Govt. Print. Off. 1975.

Illegal Aliens: Analysis and Background. Prepared for the Use of the Committee on the Judiciary by the Education and Public Welfare Division, Congressional Research Service, Library of Congress. 95th Cong., 1st sess., U.S. Govt. Print. Off. 1977.

Select Committee on Population. Report. Legal and Illegal Immigration to the United States. 95th Cong., 2d sess. Serial C., Dec. 1978, U.S. Govt. Print. Off. 1978.

Congressional Record, Extension of Remarks:
Ashbrook, John M., Swedish Immigration–Liberalism Fails Again. June 6, 1978: E3047.
_____ , Jobs and the Illegal-Alien Question. June 8, 1978: E3117.
Ford, William D., Squeezing Out Domestic Agricultural Workers. May 25, 1978: E2837-E2838.
Simon, Paul, Nutrition Problems in Latin America. Jan. 30, 1978: E227.

San Diego County, Human Resources Agency:
Illegal Aliens: Impact of Illegal Aliens on the County of San Diego, Part I. 1975. Mimeographed.
Illegal Aliens: Impact of Illegal Aliens on the County of San Diego, Part II. 1977. Mimeographed.
A Study of the Impact of Illegal Aliens of the County of San Diego in Specific Socioeconomic Areas, Final Report. 1977. Mimeographed.

Research Reports
Alvarado, Manuel De Jesus, "Slaves or Workers? Dilemmas Affecting Undocumented Mexican Farm Workers in the U.S.," Tucson, AZ. 1978. Mimeographed.

Chiswick, Barry R., "Immigrants and Immigration Policy," American Enterprise Institute, Washington, D. C., 1978. Mimeographed.

Cornelius, Wayne A., "Illegal Migration to the United States: Recent Research Findings, Policy Implications, and Research Priorities," Center for International Studies, Massachusetts Institute of Technology, Migration and Development Study Group, C/77-11, May 1977. Mimeographed.

Cornelius, Wayne A., and Juan Diez-Canedo, "Mexican Migration to the United States: The View from Rural Sending Communities," Center for International Studies, Massachusetts Institute of Technology, Migration and Development Study Group, C/76-12, June 1976. Mimeographed.

Dominguez, Virginia R., "From Neighbor to Stranger: The Dilemma of Caribbean People in the United States" (ARP Occasional Papers 5), New Haven, Yale University, Antilles Research Program, 1975.

North, David S., "Interactions between Illegal Aliens and the Social Security Tax Collection System: Some Preliminary Findings," New Trans Century Foundation, Washington, D. C., July 1976. Mimeographed.

North, David S., and Marion F. Houston, "The Characteristics and Role of Illegal Aliens in the U.S. Labor Market: An Exploratory Study," Linton & Co. Inc., Washington, D. C., March 1976. Mimeographed. (Prepared for the Employment and Training Administration, U.S. Department of Labor.)

Newspaper Articles

1970

"Crime Group Said to Smuggle Hundreds of Sicilians into U.S.," *The New York Times*, Dec. 5, 1970.

De Onis, Juan, "Job-Hunting Dominicans Devise Methods to Enter the U.S. Illegally," *The New York Times*, June 1, 1970.

1971

"Illegal Status of Dominicans Shaping Their Lives in City," *The New York Times*, Nov. 9, 1971.

Goodwin, Irwin, "Illegal Dominican Immigrants Fly to New York," *The Washington Post*, Nov. 14, 1971.

Isaacs, Stephens, "Alien Struggle in 'Paradise,' " *The Washington Post*, Nov. 14, 1971.

1972

Associated Press, "Mexicans Break U.S. Entry Ring," *The Washington Post*, Sept. 13, 1972.

Bernstein, Harry, "Employers Urging Workers to Obtain Legal Status," *Los Angeles Times*, March 25, 1972.

Del Olmo, Frank, "Crossing the Border—'I Paid $200 For a Green Card,' " *Los Angeles Times*, Dec. 17, 1972.

Waldron, Martin, "Wide Abuses Alleged in Texas Border," *The New York Times*, Dec. 19, 1972.

1973

"Four Charged Upstate in Plot to Cheat Aliens Seeking Jobs," *The New York Times*, May 2, 1973.

"125 Attend a Rally to Aid 117 Haitians," *The New York Times*, July 29, 1973.

"Report on Moving of Aliens from U.S. Stirs Mexico," *The New York Times*, May 4, 1973.

Bernstein, Harry, "60,000 Phony Immigration Cards Seized at L.A. Bus Depot," *Los Angeles Times*, Jan. 13, 1973.

Charlton, Linda, "Alien Smuggling Charged on Coast," *The New York Times*, July 10, 1973.

Del Olmo, Frank, "Illegal Aliens," *Los Angeles Times*, May 4, 1973.

Goodman, Mike, "Epidemics a Barrio Specter," *Los Angeles Times*, Sept. 16, 1973.

Keen, Harold, and Robert Kistler, "$3-Million-a-Year Mexican Alien Smuggling Ring Broken," *Los Angeles Times*, July 10, 1973.

Liddick, Betty, "Plight of the Foreign Domestic, a Critical Game of Hide and Seek," *Los Angeles Times*, June 8, 1973.

Morris, Joe Alex, Jr., "For a Price: Swiss Helps Many Flee Reds," Portland, *The Sunday Oregonian*, Sept. 23, 1973.

Shaffer, Ron, "2 in Md. Indicted in Mail Fraud Case," *The Washington Post*, July 6, 1973.

Smothers, Ronald, "Two Groups Seek a Study Here of 'Raids' on Illegal Latin Aliens," *The New York Times*, Jan. 13, 1973.

1974
"Ecuadorians Had the Will, But No Way," *The New York Times*, Aug. 18, 1974.

"Farm Union Strikers Patrol Border to Cut Illegal Alien Flow," *Los Angeles Times*, Oct. 8, 1974.

Chriss, Nicholas C., "U.S. Struggles to Control Fake Alien Wedding Racket," *Los Angeles Times*, July 7, 1974.

Del Olmo, Frank, "321 Cases Investigated in Long U.S. Border Corruption Inquiry," *Los Angeles Times*, July 5, 1974.

Farber, M. A., "Million Illegal Aliens in Metropolitan Area," *The New York Times*, Dec. 29, 1974.

Gentry, Margaret, "Aliens Buy Marriage to Avoid Deportation," *The Washington Post*, Dec. 26, 1974.

Hess, John L., "Fraudulent Marriages Rise as Aliens Seek to Circumvent Immigration Laws Here," *The New York Times*, Feb. 26, 1974.

Holles, Everett R., "Border Patrol Shifts Focus to Alien-Smuggling Rings," *The New York Times*, Dec. 24, 1974.

Holles, Everett R., "Immigration Unit in a New Inquiry," *The New York Times*, Nov. 24, 1974.

Jackson, Robert L., "Witness Says Border Agents Offered Him Girls," *Los Angeles Times*, Aug. 14, 1974.

Klernan, Laura A., "5 Deported Aliens Sue for Va. Wages," *The Washington Post*, Nov. 15, 1974.

Maxwell, Evan, "It's Door to the Promised Land–and They Keep It Hopping," *Los Angeles Times*, Aug. 19, 1974.

New York Daily News, "Hidden Among Bananas, 90 Stow Away in Hold of Ship," *Los Angeles Times*, Aug. 14, 1974.

Rawitch, Robert E., "Sentencing of 5 Ends Alien Smuggling Trial," *Los Angeles Times*, June 19, 1974.

Smith, Dave, "100 Gypsies from Europe Smuggled into U.S., Robbed," *Los Angeles Times*, Feb. 27, 1974.

United Press International, "24 Aliens Found in Truck," *The New York Times*, Feb. 3, 1974.

Walsh, Denny, "Illegal Aliens Called Duped by Lawyers," *The New York Times*, July 7, 1974.

1975

"Coast Union Aids 17 Illegal Aliens," *The New York Times*, Feb. 16, 1975.

"11 Are Indicted for Bilking Aliens," *The New York Times*, June 11, 1975.

"Employer Is Indicted over Illegal Aliens," *The New York Times*, April 6, 1975.

"More than 400 Aliens Seized in Factory Raid," *Los Angeles Times*, May 17, 1975.

"Police Giving Aid to Illegal Aliens," *The New York Times*, March 23, 1975.

"TB Rise Sparked By Illegal Aliens," *The New York Times*, May 18, 1975.

Aarons, Leroy F., "Patrol Can't Keep Aliens Out," *The Washington Post*, Feb. 3, 1975.

Associated Press, "67 Illegal Aliens Found at 2 Plants," *The New York Times*, March 7, 1975.

Bernstein, Harry, and Mike Castro, "Bid to Give Illegal Aliens' Jobs to Americans Failing," *Los Angeles Times*, July 3, 1975.

Del Olmo, Frank, "Illegal Aliens Target of Union Organizers," *Los Angeles Times*, Jan. 30, 1975.

Del Olmo, Frank, "Collusion Charged in Arrest of Aliens," *Los Angeles Times*, Feb. 7, 1975.

Del Olmo, Frank, "Immigration Consultant Receives Prison Sentence for Defrauding Illegal Aliens," *Los Angeles Times*, Oct. 25, 1975.

Gerstenzang, James, "Where the Illegal Aliens Are," *The Washington Post*, March 4, 1975.

Kins, Peter, "Puerto Rico Says Aliens Use It as Path to U.S.," *The New York Times*, March 3, 1975.

Lindsey, Robert, "Citrus Growers Hit by Worker Woes," *The New York Times*, Nov. 20, 1975.

Robinson, Timothy S., "Woman Is Indicted in Marriage Plot," *The Washington Post*, Oct. 30, 1975.

Rothmyer, Karen, "Illegal Aliens Caught in Job Squeeze," reprinted in *The Washington Post*, Aug. 17, 1975.

1976
"Foreign Workers Flood Europe," *The Thunderbolt*, Nov. 1976.

"INS Is Accused of Racist Policies," *San Antonio Express*, August 1, 1976.

"Restaurateur Held in Scheme Involving 14 Japanese Aliens," *The New York Times*, July 22, 1976.

Del Olmo, Frank, "Mexico Bars Alien Airlift," *Los Angeles Times*, June 1, 1976.

Holles, Everett R., "Bandit Gangs Prey on Mexican Aliens Crossing Border to Seek Work in U.S.," *The New York Times*, June 6, 1976.

Johnson, Thomas A., "Signatures Sought in Midtown to End Influx of Illegal Aliens," *The New York Times*, Aug. 28, 1976.

Jones, Jack, "Illegal Aliens Become Easy Prey for Thugs at U.S. Border," *Los Angeles Times*, May 15, 1976.

Kendall, John, "Bilking of Thousands of Aliens in L.A. Told," *Los Angeles Times*, Sept. 30, 1976.

Lewis, Alfred E., and Martin Well, "27 Aliens Travel Here in Small Van; 17 Seized," *The Washington Post*, Nov. 20, 1976.

Morrison, Patt, "Nun, 3 Others Face Trial for Counseling Illegal Aliens," *Los Angeles Times*, Nov. 23, 1976.

Oliver, Myrna, "Alien Assistance Firm Accused," *Los Angeles Times*, March 26, 1976.

Rawitch, Robert, "Ring Believed to Be Smuggling In Chinese," *Los Angeles Times*, Oct. 14, 1976.

Smyth, Jeannette, "With This Visa, I Thee Wed," *The Washington Post*, Jan. 6, 1976.

United Press International, "Selling of U.S. Registration Cards to Illegal Aliens Is Charged to 2," in *The New York Times*, Sept. 9, 1976.

Valente, Judith, "Ex-Ambassador Indicted in Maid's Illegal Entry," *The Washington Post*, Nov. 4, 1976.

1977

"R. Goldwater's Farm Uses Illegal Aliens, Reporters Say," *Los Angeles Times*, March 21, 1977.

"Unemployment and Underemployment Affect 56% of the Country's Labor Force" (translated by American Friends Service Committee), Mexico City, *El Sol de Mexico*, Dec. 26, 1977.

Associated Press, "Illegal Aliens Estimated at 64,000 in Grain Belt," *The New York Times*, Feb. 13, 1977.

Associated Press, "U.S. Allowing Mexicans to Aid in Onion Harvest," *The Washington Post*, June 22, 1977.

Barry, Tom, "Illegals Risk Deportation to Fight for Rights," San Francisco, Pacific News Service, Dec. 9, 1977.

Brown, Martin, "Why Does U.S. Business Need Illegal Aliens?" San Francisco, Pacific News Service, Aug. 11, 1977.

Brumbach, Deborah, "Alien Files $1 Million Suit, Alleges Employment Duress," *The Washington Post*, Feb. 16, 1977.

Callahan, Jean, "Violent Backlash Hits Illegal Aliens," San Francisco, Pacific News Service, Aug. 11, 1977.

Del Olmo, Frank, "Mexico Also Seeks Illegal Alien Solution, Leader Says," *Los Angeles Times*, April 25, 1977.

Gallup, George, "Illegal Aliens' Job Prohibition Favored 6 to 1," *The Washington Post*, April 24, 1977.

Holles, Everett R., "Police Are Accused in Wetback Attacks," *The New York Times*, Feb. 13, 1977.

Maxwell, Evan, "From Ecuador to 'Land of Plenty,' Women Rookies Break Illegal Alien Ring," *Los Angeles Times*, Jan. 31, 1977.

Maxwell, Evan, "U.S.-Mexico Smuggling: The Buying and Selling of Humans," *Los Angeles Times*, Feb. 22, 1977.

Mines, Richard, "Migratory Tide Washes Up Benefits, Too," San Francisco, Pacific News Service, Dec. 9, 1977.

Norton, Clark, "Tijuana: City of Sin, City of Hope," San Francisco, Pacific News Service, Oct. 13, 1977.

Seaberry, Jane, "Virginia Law Seeks to Oust Illegal Aliens from Job Market," *The Washington Post*, Dec. 31, 1977.

Smardz, Zofia, "Illegal Aliens, Doing the Dirty Work No One Else Will?" *Washington Star*, Aug. 8, 1977.

United Press International, "Border Patrol Raids Valley Clothing Plant," Harlington, TX. *Valley Morning Star*, May 22, 1977.

1978

"Alien Beaten and Robbed," *San Diego Union*, Nov. 5, 1978.

"Alien Report," Chula Vista, CA, *Star News*, Aug. 20, 1978.

"Alien Robbery Suspects Held," *San Diego Union*, Nov. 27, 1978.

"Alien Smuggling Charge Stems from Auto Accident," Chula Vista, CA, *Star News*, Sept. 17, 1978.

"Alien's Shooting Investigated," El Centro, CA, *Imperial Valley Press*, Aug. 2, 1978.

"Aliens Picked Up at Manufacturing Plant," Morgan Hill, CA, *Times & San Martin News*, Oct. 31, 1978.

"Arrest Illegal Aliens in Macoupin," Gillespie, IL, *Area News*, Sept. 27, 1978.

"Boatman Arrested for Cargo of Aliens," *The Miami Herald*, Dec. 1, 1978.

"Border Patrol, TJ Cops Will Hook Up 'Hot Line,' " Chula Vista, CA, *Star News*, Sept. 24, 1978.

"Burglary Probe Leads to Aliens," Hazel Crest, IL, *The Star*, Oct. 22, 1978.

"Cabbies Just Doing Their Job," Chula Vista, CA, *Star News*, July 20, 1978.

"Californian Held for Transporting Aliens," North Platte, NE, *Telegraph*, July 26, 1978.

"Changes Told in U.S. Laws on Immigration," El Centro, CA, *Imperial Valley Press*, Oct. 27, 1978.

"Chicano Sues State INS Director," *Portland Oregonian*, July 8, 1978.

"Company Cited for Child Labor Abuse," Paterson, NJ, *The News*, July 31, 1978.

"Court Action in Favor of Illegal Aliens," Los Angeles, *Mexican American Sun*, July 13, 1978.

"Fatal Alien-Smuggling Results in 3 Indictments," *San Diego Union*, Oct. 21, 1978.

"Forging a Black-Hispanic Alliance," *The Washington Post*, Nov. 18, 1978.

"14 Aliens Nabbed," Costa Mesa, CA, *Daily Pilot*, Aug. 14, 1978.

"49 Illegal Aliens Deported as 5 Others Fight to Stay," Elk Grove, IL, *Herald*, Sept. 15, 1978.

"Hospital Official Indicted," *The Washington Post*, Dec. 29, 1978.

"Illegal Alien Suspects Arrested," *Los Angeles Herald-Examiner*, Oct. 8, 1978.

"Illegal Aliens Apprehended," Grangeville, *Idaho County Free Press*, June 21, 1978.

"Illegal Aliens in the Wrong Spot Deported," Garden Grove, CA, *Orange County Evening News*, Nov. 2, 1978.

"Illegal Aliens Seek Better Life," *San Antonio Express*, July 11, 1978.

"Illegal Transportation of Aliens Charged," *St. Louis Post-Dispatch*, Oct. 6, 1978.

"Immigration Officer Demoted," *The Washington Post*, Aug. 13, 1978.

"INS Boss Hits KKK on Aliens," El Centro, CA, *Imperial Valley Press*, July 22, 1978.

"KKK Uses CB to Patrol U.S. Border," *The Detroit News*, April 16, 1978.

"Klan Warned on Border Vigil," *San Diego Union*, May 16, 1978.

"Local Inquiry Spurred by Illegal Alien Find," Reading, PA, *Eagle*, Aug. 30, 1978.

"Los Angeles Man Gets Probation For Illegally Transporting Aliens," *St. Louis Post-Dispatch*, Oct. 22, 1978.

"Man Guilty of Alien Smuggling," *San Diego Union*, Dec. 6, 1978.

"Man Held on $100,000 Bond in Alien Transport Conspiracy," *San Antonio Express*, Dec. 1, 1978.

"Man Sentenced for Transporting 5 Illegal Aliens," *Peoria Journal-Star*, June 23, 1978.

"Man Shot Crossing Border," *San Diego Evening Tribune*, Aug. 29, 1978.

"Mexico Will Open Border Office to Aid Illegal Aliens," *San Diego Union*, Aug. 19, 1978.

" 'New' Town Policies Part of Settlement," Wheatland, WY, *Record-Times*, Aug. 2, 1978.

"Passaic Company Fined on Minors," *Newark Star-Ledger*, Aug. 30, 1978.

"Petition to Stop 'Silent Invasion' of Illegal Aliens," *San Diego Daily Transcript*, Oct. 9, 1978.

"Police Stop Car, Find 6 Illegal Aliens," Corvalis, OR, *Gazette-Times*, July 31, 1978.

"Pose as Officers Alleged, 2 Held in Aliens Case," *San Diego Evening Tribune*, Nov. 27, 1978.

"Record Set in Arresting Illegals," Yuma, AZ, *The Valley News*, Aug. 16. 1978.

"Robberies of Aliens Result in 8 Arrests," *San Diego Evening Tribune*, Sept. 29, 1978.

"Robbers of Illegals Nabbed," Chula Vista, CA, *Star News*, Nov. 30, 1978.

"Seven Robbed," Oceanside, CA, *Oceanside Blade Tribune*, Dec. 14, 1978.

"Smuggling," *San Antonio Express*, Dec. 4, 1978.

"Stayton Canning Arrests Made," Salem, *Oregon Statesman*, Oct. 17, 1978.

"Suggest Fines for Firms Hiring Illegal Aliens," *Chicago Law Bulletin*, July 25, 1978.

"Suit Filed in Searches for Mexican Nationals," *The Fresno Bee*, Sept. 26, 1978.

"Suspect Taken to Federal Pen," Springfield, OR, *News*, Dec. 14, 1978.

"The VFW Opposes Influx of Aliens," *The Miami Herald*, Aug. 25, 1978.

"3 Aliens Seized for Stabbings," *San Diego Union*, Oct. 12, 1978.

"3 Held in Knifings at Border," *San Diego Evening Tribune*, Oct. 12, 1978.

"Thirty Aliens Rounded Up in Raids Here," Medford, OR, *Mail-Tribune*, Nov. 16, 1978.

"31 Illegal Aliens Arrested Near Hicks Field Complex," *Fort Worth Star-Telegram*, Aug. 12, 1978.

"2 Indicted in Fake Marriage Scheme," *The Washington Post*, Nov. 15, 1978.

"Wobbling Wheel Nets Nine Mexican Aliens," McCook, NE, *Gazette*, Sept. 20, 1978.

"Woman is Sentenced for Transporting Aliens," *Fort Worth Star-Telegram*, Nov. 18, 1978.

Aslesen, Penny, "More Illegal Aliens Are Crossing South Dakota," *Rapid City Journal*, Dec. 23, 1978

Associated Press, "Haitians Rescued from Burning Boat," *The Washington Post*, June 14, 1978.

Associated Press, "Visa Sales to Prostitutes Charged," *The Washington Post*, May 5, 1978.

Atterberry, Ann, "Texas Gold," *The Dallas Morning News*, Dec. 17, 1978.

Babcock, Charles R., "U.S. Prosecution Ruled Out in Slaying of Hispanic Boy," *The Washington Post*, July 15, 1978.

Baxton, Greg, " 'Flying Cleric' Gets Probation," *Los Angeles Herald-Examiner*, Nov. 21, 1978.

Becklund, Laurie, "Mexico to Post Officials to Aid Illegals Caught in U.S.," *Los Angeles Times*, Aug. 25, 1978.

Benson, George S., "Growing Communist Influence in Mexico," Chicago, *Hlas Naroda*, Sept. 1978.

Boodman, Sandra G., "Third World Poverty, Escaping to Washington," *The Washington Post*, May 14, 1978.

Boodman, Sandra G., and Christopher Dickey, "Police Changing Tactics to Cope in Crimes Against Illegal Aliens," *The Washington Post*, Dec. 26, 1978.

Brown, Nicholas, "All Sides Losers in Alien Dispute," *The Richmond Times-Dispatch*, Nov. 19, 1978.

Cashman, Chris, "137 Mundelein Aliens Arrested," Libbertyville, IL, *Independent-Register*, Nov. 9, 1978.

Castro, Tony, "On Both Sides of the Border . . . a Waiting Game," *Los Angeles Herald-Examiner*, Nov. 6, 1978.

Castro, Tony, "Over the Border and on the Carpet," *Los Angeles Herald-Examiner*, Nov. 28, 1978.

Castro, Tony, " 'We've Lost Control of the Border,' " *Los Angeles Herald-Examiner*, Nov. 5, 1978.

Clance, Homer, "Challenge of Alien Flow Told," *San Diego Union*, Nov. 8, 1978.

Clement, John, "Growers May Testify on Aliens," *The Richmond Times-Dispatch*, Nov. 6, 1978.

Clement, John, "34 Illegal Aliens Arrested in State," *The Richmond Times-Dispatch*, Aug. 18, 1978.

Conway, Sharon, "Labor Camp Raid Nets 71 Illegal Farm Workers," *The Washington Post*, Aug. 4, 1978.

Davis, Mike, "Tijuana's River People," *In These Times*, July 5-11, 1978.

DeSilva, Bruce, "Law, Medical Needs in Clash Over Aliens," *Providence Journal-Bulletin*, Sept. 25, 1978.

DeWyze, Jeannette and Neal Matthews, "Stoning the Border Patrol," *San Diego Reader*, Nov. 30, 1978.

DeYoung, Karen, "Doubling of U.S. Aid to Haiti Questioned," *The Washington Post*, Dec. 27, 1978.

DeYoung, Karen, "U.S. Accused of Denying Rights to Haitian Exiles," *The Washington Post*, Dec. 22, 1978.

Dewey, Jackie, "Somewhere Out There Are Hunted Human Beings," *San Jose Mercury-News*, Nov. 21, 1978.

Dickey, Christopher, "Bill on Illegal Aliens in Jobs Is Protested," *The Washington Post*, March 2, 1978.

Dickey, Christopher, "Continuing Battle, Restaurateur Auger Fumes Over Alien Raids, Plans Suit," *The Washington Post*, Nov. 23, 1978.

Dickey, Christopher, "4 at Immigration Service Sued by Blackie's Restaurant," *The Washington Post*, Dec. 13, 1978.

Dickey, Christopher, "14 Aliens Nabbed in Restaurant Raid," *The Washington Post*, Nov. 18, 1978.

Dickey, Christopher, "Illegal Alien Was Victim of His Dream," *The Washington Post*, Oct. 15, 1978.

Dickey, Christopher, "Illegal Aliens Join Armed Forces to Gain U.S. Citizenship," *The Washington Post*, July 31, 1978.

Dickey, Christopher, "Illegal Migrants: A Cyclical Drama," *The Washington Post*, Aug. 7, 1978.

Dickey, Christopher, "The Immigrant Worker Ploy; Keeping Busy Without a Card," *The Washington Post*, July 16, 1978.

Dietrich, Robert, "Two Aliens Shot at Border," *San Diego Evening Tribune*, Oct. 23, 1978.

Donovan, Judy, "Many Aliens Believed in Hiding Here," Tucson, *The Arizona Daily Star*, July 16, 1978.

Drehsler, Alex, "Deported Mexican Aliens Receive Wages," *San Diego Union*, Oct. 29, 1978.

Drennan, Christy, "City Police Instructed to Let INS Deal With Illegal Aliens," *Houston Chronicle*, Nov. 17, 1978.

Dunlap, Wayman, "Snag Hit in Alien Hearing," Oceanside, CA, *Oceanside Blade Tribune*, Nov. 30, 1978.

Durazo, Armando, "Final Step to Border Is Fatal for Some Aliens," Tucson, *The Arizona Daily Star*, Aug. 4, 1978.

Durazo, Armando, "Life Is Uneasy for Immigrants," Tucson, *The Arizona Daily Star*, July 16, 1978.

Eliaser, Elga, "Tighter Migrant Policy Urged in Norway," *The Klansman*, June 1978.

Emch, Tom, "The Other Illegal Aliens," *San Francisco Sunday Examiner & Chronicle*, Nov. 5, 1978.

Farrell, Joseph N., "18 Aliens Are Nabbed in County," Reading, PA, *Times,* Aug. 30, 1978.

Foner, Samuel P., "We Don't Need More of Their Poor," *Spotlight*, Dec. 4, 1978.

Frisbie, Al, "Alien's Dream Proves Impossible," Omaha, *Evening World Herald,* Aug. 16, 1978.

Fussman, Cal, "Haitian Alien Hopes to Find in U.S. What He Never Had at Home: Liberty," *The Miami Herald*, June 28, 1978.

Gillie, John, "Illegal Aliens Harvesting Trees," *Tacoma News Tribune*, Nov. 24, 1978.

Goldfarb, Ronald L., "Imported Farm Labor: How Growers Manipulate the System," *The Washington Post*, Aug. 2, 1978.

Golum, Rob, "Cabbie's High-Paying Fares: Illegals," Chula Vista, CA, *Star News*, July 20, 1978.

Ham, Ron, "During the Rains, We Went Hungry," Solana Beach, CA, *San Dieguito Citizen*, July 19, 1978.

Ham, Ron, "It's Easy to See Them Coming," Solana Beach, CA, *San Dieguito Citizen*, July 5, 1978.

Hatch, Katherine, "Illegal-Alien Problem Called Hemispheric," *San Diego Evening Tribune*, Aug. 12, 1978.

Heintzman, Tom, "Team Corrals Illegal Aliens," Reading, PA, *Times*, Nov. 17, 1978.

Henderson, Bob, "Illegal Immigration Linked to Over-Population," Pasadena, TX, *The Pasadena Citizen*, Nov. 9, 1978.

Homan, Carolyn, "Grower Says Everyone Hires Aliens—Only Ones Who'll Work," Salem, *Oregon Statesman*, Oct. 17, 1978.

Howard-Jones, Marje, "Gang Nabbed Robbing Illegal Aliens," Carlsbad, CA, *Carlsbad Journal*, Oct. 14, 1978.

Hunter, Gordon, "Illegals Fatten Cash Registers in Expanding East End of City," *Houston Chronicle*, Nov. 19, 1978.

Jones, Jack, "Border Patrol Denies Charges of Harassment," *Los Angeles Times*, June 27, 1978.

Jones, Jack, "Border Patrol: More Fingers in the Dike," *Los Angeles Times*, Aug. 9, 1978.

Kelly, Nicki, "Bahamians Deporting Haitians," *The Miami Herald*, June 28, 1978.

Korewick, Kathryn, "Border Patrol Nabs, Deports Mexican Nationals," Blackfoot, ID, *News*, July 24, 1978.

Kotkin, Joel, "2 Labor Unions Openly Aiding Illegal Aliens," *The Washington Post*, Sept. 11, 1978.

Lattin, Don, "Concord: Rare Find in 'Green Card' Bust," *San Francisco Examiner*, Aug. 28, 1978.

Lemmons, John, "US-Mexico in Crackdown on Alien Smuggling Racket," Nogales, AZ, *International*, July 12, 1978.

Livernois, Joe, "All American Canal's Perilous Ways," El Centro, CA, *Imperial Valley Press*, Oct. 12, 1978.

McClure, Rosemary, "Davy Crockett: Alive and Well in Yuma," *San Bernardino Sun-Telegram,* July 2, 1978.

McLemore, David, "Aliens Hard at Work in S.A.," *San Antonio Express-News*, July 8, 1978.

McLemore, David, "Status is Goal, Undocumented Aliens Seek Documents," *San Antonio Express*, July 11, 1978.

McClure, Rosemary, "Davy Crockett: Alive and Well in Yuma," *San Bernardino Sun-Telegram*, July 2, 1978.

MacNitt, Ben, "Even Desert Can be Cold for Illegal Aliens," *Tucson Citizen,* June 22, 1978.

Mack, Don, "Is Springfield Fugitive 'El Abuelo'?" Eugene, OR, *Register-Guard*, Dec. 6, 1978.

Mahoney, Robert, "Zapata Warns of Friction Caused by Illegal Aliens," *Fort Worth Star-Telegram*, Nov. 5, 1978.

Marcotte, Paul, "America a Mecca for Illegal Aliens," Des Plaines, IL, *Herald*, Dec. 31, 1978.

Mark, Susan, "Shipment of 13 Mexican Aliens Ends on Rte. 80," Hackensack, NJ, *Record*, Nov. 1, 1978.

Meyer, Jeff, "Illegal Aliens Sent on Taxpayer Busride," *Las Vegas Sun*, Oct. 20, 1978.

Mintz, Bill, "Virginia Tobacco Farmers Called in Alien Labor Probe," *San Antonio Express*, Nov. 10, 1978.

Moran, Tim, "145 Arrested As Illegal Immigrants," Mundelein, IL, *Herald*, Nov. 8, 1978.

Morrison, Patt, "Border Paradox: Witnesses Jailed—Aliens Held, Smuggler Suspects Get Bail." *Los Angeles Times*, Sept. 4, 1978

Morrow, Thomas J., "Border Patrol Holds Watch for Aliens," Escondido, CA, *Daily Times-Advocate*, Aug. 9, 1978.

Morrow, Thomas J., "Close Call Convinces 'Coyote' to Quit," Escondido, CA, *Daily Times-Advocate*, Aug. 27, 1978.

Morrow, Thomas J., "Fugitive Aliens Feel Fortunate," Escondido, CA, *Daily Times-Advocate*, Aug. 8, 1978.

Morrow, Thomas J., "Growers, Illegal Aliens, Caught in Double Bind," Escondido, CA, *Daily Times-Advocate*, Aug. 7, 1978.

Morrow, Thomas J., "Mexico May Organize Its Own Border Patrol," Escondido, CA, *Daily Times-Advocate*, Aug. 20, 1978.

Moss, Ellison, "Five Charged in Alien Marriage Scheme," *Baltimore News American*, Nov. 15, 1978.

Murtha, Don, "Border Officer Says Aliens Victims of Racket in Labor," Silverton, OR, *Appeal-Tribune*, Nov. 2, 1978.

Neumeier, Larry, "Hoping for Work, He Winds Up Shot," El Centro, CA, *Imperial Valley Press*, Aug. 7, 1978.

Norton, Clark, "Illegal Alien Smuggling a Nationwide Business," San Francisco, Pacific News Service, June 12, 1978.

Oglesby, Joe, "Haitians Making Themselves at Home," *The Miami Herald*, July 31, 1978.

Ott, Bill, "2 Men Indicted on Charges of Violating Alien's Rights," *San Diego Union*, Nov. 4, 1978.

Parsons, Jim, "Good News: Free Trip to Mexico. Bad News: You Can't Say No," *Minneapolis Star and Tribune*, Nov. 18, 1978.

Perskie, James, "Arrest Reveals: An Alien Way of Life," Pleasantville, NJ, *Atlantic Sun*, Sept. 6, 1978.

Pinkerton, James, "100,000 Illegal Aliens Living in Metroplex," *Fort Worth Star-Telegram*, July 5, 1978.

Pinkerton, James, "62 Illegal Aliens Nabbed in Check at Plant," *Fort Worth Star-Telegram*, July 7, 1978.

Polk, William, "Authorities Probe Shooting of Alien by Border Guard," *San Diego Evening Tribune*, Aug. 4, 1978.

Price, Joyce, "Illegal Aliens Find Haven in Wedding Belles," *Baltimore News American*, Oct. 27, 1978.

Quale, Alan, "Illegal Aliens—Their Dreams, Disappointments," San Mateo, CA, *San Mateo Times*, Nov. 17, 1978.

Ramos, Manny, "Brutalidad de Inmigración," *San Diego Newsline*, Nov. 22, 1978.

Reyes, David, "Immigration Arrests 100 at Woodburn," Salem, *Oregon Statesman*, Oct. 17, 1978.

Reyes, David, "NAACP Delegate Claims Illegal Aliens Steal Jobs From Blacks in California," Salem, *Oregon Statesman*, July 6, 1978.

Reyes, Raul, "Sanctions for Knowingly Hiring Illegals Suggested," *Houston Chronicle*, Sept. 14, 1978.

Reyes, Raul, "Latin Woman Testifying Before Unit Learns She Might Avert Deportation," *Houston Chronicle*, Sept. 15, 1978.

Rodriguez, Eliott, "Haitians March in Miami for Political Asylum," *Miami News*, Aug. 4, 1978.

Rosentiel, Paul, "Plenty of High Skill Jobs, Lots of Unskilled Workers," San Francisco, Pacific News Service, April 6, 1978.

Rosentiel, Paul, "Workers Risk Unemployment for Survival Wages," San Francisco, Pacific News Service, April 13, 1978.

Saldana, Frank, "Detectives Question Aliens in Slaying," *San Diego Evening Tribune*, Dec. 6, 1978.

Sandoval, Moises, "Geese Thrive, Families Fail in Colorado Farmlands," San Francisco, Pacific News Service, March 23, 1978.

Schauble, Chris, "Nine Stowaways, Caught from Ship in Baltimore," *The Washington Post*, June 28, 1978.

Simons, Marlise, "Mexican President Surprises Many in Campaign Against Corrupt Officials," *The Washington Post*, July 9, 1978.

Smith, Bill, "Firm 'Didn't Know Employees Were Illegal Aliens' " *Peoria Journal-Star*, Oct. 19, 1978.

Smith, David S., "Officers Probe Death of Two Aliens on Int. 10," *Palm Springs Desert Sun*, Oct. 7, 1978.

Smith, Doug, "The Coyote and the Pollos: Not a Fable," *Los Angeles Times*, Sept. 3, 1978.

Smith, Rodney, "Police Identify Suspects in Extortion of Spanish-Speaking Illegal Aliens," *Washington Star*, Nov. 16, 1978.

Smollar, David, "Troubles by the Trainload . . . Illegal Aliens Load Up for L.A.," *Los Angeles Times*, Aug. 13, 1978.

Staats, Craig, "Illegal Aliens Are After Work, Not a Home," *San Bernardino Sun Telegram*, Oct. 1, 1978.

Trahan, Ellen, "Lopez Goes Home Minus Leg, Wife," Freemont, NE, *Tribune*, Aug. 16, 1978.

Waters, Pat, "Man Arrested in Freemont Is Indicted; Charge Is Transporting Illegal Aliens," Freemont, NE, *Tribune*, Aug. 4, 1978.

Watson, Stu, "Firm to Recruit Foreign Workers," Medford, OR, *Mail Tribune*, Aug. 2, 1978.

Weathersby, Jeff, "Bell Wants Only INS Agents Capturing Them," Yakima, WA, *Herald Republic*, Aug. 21, 1978.

Weinstein, Rob, "An Alien Tells How She Came to U.S.," Healdsburg, CA, *Healdsburg Tribune*, Dec. 7, 1978.

Wicker, Jim, "Penniless Aliens Dumped Here," *Greensboro Record*, Oct. 5, 1978.

Williams, Bob, "Illegal Aliens Winning Third World Beachhead," *Los Angeles Times*, Sept. 3, 1978.

Zacchino, Narda, "Union Sues over Garment Factory Raids," *Los Angeles Times*, Aug. 23, 1978.

1979

"Alien Beating Probe Opposed," *The Washington Post*, Feb. 24, 1979.

"Alien Pays in Loneliness for a Living Wage," *The New York Times*, Feb. 12, 1979.

"Alien Smuggling Ring Exposed," Chula Vista, CA, *Star News*, March 15, 1979.

"Alien Workers' Rights Violated," *Los Angeles Herald-Examiner*, Jan. 26, 1979.

"Aliens Apprehended Near Mt. Vernon," Bellingham, WA, *Herald*, July 27, 1979.

"Aliens in Vista Raid Queried," *San Diego Union*, Jan. 21, 1979.

"Alleged Smuggler of Aliens Arrested," El Centro, CA, *Imperial Valley Press*, Jan. 26, 1979.

"Chicano Rights Committee Urges Border Patrol Probe," *San Diego Union*, March 22, 1979.

"Circulation of Illegal Alien Ballot Measure Approved," *Los Angeles Times*, April 10, 1979.

"County Pays $1,000 to Man Jailed as Alien," Pendleton, *East Oregonian*, Feb. 24, 1979.

"Eight Indicted in Area Alien-Smuggling Setup," *San Diego Evening Tribune*, Feb. 22, 1979.

"Feds to Return Mexicans Arrested Near Morrilton," *Arkansas Democrat*, Feb. 4, 1979.

"Four Arraigned for Smuggling," Covina, CA, *San Gabriel Valley Tribune*, Jan. 20, 1979.

"4 Deny Smuggling Illegals," *Los Angeles Herald-Examiner*, Feb. 8, 1979.

"4 Indicted in Illegal Alien Scheme," Union City, NJ, *Hudson Dispatch*, Feb. 1, 1979.

"57 Illegal Aliens Held," Oceanside, CA, *Oceanside Blade Tribune*, Feb. 19, 1979.

"Firm Accused of Urging Aliens to Evade Law," *San Jose Mercury-News*, Jan. 13, 1979.

"Five Suspected Alien Smugglers Plead Innocent," Covina, CA, *San Gabriel Valley Tribune*, Feb. 8, 1979.

"Harassment Complaints Registered," Covina, CA, *San Gabriel Valley Tribune*, Jan. 24, 1979.

"Illegal Alien Raid Made," Fullerton, CA, *Fullerton Tribune*, April 3, 1979.

"Illegal Alien Smugglers Sentenced," *Los Angeles Herald-Examiner*, March 27, 1979.

"Illegal Alien Sweep Yields 29 in City," *West Chicago Press*, March 22, 1979.

"Illegal Aliens' Claims Probed," Nacogdoches, TX, *Sentinel*, Feb. 27, 1979.

"Illegal Aliens on His Farm, Virginian Charged as Smuggler," *The Washington Post*, April 7, 1979.

"Illegal Aliens Pose Problems, Prof Says," Espanola, NM, *Rio Grande Sun*, Feb. 8, 1979.

"Illinois Law Officers Given Alien Search Warrants," Carbondale, *Southern Illinoisan*, March 12, 1979.

"Immigration Agent Indicted in Theft of $540 from Mexican Illegal Alien," *Dallas Morning News*, March 13, 1979.

"Immigration Now: No Room for A. P. Giannini," Walnut Creek, CA, *Contra Costa Times*, Feb. 19, 1979.

"INS Didn't Tell Suspected Aliens of Available Aide, ACLU Charges," Covina, CA, *San Gabriel Valley Tribune*, Jan. 5, 1979.

"INS Officer Charged in Bribes," *Los Angeles Herald-Examiner*, March 25, 1979.

"INS Officials Reportedly Probed," *The Washington Post*, Jan. 8, 1979.

"Klansman Pleads Guilty in 'Arrest,'" *San Diego Evening Tribune*, Jan. 30, 1979.

"Man Enters Guilty Plea in Alien-Transport Deal," *San Antonio Express*, Feb. 6, 1979.

"Many Illegal Aliens in Hudson, Essex," Jersey City, NJ, *Jersey Journal*, Feb. 15, 1979.

"Nebraskans Give Hope, Artificial Leg to Man," Freemont, NE, *Tribune*, Feb. 13, 1979.

"New Illegal Alien Guidelines," *Chicago Sun-Times*, March 13, 1979.

"19 More Aliens Arrested," Sidney, NE, *Telegraph*, March 14, 1979.

"Officials Push Search for Suspect in Alien Smuggling," *San Antonio Express*, Feb. 6, 1979.

"Police Seek Couple for Aliens' Abuse," *Fort Worth Star-Telegram*, Jan. 11, 1979.

"Seventeen Aliens in Van Held for Authorities," Kimball, *West Nebraska Observer*, March 8, 1979.

"Talking to Car Leads to Arrest," Santa Paula, CA, *Daily Chronicle*, Feb. 5, 1979.

"Texas Man Sentenced for Transporting Aliens," *Tulsa Tribune*, Jan. 8, 1979.

"3 Aliens Smugglers Jailed; Tied to Biggest '78 Ring," *San Diego Evening Tribune*, Jan. 16, 1979.

"Three Illegal Alien Smugglers Convicted," *Los Angeles Herald-Examiner*, Feb. 27, 1979.

"Three Illegal Aliens Holdup Victims," *San Diego Union*, Jan. 22, 1979.

"Tuberculosis Rate Disturbs Merced," *Fresno Bee*, Jan. 16, 1979.

"Two Charged," *Laredo Citizen*, Jan. 11, 1979.

"U.S. Officers Bail Set in Alien-Bribery Case," *San Diego Evening Tribune*, April 12, 1979.

Adler, Michael, "Investigator Chops Chinatown Exploitation of Illegal Aliens," *New York News World*, Feb. 14, 1979.

Akst, Daniel M., "Illegal Aliens: Society's Shadows," Paterson, NJ, *The News*, March 21, 1979.

Akst, Daniel M., "Legal Residents Seek Help," Paterson, NJ, *The News*, March 21, 1979.

Akst, Don, "Raid on Clifton Company Grounds 3 Illegal Aliens," Union City, NJ, *Hudson Dispatch*, March 6, 1979.

Alberta, Paul, "Illegal Aliens Scheme Results in Probation," *Passaic Herald News*, April 3, 1979.

Alberta, Paul, "Travel Agency Head Admits Illegal Payoffs," *Passaic Herald News*, March 19, 1979.

Alex, Tom, "Cicero Wants Smuggling Suspect Here," *Des Moines Tribune*, March 29, 1979.

Alex, Tom, "How 9 Aliens Were Nabbed," *Des Moines Tribune*, March 28, 1979.

Ball, Neil, "Bus Driver's Tip Leads to 43 Illegal Aliens," *San Diego Union*, March 24, 1979.

Blum, Howard, "Illegal Aliens in New York: A Life of Fear, Costly to All," *The New York Times*, March 18, 1979.

Blum, Howard, "Unrecorded Aliens Cost New York City Millions," *The New York Times*, March 19, 1979.

Buder, Leonard, "Illegal Alien Is Seized on 'Green Card' Sales of $100,000 a Month," *The New York Times*, April 5, 1979.

Caleca, Vic, "The Illegals of Elgin," Elgin, IL, *Courier-News*, Feb. 4, 1979.

Campbell, Richard, "Record Number of Illegal Aliens Seized in Bar Raids," *Los Angeles Herald-Examiner*, Jan. 8, 1979.

Clance, Homer, "Alien Slain, 2nd Shot in Border Arrest," *The San Diego Union*, March 19, 1979.

Clifford, Frank, "INS Continues Crackdown on Illegal Aliens," *Dallas Times Herald*, Jan. 1, 1979.

Cramer, Jim, "Should Illegal Aliens Know Their Rights?" *Los Angeles Herald-Examiner*, Jan. 5, 1979.

Crewdon, John M., "The Border Patrol, a Job Without End," *The New York Times*, Feb. 19, 1979.

DeYoung, Karen, and Christopher Dickey, "Divorce, Intipuca Style," *The Washington Post,* April 3, 1979.

Del Olmo, Frank, "New Tactics Being Used in Behalf of Aliens," *Los Angeles Times*, Feb. 8, 1979.

Dickey, Christopher, "British Journalist Henry Fairlie Termed Illegal Alien by Immigration," *The Washington Post*, Feb. 24, 1979.

Dickey, Christopher, and Karen DeYoung, "Illegal Entry: A People's Terrifying Survival Tradition," *The Washington Post*, April 2, 1979.

Dickey, Christopher, and Karen DeYoung, "The Long Journey to Find Work Here," *The Washington Post*, April 1, 1979.

Dickey, Christopher, and Tom Grubisich, "First Test of Alien Law Ends in Dismissal in Va.," *The Washington Post*, Jan. 31, 1979.

Dietrich, Robert, "Alien Shooting Being Probed," *San Diego Evening Tribune*, Feb. 17, 1979.

Dietrich, Robert, "KKK Prowls Border, Protests Mexico Talks," *San Diego Evening Tribune*, Feb. 17, 1979.

Dietrich, Robert, "Officer Fired in Self-Defense, Investigators Say," *San Diego Evening Tribune*, March 20, 1979.

Disbie, Patricia, "Probers Collect Pay for Illegal Aliens," *San Diego Evening Tribune*, Feb. 2, 1979.

Drehsler, Alex, "Bidder for Mexican Gas Linked to Illegal Aliens," *San Diego Union*, Jan. 14, 1979.

Drehsler, Alex, "MCOP Looks Out for Farm Workers, Illegal Aliens," *San Diego Union*, Jan. 21, 1979.

Drehsler, Alex, "Nun Says Fear Is Common Denominator in Arizona's Citrus Groves, Basque Homeland," *San Diego Union*, Jan. 21, 1979.

Drehsler, Alex, "They Must Shiver in Valley of Sun," *San Diego Union*, Jan. 14, 1979.

Dusek, Ron, "Mexicans Protest at Border," *The Washington Post*, March 12, 1979.

Endicott, William, "Firm Accused of Deceiving Aliens," *Los Angeles Times*, Jan. 13, 1979.

Ewell, James, "Immigration Agent Charged with Theft," *Dallas Morning News*, Feb. 20, 1979.

Fritcher, Gary, "Aliens Said Important to Erath Dairy Industry," Stephenville, TX, *Empire-Tribune*, March 6, 1979.

Futterman, Ellen, "Undocumented Workers Hold Rally," *Los Angeles Herald-Examiner*, March 11, 1979.

Gay, Lance, " 'Undocumented' Aliens Sign Farm Labor Pact," *Washington Star*, Jan. 30, 1979.

Hamill, Denis, "What About All the Other Illegals?" *Los Angeles Herald-Examiner*, Feb. 21, 1979.

Harrigan, John J., "Ranch Signs Union Pact Including Illegal Aliens," *Phoenix Republic*, Jan. 31, 1979.

Herbers, John, "Changes in Society Holding Black Youth in Jobless Web," *The New York Times*, March 11, 1979.

Houston, Robert, "Hispanics Continue Fight in Tucson Alien-Beating Decision," Mesa, AZ, *Mesa Tribune*, Jan. 21, 1979.

Humphries, John, "Border Agents Arrest Illegal Aliens in Cenla," Alexandria, LA, *Town Talk*, Feb. 16, 1979.

Hutcheson, Jus Nyla, "La. Aliens May Total 30,000," *New Orleans Times-Picayune*, Jan. 27, 1979.

Kelly, Dennis, "27 Aliens Rescued, Arrested," *San Bernardino Sun*, Feb. 13, 1979.

Kendall, John, "Youths Tell of Privations as Pickers, Claims Are Basis of $3.85 million Suit Against Grower," *Los Angeles Times*, April 10, 1979.

Kenny, Steve, "Agents Arrest Pair in Plot to 'Sell' 300 Aliens," *Dallas Morning News*, Feb. 28, 1979.

Kenny, Steve, "Illegal Aliens Discover Housing as Hard to Find as Work," *Dallas Morning News*, Feb. 18, 1979.

Kenny, Steve, "Illegal Aliens 'Ride Rail' To Dallas," *Dallas Morning News*, Feb. 26, 1979.

King, Larry, "Commission Supports Illegal Alien Measure," *Omaha Morning World-Herald*, March 24, 1979.

Krause, Charles A., "Argentines Bust Ring Supplying Fake U.S. Visas," *The Washington Post*, April 2, 1979.

Kriz, Margaret, "Campaign Spotlight on Illegal Aliens, Hinsdale, IL, *Suburban Trib*, March 30, 1979.

Lindsey, Robert, "Rights Workers Allege Exploitation of Mexican Aliens," *The New York Times*, Jan. 28, 1979.

Lowe, Bob, "Backers Say Citrus Accord Will Protect Illegal Aliens," Tucson, *The Arizona Daily Star*, Jan. 31, 1979.

Maxwell, Evan, "LAPD Eases Policy Toward Illegal Aliens," *Los Angeles Times*, March 21, 1979.

McDaniel, Ann, "Texas Farmers 'Need' Mexicans," *Dallas Times Herald*, March 8, 1979.

Molnar, Jim, "Alien Smuggler Raid Only One of Series Here," Escondido, CA, *Daily Times Advocate*, Jan. 21, 1979.

Morgan, Skip, "Alien Smuggling Suspects Set Free," Vista, CA, *Vista Press*, March 1, 1979.

Morgan, Skip, "New Charges Added in Alien Smuggling Case; Trial Put Off," Vista, Ca, *Vista Press*, Feb. 21, 1979.

Morgan, Skip, "New Charges Added in Alien Smuggling Case; Trial Put Off," Vista, CA, *Vista Press*, Feb. 11, 1979.

Moriwaki, Lee, "Citizen-Migrant Suit Could Be Landmark," Seattle, WA, *Times*, April 1, 1979.

Nelson, Jack, "Castillo To Study Alien Border Toll," *Los Angeles Times*, March 22, 1979.

Nunez, John, "Growers Must Pay Aliens Back Wages," Escondido, CA, *Daily Times-Advocate*, Jan. 28, 1979.

Ott, Bill, "Alien Smuggling Rings Target of Area Crackdown," *San Diego Union*, Jan. 14, 1979.

Pool, Maurine, "High Rate of TB Found in County," Los Banos, CA, *Enterprise*, Jan. 17, 1979.

Proctor, Brent, "Alien Smugglers Find that Rain Is Their Most Helpful Ally," Oceanside, CA, *Oceanside Blade Tribune*, Feb. 22, 1979.

Raab, Selwyn, "Paraguayan Tied to Murders Is Ordered Deported," *The New York Times*, April 6, 1979.

Redfern, James, "Baja Police Raid Border Area," *San Diego Evening Tribune*, March 26, 1979.

St. John, Bob, "Easy In and Easy Out," *Dallas Morning News*, March 3, 1979.

Unger, Nancy, "Officials Nab 8 As Illegal Aliens," *Yonkers Herald Statesman*, March 6, 1979.

Washington, Betty, "Job Program Director Charged with Smuggling Aliens," *Chicago Sun Times*, Feb. 1, 1979.

Washington, Betty, "Recruiter, Aides, Indicted for Alien Smugglings," *Chicago Sun Times*, Feb. 28, 1979.

Weber, Mark, "Illegal Aliens: Worst Threat to America," *National Vanguard*, Jan. 1979.

Williams, Bob, and Leo C. Wolinsky, "5 Suspended by Army for Enlisting Aliens," *Los Angeles Times*, Feb. 13, 1979.

Wyckoff, James, "Illegal Aliens Filling Building Jobs Here," *Tucson Citizen*, Jan. 12, 1979.

INDEX

Oregon: H-2 workers in, 174; undocumented workers in, 8, 46, 66, 69, 177

Overpopulation, attributed to Hispanic illegals, 140, 187

P

Pakistan, student visa issuance in, 34

Panamanian illegal immigrants, 29

Paraguayan visa abuser, 33

Pasadore, role in smuggling operations, 44-45, 66

Payment schemes, in smuggling operations, 47, 71

Peruvian illegal immigrants, 30

Philadelphia, Pennsylvania, undocumented workers in, 7, 28, 107

Philippines, effects of American activities in, 27-28, 187

Phoenix, Arizona, undocumented workers in, 68, 69

Piore, Michael J., 152, 164

Police departments: changing policy of, toward immigration law enforcement, 126-127; racist treatment of Hispanic people, 138-139

Polish illegal immigrants, 7, 37, 145, 177

Polish laborers, 4, 15, 16

Polleros, role in smuggling operations, 44-45

Population estimates, of illegal immigrants, 6, 7, 31-32, 36-38

Portillo, Pres. Jóse López, 125, 133; and border violence, 57, 58; and smuggling operations, 48, 49

Prostitutes: hustling of undocumented workers, 112; immigration laws barring, 14; INS involvement in rings of, 98, 99, 102

Poverty level peoples, immigration laws barring, 5, 15, 26, 30

Puerto Rico, employer sanctions in, 168; INS discrimination against workers from, 98

Public services: illegal immigrants using, 154-159; legal immigrants using, 167

R

Racism, and illegal immigrants: of American media, 139-141; and community tensions, 144-147; of INS, 98, 101, 136-139; of local police departments, 126-127, 138-139; of nativist organizations, 141-144

Rape, of illegal immigrants, 11, 40, 56, 105, 178

Trujillo, Dr. Xavier Manrique, 41
Twin plants, on U.S.-Mexican border, 53-54